Comparative Politics and Government of the Baltic States

Comparative Politics and Government of the Baltic States

Estonia, Latvia and Lithuania in the 21st Century

Daunis Auers
Department of Political Science, University of Latvia

First published 2015 by
PALGRAVE MACMILLAN

Palgrave Macmillan in the UK is an imprint of Macmillan Publishers Limited, registered in England, company number 785998, of Houndsmills, Basingstoke, Hampshire RG21 6XS.

Palgrave Macmillan in the US is a division of St Martin's Press LLC, 175 Fifth Avenue, New York, NY 10010.

Palgrave Macmillan is the global academic imprint of the above companies and has companies and representatives throughout the world.

Palgrave® and Macmillan® are registered trademarks in the United States, the United Kingdom, Europe and other countries

ISBN: 978–1–137–36996–3

This book is printed on paper suitable for recycling and made from fully managed and sustained forest sources. Logging, pulping and manufacturing processes are expected to conform to the environmental regulations of the country of origin.

A catalogue record for this book is available from the British Library.

A catalog record for this book is available from the Library of Congress.

Zintai, Markusam un Annai
Aijai un Valdim
Daigai un Andrim

Contents

List of Figures and Tables

Figures

Tables

Preface and Acknowledgements

The Baltic states have been fundamentally transformed since they finally broke away from the Soviet Union in August 1991. The extraordinary politics of the early 1990s has been replaced by the mundane, but important, issues – such as voter apathy and rising inequality – that plague contemporary European democracies. Russia's annexation of Crimea and support for insurgents in eastern Ukraine in 2014 reminded the Baltic states and the international community how far they have come over the past quarter century.

This book compares the contemporary political systems of the three Baltic states of Estonia, Latvia and Lithuania. Three admirable comparative histories of the Baltic states have been published in recent years (Kasekamp, 2010; Plakans, 2011; Purs, 2012), but no single volume covering the politics and governments of the Baltic states has been published since the mid-1990s (Lieven, 1994; Norgaard, 1995). I hope that this volume at least partially fills this gap.

Although I was born, raised and educated in the United Kingdom, I have spent more than two decades – most of my professional career – in Latvia, with regular travel (both work and pleasure) to Estonia and Lithuania. I have been fortunate enough to witness first-hand the significant changes and challenges that the political systems of the Baltic states have undertaken since the early 1990s. To be sure, they remain poorer and smaller than most of their European Union partners, and they have worrying and unstable authoritarian neighbours to the east, a challenge that is typically underrated because it is shared by so few European states. Nevertheless, all three are consolidated democracies where true political competition has become 'the only game in town'.

In writing this volume I have drawn on the rich number of resources now available to scholars studying the Baltic states. In addition to the long-standing academic journals that have regularly published articles on the politics and government of the region, particularly the *Journal of Baltic Studies*, *Europe-Asia Studies* and *East European Politics and Societies*, there are also a significant number of academic volumes dealing with specific dimensions of Baltic politics. For example, a 2010 volume edited by Bengt Jacobsson (*The European Union and the Baltic States: Changing forms of governance*) examined the impact of negotiating accession to the European Union, while an admirable 2012 volume by Richard C.M. Mole (*The Baltic States from the Soviet Union to the European Union: Identity, Discourse and Power in the Post-Communist Transition of Estonia, Latvia and Lithuania*) focused on the changing identity politics of the three states. Most edited volumes dealing with European government, elections, parties and other dimensions of politics now typically include chapters covering the Baltic states. Scholars can now also draw on the rich empirical data produced by Eurobarometer, the World Values Survey, the European Social Survey, and other comparative data sets. Accession to the European Union and other international organisations, as well as the ever-increasing research and publication activities of both national and international non-governmental organisations, has led to a rich bounty of data and reports on many different dimensions of the Baltic states. All three Baltic states now have an established community of political scientists writing both in their own languages and in English, the new lingua franca of the region. There are political science departments in all the major Baltic universities, and a steadily growing number of think-tanks, pollsters, state-funded research services and other organisations produce valuable data and research. I have tried to balance the space given to each Baltic state in the text. However, my Lithuanian language skills could charitably be described as poor. My Estonian is poorer still. As a result, I have used Latvian language texts most extensively and, despite my best efforts, this is likely to be reflected in the text.

I was able to draw on the expertise of my friends in the Baltic social sciences community who read early drafts of the chapters. My thanks go to Kjetil Duvold, Morten Hansen, Mindaugas Jurkynas, Aldis Purs, Toms Rostoks, Allan Sikk and Ken Smith for their comments. Any mistakes or omissions are, of course, my own.

I would like to thank the Baltic American Freedom Foundation for a research grant that took me away from my daily routine at the University of Latvia in the first half of 2014. The Department of Political Science at Wayne State University, Detroit, was kind enough to provide me with an office and access to university resources. Many thanks go to Daniel Geller and Kevin Deegan-Krause for looking after me and to my colleagues at the University of Latvia for approving my sabbatical request. This book would not have been written without this opportunity to put my administrative and lecturing duties to one side.

Introduction

On 21 August 1991 an attempted putsch by reactionary communists in Moscow collapsed. The Baltic states seized this unique historical opening to declare de facto independence from the Soviet Union and reaffirm the statehood they had lost during the Second World War. International recognition, beginning with Iceland, swiftly followed. Both the United States and the remaining parts of the Soviet Union had recognised Baltic independence by the end of September 1991.

The early days, months and years of renewed independence were marked by political, economic and social uncertainty. In the foreword to his masterly account of the Baltic states' struggle for independence and the subsequent early travails of independent statehood, Anatol Lieven (1994, p. xiii) argued that in the early 1990s 'the Baltic states continue[d] to wrestle with problems and dangers on a scale unknown to any [W]estern government'. The three countries had inherited a large Russian military presence as well as enormous fiscal problems caused by the break with the Soviet Union. Their societies were enveloped by crises as inflation soared, public salaries went unpaid, and government services collapsed. Many Western analysts feared that armed conflict would erupt between the ascendant majority titular and the minority Russophone communities in Estonia and Latvia. The likelihood of a successful transition to democracy, market economy and integration with the West was in the balance.

A quarter century later the situation is very different. Estonia, Latvia and Lithuania have been members of the two pillars of European security and prosperity – the European Union (EU) and NATO – since 2004. As of 2015 all three had adopted the euro as their currency. Estonia is one of the 34-member countries in the Organisation for Economic Cooperation and Development – sometimes known as the rich countries' think tank – and Latvia and Lithuania are negotiating to join. Estonia and Latvia have even won the Eurovision Song Contest (although this may not be something to boast about). The three have moved far beyond their post-Soviet roots. Since 2006 they have hovered between 33rd and 48th place in the 167-state Economist Democracy Index (of the three, Estonia has consistently scored highest and Latvia lowest). Their democracy scores in the Freedom House Index have been on an upward trajectory since the 1990s. This is not to say that the situation is ideal. The Economist Democracy Index categorises all three as 'flawed democracies' (alongside Portugal, France and Italy) and they face issues that test the quality of democracy in their states – corruption, minority relations and inequality are particularly ticklish challenges. However, there can be no doubt that democracy has become 'the only game in town'. All have come through challenges to the democratic order. The Estonian government resigned in 1995 after Interior Minister Edgar Savisaar admitted to secretly recording high-level political meetings and passing them on to a shadowy security company with alleged links to the local mafia. Lithuania and Latvia have faced down still more serious challenges. In 2004 the Lithuanian parliament impeached and removed president Rolandas Paksas, and in 2011 the Latvian president called a referendum on the dissolution of parliament, leading to early elections. These and other crises were resolved through peaceful constitutional mechanisms, which sharply contrasts with the erosion of democratic institutions in the other 12 post-Soviet states.

Table 0.1 Contemporary Baltic states. Basic indicators

	Estonia	Latvia	Lithuania
Population size	1,324,814	2,023,825	2,971,905
Capital (population)	Tallinn (400,000)	Riga (703,000)	Vilnius (557,000)
2012 GDP per capita in PPS (EU 28=100)	71	64	72
UNDP HDI Ranking (2013), of 187 states	33	44	41

Source: Eurostat (2014).

Nevertheless, significant differences with the Baltic states' western neighbours persist. Although fast rates of growth, both before and after the severe economic crash of 2008–2010, have led to some convergence with the West, the Baltic states remain much poorer than their western and northern partners in the EU. The comparison with their Nordic neighbours across the Baltic Sea is particularly painful. However, the Nordic countries comprise a region regarded as among the most developed in the world. In contrast, the Baltic states were occupied by the Soviet Union from 1944 to 1991 with all the economic, political and social distortions that this brought.

This volume analyses the contemporary politics and governments of the three Baltic states. Although the political systems of all three are changing and evolving, this is the case in all democracies. The era of extraordinary politics has ended, and the Baltic political systems have stabilised and consolidated. This is not to say that the Soviet era has not left a significant mark on the region or that the Soviet inheritance has completely disappeared. However, continuing Europeanisation, rather than the Baltic states' post-Soviet past, has a far greater impact on their political systems today. The visual impact of the Soviet era is obvious to any visitor driving into rural Baltic towns and villages, or to those who stray from the cosmopolitan and developed urban centres. The economic policies of the Soviet years are still felt in the Baltic states' relative economic backwardness. However, Brussels, Strasbourg and the domestic legislatures shape the Baltic states more than does the communist experience that ended a quarter century ago.

Why the Baltic states?

Estonia, Latvia and Lithuania are analysed together because the three do make up a common European micro-region, sharing a similarly painful modern history and, in more recent years, a trajectory from the Soviet Union to the European Union. Naturally, there are key differences. Lithuanians are Catholic and often consider themselves Central European, while the Estonians are Lutheran (or actually agnostic according to the latest data) and increasingly Nordic; and Latvia has considerable Catholic, Lutheran and Orthodox communities. The Estonians are a bit richer (although Lithuania has caught up), and the Latvians more corrupt (although Lithuania has again caught up). With the exception of defence, the Baltic states cooperate little. However, the region has many commonalities. Between 2008 and 2010 all three Baltic states experienced sharp economic contractions followed by speedy returns to high economic growth. This was an unambiguously Baltic pattern not seen elsewhere in Europe.

Structure of the book

The book is divided into six chapters. Chapter 1 focuses on the political history of the Baltic states, particularly the historical events that continue to have contemporary political salience. It describes the centrality of language to Baltic culture, which largely explains the harsh language laws adopted after 1991. It also describes the contested events of the Second World War, and the issue of whether the Baltic states were occupied, annexed or willingly joined the Soviet Union, which continues to divide Estonians, Latvians, Lithuanians and their Russophone communities and also impacts foreign and economic relations with Russia. Finally, this chapter examines the impact of Soviet occupation on the Baltic states and the brave drive for independence in the 1980s.

Chapter 2 considers the key political institutions adopted by the post-1991 states. The first part compares basic constitutional choices before moving on to consider the main elected and executive institutions: legislatures, executives, presidents and local government. The second part looks at the key unelected institutions: public administration, courts and judges and the security services. The organisational rigour of these institutions has been tested on many occasions over the last quarter century, and the institutions have emerged strengthened and largely unscathed.

Chapter 3 focuses on elections and parties. The Baltic states have had a great number of regular elections at local, national and European levels. Latvia and Lithuania have also held many referendums triggered by both political actors and citizens' initiatives. However, electoral participation has greatly fallen since the highs of the early 1990s, and the Baltic states face the challenge of getting more voters into polling booths. Estonia has long led the world in Internet voting, despite occasional international concerns over the security of the system, while Latvia and Lithuania have put voting booths in shopping centres in order to entice voters. The party systems of Estonia and Latvia have moved from extreme fragmentation to ever-increasing stability, but the Lithuanian party system has moved in the opposite direction. Changes in party financing and campaigning laws have forced the Baltic states' parties to strengthen their organisations and reach out to the public, especially in Estonia where parties have a higher membership than the European average. However, the ideological roots of parties remain weak, as do their policy-creation capacities.

Chapter 4 turns to look at civil society, a crucial dimension of democratic consolidation. The multiple cultural, sectoral and other organisations as well as citizen groups that compose civil society were very active (including holding ad hoc rallies) in the drive for independence from the Soviet Union but then participation collapsed as the economic, political and social transformation took hold. Corruption also took hold in all three states. Latvia saw the development of a particularly pernicious state capture form of corruption. However, the 2000s saw a resurgence of civil society and a decline in corruption as powerful new institutions, created in the race to join the EU and NATO, increasingly proved equal to the challenge of fighting corruption. At the same time, the Estonian and Latvian political communities remain divided between Russophones and titulars, with social-integration initiatives having done little to eradicate this gulf.

Chapter 5 compares economic and social developments in the three states. It recounts the traumatic economic transformation of the 1990s and the rapid economic development of the 2000s that eventually led to overheated economies and, between 2008 and 2010, deep recessions. However, the Baltic states quickly bounced back and enjoyed renewed rapid economic growth despite the malaise elsewhere in Europe. The second half of the chapter compares social policy in the three states and describes the distinct Baltic social welfare model that has emerged in the region.

Chapter 6 turns to look at the foreign and security policy of Estonia, Latvia and Lithuania. This is the area that has seen the deepest and longest Baltic cooperation, stretching back to the late 1980s as the three states lobbied Western countries together. Defence is an area in which the Baltic states have long successfully pooled their resources despite their having differing defence models. Broadly speaking, they have opened their western borders, joining the EU, NATO and participating in a whole host of other western organisations, while attempting to shut the door on neighbouring Russia. This began to change in the 2000s as economic cooperation with Russia increased, and Russian businessmen became major investors in the region. However, Russia's annexation of Crimea in early 2014 led to the Baltic states pushing once more for ever closer links with the West and successfully arguing for an increased NATO presence in the region. As small states with a large, belligerent neighbour, it will be diplomats and foreign policies that will ultimately decide the long-term viability of Estonia, Latvia and Lithuania as sovereign states.

Note on language

Throughout this book I have used the Estonian, Latvian and Lithuanian spelling, and diacritical marks, for names. When possible, financial data are presented in euros. I also refer to the Russian-speaking communities in all three states as Russophones, by which I mean those who use or prefer to use the Russian language in their personal and/or professional lives.

1
A Brief Political History of the Baltic States

Political discourse in the Baltic states is marked by debates on the past as much as on the future. The 1980s drive to break from the Soviet Union, driven by an overwhelming sense of historical injustice, began with small 'calendar demonstrations' marking significant dates in Baltic history. Key domestic and international disputes are based on contested interpretations of history. This is particularly visible each spring in Latvia. On 16 March a shrinking number of Latvian Waffen SS Legion veterans, along with several hundred nationalist supporters, march from the historic Dom Church in the Old Town of Riga to the towering Freedom Monument, the symbol of Latvia's independent statehood. There they are confronted by counter-demonstrating Russophone 'anti-fascist' protesters. A few months later, on 9 May, the positions are reversed as Latvia's Russophone community celebrates Victory in Europe day (which marks the end of the Second World War for the Soviet Union) at the Soviet-era Victory Monument. Protesting Latvians accuse participants of honouring totalitarian communism.[1] There is no common ground between the two groups. History lives, breathes, provokes and mobilises Baltic publics to an extent almost unimaginable in neighbouring Western European democracies.

Evidently, a study of the Baltic states' political systems must begin with a discussion of the complicated and contentious history of the region. Rather than duplicate the many available excellent comparative and single-country histories of the Baltic states, I will sketch the broad sweep of comparative Baltic history and focus on the controversies that touch and shape the political systems of modern Estonia, Latvia and Lithuania.[2] The first section briefly considers the geography and climate that shaped the comparatively late modernisation of the region and then discusses the emergence of Baltic national movements in the nineteenth century. The next part covers the First World War, the collapse of the Russian Empire and the following vicious battles for autonomy and independent statehood. The third part covers the rise and fall of the democratic inter-war states. The fourth part discusses the Second World War and the three brutal occupations that it brought. I then deal with the impact of four decades of sovietisation. Finally, I consider the emergence of opposition to the Soviet regime in the second half of the 1980s and the successful non-violent revolutions that led to the re-emergence of independent, democratic Baltic states in August 1991.

1.1 Three nations survive and awake

Geography and the relatively small size of the Baltic nations, located at the eastern edge of the Baltic Sea, explain much of the turbulence of Baltic history. Samuel Huntington (1996, p. 159) defined the Baltic states–Russian/Belorussian border as the 'eastern boundary of western civilization'. While Huntington gives an overly simplistic vision of a complicated, multi-layered and bitter cultural history, he does capture the geographic vulnerability of the small Baltic nations, located in a flat, boggy, forested and sparsely populated region fought over by larger, more powerful neighbours for more than eight hundred years.[3] This history also explains why the languages, the key to the construction of the three Baltic nations, survived. This is the 'Windy Land – a zone where conquerors alternated sufficiently often, so that their languages could not take root[, this]...inadvertently gave the local language breathing space' (Taagepera, 2011, p. 126).

In the early thirteenth century the territory that makes up much of modern Estonia and Latvia was conquered by Teutonic Knights, shielding the clerics, missionaries and merchants that accompanied them. The order was also charged with eradicating the pagan customs still practiced by the indigenous people, who had started settling in the region around 11,000 BC, and with protecting the new native converts to Christianity. This is the bitter-sweet beginning of European culture encroaching on the peoples of the area and the eradication of the indigenous Baltic societies that were already organised into hierarchical, actively trading communities. It is also what Aldis Purs (2012, p. 25) has described as the 'opening salvo of the "700 years of German oppression" myth' that nationalists use to account for the late emergence of the Baltic nations. On the one hand, this is the moment at which the Baltic states began their long and slow integration with the ideas, economies and politics of the European continent to the west, south and (later) north. On the other hand, this is the point at which they began to have their unique pagan traditions, lifestyles and control of the land stripped away from them. Relations with Western Europe still prompt mixed emotions.

This is the stage at which the history of the modern Baltic states begins. Danish, Swedish, Polish and Russian empires later invaded and occupied the Baltic lands, but throughout the Baltic, the Germans – often the direct descendants of the first Crusaders – remained the effective governors of the Estonian and Latvian lands. Lithuania, however, resisted the Teutonic Knights long enough to become the last remaining pagan nation in Europe (only converting to Christianity in the late fourteenth century, following dynastic union with Poland). Lithuania grew into the Grand Duchy of Lithuania, stretching into modern Ukraine, and raised a clutch of heroic leaders on whom nationalists could later draw in the nineteenth and twentieth centuries. Vytautas and Mindaugas, Lithuanian grand dukes, remain popular boys' names in modern Lithuania. Following the dynastic union, Poles, rather than Germans, emerged as the ruling class in the Lithuanian lands. Crucially, Lithuania also acted as a buffer between the German lands to the west and Estonia and Latvia to the northeast, preventing what could otherwise have been a mass migration of ethnic German peasants to the lands controlled by German nobility.

Nevertheless, the Baltic lands became increasingly multinational. While the Baltic Germans long ruled the region, and the three titular nations made up most of the peasant population: Poles lived in Lithuania's Eastern Marshes; Jews (also known as Litvaks in Lithuania, where Vilnius was a major centre of Yiddish culture) lived in Lithuania and, to a lesser extent, Latvia; Russian Old Believers were in eastern Latvia and small Roma communities were scattered around the country. The rapid post–Second World War influx of Russophones created large new minorities in Estonia and Latvia.

There is little recorded information about the detailed rhythm of life enjoyed by the native Baltic peasants who lived under varying degrees of serfdom until the early nineteenth century (and later in Lithuania and Latgale in what is now the eastern region of Latvia). Life was likely particularly 'solitary, poor, nasty, brutish, and short' (Hobbes, 1651, p. 89). Their cultures were ignored and neglected by the ruling Germans, allowing them to maintain distinct primordial identities based on their unique (and difficult-to-master) languages, ancient pagan rituals and traditions that were never entirely eradicated despite eventual mass conversion to Christianity.[4] As Anatol Lieven (1994, pp. 110–111) points out, 'until the early nineteenth century, peasant folk songs and legends were, to all intents and purposes, the essence of Latvian and Estonian culture'.

Just as the Baltic Sea is the youngest sea in the world, formed only 10–15,000 years ago, the three Baltic nations are among Europe's youngest, created at the tail end of Central Europe's arc of nation awakening. European trends take longer to reach the Baltic periphery of the region. They do eventually arrive, however, and such was the case with the Enlightenment. In Miroslav Hroch's (1985) terms, it arrived 'belatedly' but took hold furiously fast.[5] As elsewhere in nineteenth-century Europe, the Enlightenment contributed to a national awakening (*ärkamisaeg* in Estonian, *atmoda* in Latvian and *atgimimas* in Lithuanian) of the Baltic nations, which began as the region modernised through socio-economic change, resulting in increased educational attainment (Gellner, 1983). National awakening describes the resulting discovery, codification and mass communication of distinctive Baltic identities by the first wave of modernised and educated Estonian, Latvian and Lithuanian professionals in the mid-nineteenth century. It remains a key concept, linking the contemporary Baltic states with the (slumbering) ancient communities of the region as well as with early Baltic nationalists in the nineteenth century (the first awakening), the statesmen and soldiers who led Estonia, Latvia and Lithuania to statehood at the end of the First World War (the second awakening) and with the national movements of the late Soviet era (the third awakening). Indeed, contemporary nationalist politicians have talked of the need for a twenty-first century fourth awakening to allow the Baltic nations to rediscover and return to their core national values (Dzintars, 2010).

Modernisation began with the emancipation of Estonian and Latvian peasants in 1816 and 1819, well before the rest of the Russian Empire (including Lithuania and Latgale) in 1861. The first significant changes in social structure began in the 1840s and 1850s when legislative reforms allowed ethnic Estonians and Latvians to purchase agricultural land (often funded by loans from state mortgage banks) and removed restrictions on migration to urban areas. The resulting increases in agricultural efficiency and productivity led to higher incomes, educational opportunities and social mobility, while industrialisation meant increasing blue-collar and professional urban job opportunities. The sons of Estonian and Latvian peasants were capable of seizing the opportunity to enter higher education thanks to the earlier efforts of rural Lutheran German clerics following the teachings of Martin Luther, who had encouraged the reading of the Bible in native tongues. Indeed, Baltic Germans played a key role in developing early Baltic culture. The German cleric and intellectual Johann Gottfried Herder lived in Riga from 1764–1769 and developed a fascination with Latvian peasant folklore and poetry that, he argued, revealed a distinct national culture. Baltic Germans authored and published the first Latvian-language grammar book in 1761, financed the first Estonian-language teaching post at the University of Tartu (then Dorpat) in 1803 and founded the Estonian Learned Society in 1838. By 1897 the Russian census records that 95 per cent of the total population of Estland (Estonia) and 92 per cent of Livland (Latvia minus Latgale) could read, while the average in the Russian Empire as a whole was just 28 per cent (Raun, 1979, p. 115).

By 1885 Estonians had 'evolved into a nation with newspapers, theatre, poetry, and mass cultural events, expressing themselves in a rapidly modernizing language and sustained by a vigorous farm economy' (Taagepera, 1993, p. 31). This was equally true of Latvians and, a few decades later, of Lithuanians, whose national movement only emerged in the 1880s (Balkelis, 2009). Rapid industrialisation of the port cities of Riga, Liepaja and Tallinn, connected to the rest of the Russian Empire through newly constructed rail links, saw a corresponding growth in economic activity, jobs and population. Riga grew from 75,000 in 1860 to 500,000 by 1910. A significant part of this growth was made up of Latvian migration from rural to urban areas: in the 1867 census Latvians made up 23.6 per cent of the population of Riga, but by 1897 this proportion had risen to 45 per cent (Ābols, 2003, p. 98). In the same year Estonians were almost two-thirds of the population of Tallinn. In contrast, the same census revealed that only 2 per cent of the population of Vilnius, the city that would (briefly) become the capital of Lithuania just two decades later, were ethnic Lithuanians. 93 per cent of ethnic Lithuanians remained peasants (Balkelis, 2009, p. 2). Many Lithuanians migrated to North America seeking opportunities to make a better life and by the First World War it was estimated that roughly one-third of all ethnic Lithuanians lived in the United States or Canada. Others found work elsewhere in the Russian Empire – the 1897 census revealed that one-third of educated Lithuanians worked in a different place in the Empire (Balkelis, 2009, p. 24). Lithuanians were hampered by limited professional opportunities and a comparative lack of industrialisation in their part of the Russian Empire – as a buffer zone between Tsarist Russia and Germany, the regime was reluctant to invest in industrialising the Lithuanian lands.

By the mid- to late-nineteenth century, Balts no longer needed to assimilate into the Baltic-German community in order to progress socially. At the end of the nineteenth century, however, Russian authorities, worried by the impact of the unification of Germany on Baltic-German attitudes to the region, attempted to rein in the Baltic nations through a Russification programme. However, it was too little, too late. Indeed, it even promoted the Baltic cultures as the switch to Russian-language teaching in schools and universities increasingly drove Baltic Germans away from the region and increased opportunities for the titular populations.

Creeping liberalisation of political activity in the Russian Empire allowed ethnic Estonians, Latvians and Lithuanians to form associations guarding their own cultural interests. Early organisations were formed in educational institutions. The only university-level institution in the Livonia administrative region, the University of Dorpat (Tartu), attracted Estonians and Latvians, while Lithuanians typically went to St. Petersburg or Moscow. Krišjānis Valdemārs organised 'Tartu Latvian student evenings' and, in 1862, part of the same group, now based in St. Petersburg, began publishing a Latvian-language newspaper, *Pēterburgas Avīze* (*The Petersburg Newspaper*), reaching a circulation of 4,000 within a few years (Page, 1949, p. 25). This group, which came to be known as the *Jaunlatvieši* (Young Latvians[6]), proved the catalyst for a rapidly increasing output of Latvian literature. The group also founded the student fraternity *Lettonia*, the first elite Latvian organisation. A later rival, the Latvian *Jaunstrāvnieki* (New Current) movement was more explicitly political and left-wing, and its leaders were eventually forced into exile (primarily in London and Zurich), largely because they were perceived as a direct political threat to the Tsarist order, unlike the *Jaunlatvieši* who initially focused on cultural, rather than political, autonomy. There was no such deep division between Estonian nationalists – perhaps reflecting the lower level of industrialisation in Estonia. Rather, the emerging Estonian nationalist movement was split between those who pivoted westwards (such as Johannes Voldemar Jannsen, the founder of *Eesti Postimees*), believing that Estonians had a Western European cultural identity tied to Baltic German traditions and to the 'Saint Petersburg patriots' group, which looked to the east because Baltic Germans were seen as oppressors (Smith, 2002). The much smaller Lithuanian national movement – estimated by Miroslav Hroch (1985) at just 290 individuals in 1890 – was also less divided than were the Latvian activists. This indicates the developing sophistication of the Estonian and Latvian national movements, as they developed conflicts and cleavages. However, at this point a key difference emerged between the two northernmost Baltic nations and Lithuania. The Catholic Church, rather than Lutheranism, was key in building

Lithuanian identity and – rather than urban, cosmopolitan students – rurally based priests were the early nationalists.

A wider Estonian, Latvian and Lithuanian civil society also continued to develop: 'funeral savings groups, friendship associations, and cultural associations' began to mushroom, and farmers, teachers and other professions banded together, not least because Balts were still excluded from similar Baltic-German and Russian groups (Freivalds, 1961, p. 26). In the late nineteenth and early twentieth centuries, Estonian Jakob Hurt and Latvian Krišjānis Barons collected and codified existing Estonian and Latvian folklore, the foundation of traditional Baltic culture. A key Latvian organisation was the Riga Latvian Association (*Rigas Latviešu Biedrība*). Founded in 1868, it represented the conservative urban middle class that considered both the *Jaunlatvieši* and the *Jaunstrāvnieki* far too confrontational. It focused on developing Latvian culture, organising the first Latvian theatre in 1868 and published a series of books on topics ranging from popular science to fiction. Its most significant initiative was the first Latvian song festival in 1873, which gathered together Latvians from all regions and acted as a highly visual, emotional demonstration of the existence of a broad Latvian nation – a people with a common culture and language spread across the Latvian lands. Similarly, the Alexander School (*Eesti Aleksandrikool*) mobilised Estonians to finance an Estonian-speaking secondary school, and the first Estonian song festival was organised by Johann Voldemar Jannsen's Vanemuine Choral Society in 1869. These song festivals are still the key public events in the Estonian and Latvian cultural calendars. Lithuanian civil society organised later (and no song festival was held until 1924), largely because so few Lithuanians lived in urban areas. However, song festivals are now also central to Lithuanian cultural identity. A Lithuanian Learned Society was only founded in 1907. Indeed, Lithuanian civil society at that time was largely built on the personal generosity of a single wealthy benefactor, Petras Vileišis, who funded newspapers, published books and supported national organisations based in Vilnius. At one point, he was estimated to have financially supported up to one-third of the Lithuanian community in Vilnius (Balkelis, 2009, p. 43).

Industrialisation allowed left-wing ideas to quickly spread beyond student debates in the universities and, by the turn of the century both urban and, to a lesser extent rural, Baltic territories were dotted with small, illegal groups of social democrats, who were active not just in discussing socialist literature, but also organised demonstrations and even festivities. Debate and discussion eventually led to the formation of political parties. The Lithuanian Social Democratic Party (LSDP) was founded in 1896, the Latvian Social Democratic Workers Party (LSDSP) in 1904 and the Estonian Social Democratic Workers' Association (ESDTU) in 1905. The Russian Social Democratic Workers Party also had supporters in the Baltic territories, as did the Jewish Bund. The key cleavage between Baltic and Russian socialists at this time was national: In contrast to the Russians, the Baltic social democrats supported the creation of some form of autonomous political Baltic units within the Tsarist state.

The social contours of the region had completely changed by the early twentieth century. From the 1866 local parish council elections onwards, Latvians, Estonians and later Lithuanians began gaining valuable political experience. The Baltic region now had a visible, increasingly assertive native Baltic middle-class. The number of Baltic university graduates in medicine, law and other professional programmes rose in tandem with demographic increases in the native Baltic population. A crucial turning point came with the upheavals and disorder of the 1905 revolution, which saw ethnic Estonians, Latvians and Lithuanians (mobilised by economic, social and national concerns) turn on the regional ruling classes. Social democrats played a key role in organising strikes and disturbances in the cities, although they were less influential in the countryside, where 'the peasants rose with savagery against their former masters' (Hiden and Salmon, 1994, p. 21). National assemblies called for autonomy for the Baltic peoples. Acts of aggression against the Baltic Germans in the Estonian and Latvian territories and against local government offices in Lithuania were followed by acts of repression by the Tsarist regime against the peasants. While many of the leading national figures were arrested or fled into exile, this was but a temporary set-back. The risings of 1905 had revealed that Balts could be mobilised en masse. Moreover, post-1905 Duma elections and the resulting legislative experience 'provided a training ground for parliamentary debate and procedure, which stood many of the non-Russian delegates in good stead at a later date' (von Rauch, 1974, p. 15). At the same time, the Baltic nations – and there is no doubt that by this point they were *nations* that shared 'myths and memories, a mass public culture, a designated homeland, economic unity and equal rights and duties for all members' (Smith, 1991, p. 43) – continued urbanising, educating and socialising in addition to accruing valuable democratic and organisational experience that would be utilized as the First World War unexpectedly opened up the opportunity for the Baltic states to first seize political autonomy and then, remarkably, grab a unique opportunity for independent statehood.

1.2   From autonomy to independence: 1914–1920

The heroic, and ultimately successful, battles for independence are central to the national narrative of all three Baltic states. However, while the bravery of statesmen and soldiers is beyond question, the opportunity for independence came from the dual collapse of Tsarist Russia and Imperial Germany. As a result, 'these states were created neither by the foresight of their own leaders nor by any vision of the victorious western allies. They were the product of ruin and disintegration, and only secondarily of positive effort' (Eksteins, 1999, p. 59).

Lithuania and Latvia were swiftly drawn into the First World War's bitter fighting, although Estonian soil escaped military action until the last year of the war. There were two important early developments for Baltic national political identity. First, the German attack led to the formation of Latvian military units, initially part of the Tsarist army, but later organised along national lines and operating in the Baltic languages. Soldiers and officers from these units eventually played a key part in the wars for independence and the subsequent construction of the national Baltic militaries. Second, a significant part of the Baltic populations were evacuated from German-occupied territories to the Russian heartland, where they were neglected by central authorities focused on the war effort. Half a million Lithuanians and 800,000 Latvians (60 per cent of the entire ethnic Latvian population) were evacuated. The administrative vacuum was filled by grassroots organisations such as the Latvian Central Refugee Committee and the Lithuanian War Relief Committee, which proved to be valuable training grounds in political coordination as well as in executive and public management: '[T]he elites that staffed and managed "national committees" for refugee relief evolved (not always smoothly) into the national leadership that clamoured for independent statehood' (Purs, 2007, p. 480).[7] Indeed, the large United States-based Lithuanian diaspora also established in Paris a Lithuanian Information Bureau, which as early as 1916 adopted a resolution calling for an independent Lithuania, although this ambition only appeared on the mainstream Baltic agenda in late 1917.

This political and military experience proved crucial when the tsarist empire collapsed and the Baltic lands found themselves fought over by a combination of Whites (pro-Tsarists), the Red Army, German freebooters, and Baltic nationalists. White forces battled against the Bolsheviks and for the reinstatement of the Russian Empire on pre-1914 lines.[8] The Red Army (including a sizeable unit of Latvian Red Riflemen) fought for the incorporation of the Baltic states into Red Russia (or the Soviet Union as it was later named) and a bewildering number of German freebooters fought for the federation of the Baltic lands into a greater Germany, as well as simply against the Bolsheviks and independence-seeking Balts. At one point *eight* different forces were fighting on Estonian and Latvian soil.[9] This combination of forces led to huge rural and urban destruction that would later hamper the Baltic states' efforts at post-war reconstruction.

Equally disorienting was the flurry of new democratic activity, as a series of competing regional and local councils, congresses and other governing authorities formed and then disintegrated in attempts to fill the administrative vacuum caused by the to and fro of the battling armies. Baltic leaders initially had limited ambitions, calling for autonomous status within a larger Russian federation. At that time there was no substantial international support for independent Baltic states. However, in 1917 the provisional government ceded increased autonomy to the Baltic provinces, recalling the Russian governors and replacing them with ethnic Estonian and Latvian 'government commissars' (von Rauch, 1974, p. 27).

In November 1917, the Estonian Provincial Assembly declared itself the representative of Estonian interests, and the Council of Lithuania in Vilnius represented Lithuanian interests. Two unelected organs initially claimed to represent the Latvian territories: the Provisional National Council, which held meetings in north-east Latvia (controlled by the Red Army) and in Russia, and the Democratic Bloc which operated in Riga and in the western region dominated by German forces. The two merged into the Latvian National Council in 1918. Through the promise of land, these institutions created peasant armies, and they declared independent statehood. However, they did not yet control their territories. At one point almost the entire Latvian government was working from a British warship in the port of Liepaja. International support was critical for Baltic ambitions in the battle against Soviet Russia, with the British also supplying arms and naval support to the Baltic forces, Finland providing men to help the Estonians and the Americans supplying humanitarian relief for the liberated parts of the Baltic lands. Peace treaties with Soviet Russia were signed in 1920, and economic reconstruction began, alongside political construction. The following 20 years saw an initial flowering of democracy, along with economic and political modernisation, although all three states eventually succumbed to relatively mild authoritarian rule.

1.3   The inter-war years

Estonia, Latvia and Lithuania all initially tackled the monumental challenges of constructing new states. They were not alone in this, of course, and the new post-war states in Central and Eastern Europe copied and innovated in equal measure. A new political order was built with written constitutions and national identities constructed through the adoption of flags, anthems, national holidays, monuments, medals and awards, street names and other key national symbols. Different regional dialects were harmonised and codified into distinct Estonian, Latvian and Lithuanian languages (only the Lattgalian dialect still lives to indicate the diversity of the Baltic languages that existed a hundred years ago). Lithuania's political leaders particularly focused on higher education in order to increase titular representation in the professions and urban areas that were initially dominated by Germans, Poles and Jews. Latvia and Lithuania founded two new national universities – the University of Latvia in Riga in 1919 and Kaunas University in 1922. The University of Tartu in Estonia (founded in 1632) began teaching in Estonian for the first time. However, all three were initially hampered by a lack of qualified titular faculty. Perhaps most importantly, the war-ravaged Baltic states needed to construct economic systems capable of providing economic growth and popular legitimacy.

National symbols posed a particularly ticklish challenge. The most visible symbols of the state – flags and national anthems as well as heraldry, state buildings, statues and street names – had to be rapidly created and adopted. Flags are an interesting case study of the different approaches and sources of inspiration open to these state builders. The Estonian blue-black-white tricolour flag had initially been used as a national symbol by the first Estonian student society in the early 1880s and then as the official state flag after the 1918 declaration of independence. However, between 1918 and the adoption of the 1922 Law on the National Flag, its status was disputed and a number of colourful new designs were proposed, many with Nordic themes, as well as one attention-grabbing rising sun motif with a strong resemblance to Japan's flag (Riigi Arhiiv, 2014). Indeed, as late as 2001 a leading Estonian civil servant proposed that Estonia cement its identity as a Nordic, rather than a Baltic, state and adopt a Nordic cross flag in place of a tricolour (Sakkov, 2014, p. 160). The narrative of the red-white-red Latvian flag dates back to the native thirteenth-century warriors who fought the Teutonic knights and purportedly carried a red-white-red flag into battle (having copied the use of this symbol from their opponents). The colours of the flag were readopted by the first Latvian fighting units in the First World War (although some Latvians also supported adopting the first Latvian student fraternity's green-blue-yellow tricolour flag – *Lettonia* – as Estonia did). Lithuania adopted a yellow, green and red tricolour at a 1905 national meeting (the Great Seimas) and did so again at meetings held in 1917 and 1918. The design was put together in imitation of contemporary European flag traditions and with an agreeable set of colours rather than as any explicit link to the past. This combination of looking to the ancient (often imaginary) past, to the national awakening era and Western Europe, as well as straightforward personal taste could also explain the different constitutional combinations that emerged in the new sovereign states.

Economic reconstruction was an immediate concern. The Baltic states had seen much of their manufacturing infrastructure dismantled and moved east during the First World War, and what remained was ravaged by conflict. The Baltic states' population had sharply fallen. On the other hand, the region had been at least partly integrated with capitalist Western Europe and did not face fundamental reforms of the economy as in 1991. The Baltic states suffered from a lack of foreign direct investment in this period, stunting major development opportunities. One important exception was the construction of the Ķeguma Hydroelectic Power station, completed in 1939, constructed with strategic Swedish investors (*Svenska Entreprenad Aktiebolaget* and *Aktiebolaget Elektro-Invest*). As with the economic transition of the early 1990s, trade was redirected away from the Soviet Union, where, of course, the Baltic states had long-standing economic ties as former constituent parts of the Russian Empire. This was done for primarily political reasons – the wish to build closer ties to the West through economic relations, as well as the practical reality that the Soviet Union simply did not want to trade with the Baltic states in the 1920s and 1930s. By the late 1930s, the Baltic economies were closely integrated with the West while trade with the Soviet Union ran at just a few percentage points of the total. Exports were mostly agricultural products, paint and alcoholic beverages as well as textiles and timber, cameras and radios. Although economic recovery was in full-swing by the mid-1920s, it would likely be an exaggeration to state, as some histories have claimed, that living standards and income were broadly similar to those in the Nordic states. In post-war histories this claim often seems to have been made to serve the political purpose of aligning the Baltics with Western Europe, rather than actually being based on data. One of the few detailed comparisons of the Nordic and Baltic economies found that Finland, the poorest of the Nordic states at that time, developed far more quickly than did Estonia in the inter-war era (Myllyntaus, 1992). Nevertheless, although the economies certainly grew in the 1920s, Baltic popular memory remembers the authoritarian years of the 1930s as the golden era of economic development.

All three states elected constituent assemblies to carry out the task of writing the basic law. Estonia adopted a constitution in 1920 with Latvia and Lithuania following in 1922. These constituent assemblies are best conceptualised as the first legislatures rather than as mere transitional bodies. They were both a campaigning and legislative training ground for the Baltic political parties and passed a number of important laws, particularly land reform, while also writing the new constitutions. Land reform law was particularly important in fulfilling a promise to redistribute land to soldiers who had fought for the new states, as well as creating a more equitable society and a new class of stakeholders to support the new regime. This law also undermined the social and economic status of the established Baltic elites in favour of ethnic Balts.

The new constitutions were extremely liberal. The distinguished Estonian-American political scientist Rein Taagepera (1993, p. 53) describes the resulting Estonian political system, largely based on the Swiss constitution, as an 'ultrademocracy'. The State Elder (*Riigivanem* – effectively prime minister but also fulfilling the ceremonial functions of the president, hence the distinctive title to avoid being confused with a mere prime minister) was elected by parliament (*Riigikogu*), but had no power of veto over the legislature. The Estonian constitution placed all political power in the hands of the parliament, with no independent executive or president's office. The only check was a liberal initiative law that allowed 25,000 citizens to put forward or veto new legislation. While the Latvian and Lithuanian constitutional orders were rather more traditional in foreseeing a president with certain veto powers over the executive, parliaments did maintain outsize influence over the executive.

The contours of the new Baltic party systems were shaped by the three major cleavages of the inter-war era. First, a nationalism versus communism divide that was effectively a continuation of the initial independence cleavage (between those who had supported or acted against the independence movement). The second urban versus rural cleavage emerged from both long- and short-term trends: the long-term migration of workers from rural areas to industrial centres, and the post-war break-up of the Baltic-German baronial estates into smaller farms. More than 30,000 new farms were established in Estonia in the 1920s, and three-quarters of the Baltic populations remained employed in the agricultural sector. Moreover, the agrarian parties reflected not just the central role of agriculture in the Baltic economies, but also characterised the roots of Baltic nationalism and also served as conservative parties in the Estonian and Latvian party systems. Farmers did not constitute an entirely cohesive bloc. A core division existed between the 'old' farmers and the 'new' farmers (those who had gained land through the territorial reforms). Their interests did clash and led to a fracturing of the agricultural vote in the second half of the 1920s. The third owners-versus-workers divide was operationalised through the social democratic parties (which were particularly strong in Estonia and Latvia) and the smaller liberal centre parties that represented professionals and the middle class. Estonia and Lithuania, in sharp contrast to Latvia, were relatively homogenous states: 88 per cent of the Estonian population was ethnically Estonian, and many Russians in Estonia (8.2 per cent of the population) were Lutherans rather than Russian Orthodox. Latvia was far more diverse, with Russians, Germans, Byelorussians and Jews representing around a quarter of the population (Plakans, 1995, p. 132). Thus, Latvia's ethnic heterogeneity led to a fourth salient titular versus minority cleavage. Minority parties represented Germans, Russians, Jews and Poles and consistently won 15–17 deputies out of 100 deputies in each parliamentary election and formed a reasonably cohesive bloc. Latvia did not adopt the second 'rights' part of the constitution in 1922, but the 1919 schooling law granted autonomy and state funding to minority schools that contributed to a thriving minority culture.

The Estonian and Latvian party systems were broadly similar, dominated by social democrats on the left, agrarians on the right and smaller liberal, minority and single-issue parties in the middle. Communists were banned, although they often ran behind 'front' parties, doing particularly well in the 1931 Latvian parliamentary election. In Estonia they were further discredited and forced deeper underground after a failed coup on 1 December 1924. Social democrats tended to be the largest and most powerful parliamentary bloc, but the agrarians, typically in coalition with the smaller parties of the centre, dominated the executive office. The Latvian Farmers Union (LZS) was a coalition partner in 11 of the 13 coalition governments, providing 10 of the 13 prime ministers, as well as three of the four presidents (including, of course, Kārlis Ulmanis, who was to lead the coup against the parliament in 1934 and use his powers to appoint himself president).[10] Similarly, the Estonian Farmers

Party (*Maaliit*, subsequently *Põllumeeste kogud*) provided 10 of Estonia's 17 'state elders'. However, the agrarians' share of the vote was gradually chipped away by new farmers' parties. In 1925 the Latvian Smallholders Party was created to specifically look after the interests of the new, small-holding farmers who had benefited from the land reform. And in 1931 the LZS splintered as the New Farmers Party (*Jauno Zemnieku Partija*) was formed and appealed to the same basic constituency. In contrast, the LSDSP participated in only two Latvian government coalitions, although throughout the inter-war era it held the post of parliamentary speaker (a largely symbolic position, although officially the second-ranking statesman in Latvia after the president). Similarly, the Estonian social democrats only once held the prime minister's post and were rarely in executive office. Lithuania's 1926 authoritarian coup ensured that its party democracy was much shorter lived. However, its party system had broadly similar contours to its northern neighbours, with a left-wing bloc rooted in urban areas and an agrarian right wing with large rural support. The biggest difference lies in the centrist parties which, due to the lack of a substantial middle-class vote, were rooted in populism rather than liberalism. Another key difference was the greater role of the Catholic Church in shaping party ideology. However, all three party systems were plagued by fragmentation and instability, with governments typically lasting about one year. Indeed, the limited public opposition to the anti-democratic coups hints at the underlying weakness and lack of deep support for these parties.

Civil society, as well as political parties, initially flourished in the new democracies. Ādolfs Šilde (1976, pp. 544–545) observed that by 1928 Latvia had well over 6,000 different independent organisations. Trade unions were comparatively small and fragmented and, because they were closely affiliated to the social democrats and communists, they had little political influence.[11] Perhaps the most influential non-governmental organisations (NGOs) were the student fraternities, but in a very indirect, opaque way because while many deputies and ministers were members, their affiliation remained hidden from public view (Ščerbinskis, 2005).

Political corruption was a major issue throughout the parliamentary years. Political parties were frequently implicated in corruption scandals that undermined public support for parties and the democratic system (Zirnis and Veveris 2005, 9).[12] Scandals, particularly inappropriate relationships between political elites and the private sector were frequently uncovered by the press. Ādolfs Šilde (1982, p. 268) argued that all Latvian parties in this era had 'grey wallets' (illegal or hidden income), but that the smaller parties, especially the parties with just a few or even just one deputy, were the most open to corruption (particularly selling their votes, or lobbying private interests).[13] Alfrēds Bērziņš (1963, pp. 124–125), a deputy in the final parliamentary calling, recounted his experience in constructing the Latvian government coalition just before the 1934 coup:

> In forming the final Ulmanis government in March 1934, I had the opportunity to talk with the single-deputies about the vote approving the new government. The deputy representing the 'Bank Depositors and Other Aggrieved Party' asked for 60,000 Lats in cash for his vote.

Political corruption certainly contributed towards the malaise that made the authoritarian coups possible. However, there were also a number of additional factors that hastened the 1934 coups. A crisis of confidence in the political system (prompting calls for a new constitutional settlement) as well as the rise of anti-systemic parties and the belated impact of the global economic depression on the Baltic states, all undermined the existing order and created an opportunity for Estonian and Latvian political leaders.

All three states had large right-wing, anti-systemic movements. The first, Iron Wolf (*Geležinis Vilkas*), emerged in Lithuania after the 1926 authoritarian coup and was allied with Prime Minister Augustinas Voldemaras. It was forced underground after Voldemaras was dismissed from his post by President Antanas Smetona in 1929. The groups that emerged in Estonia and Latvia in the early 1930s proved to be far more influential. Latvia's Firecross (*Ugunskrusts*) was formed in January 1932 and then renamed Thundercross (*Pērkoņkrusts*) after Firecross was banned in April 1933. It claimed a membership of 6,000 at its peak in 1933 (von Rauch, 1974, p. 153). However, Estonia had perhaps the most influential right wing group in the Estonian War of Independence Veterans' League (*Eesti Vabadussõjalaste Liit* – popularly known as 'Vaps'). Founded in 1929, it garnered sufficient support in the early 1930s to block attempts by the government to adopt a new constitution, while also gathering public support for its own constitutional plan creating a popularly elected president with strong executive powers. Vaps attacked the whole democracy experiment, pushing for a strong executive and 'democracy without parties' (Kasekamp, 1993, p. 264). In terms of organisation, uniform and symbols they looked like the fascist parties of central Europe and Italy but claimed they were not national socialists and 'that [their] ideas were purely the products of their native soil' (Kasekamp, 1999, p. 594).[14]

The political systems of all three proved unable to deliver stable government, and the new democratic order was left vulnerable. The economic depression of the 1930s further undermined public confidence in the Estonian and Latvian political systems, leading to a radical fall in exports, the exit of foreign capital and a rise in unemployment. The political elite initially offered constitutional reforms aimed at strengthening the presidency and weakening the parliamentary system.[15] Social democrats, however, opposed strengthening the presidency, largely because they realised that there was very little possibility of a left-wing presidential candidate winning the poll.

Lithuania's authoritarian era began after a coup d'état in December 1926. It was of a nature different to the later Estonian and Latvian coups in that it was instigated by the Lithuanian military and targeted an incumbent left-wing government that was granting concessions to Poles in the field of education as well as threatening cuts to the defence budget. However, the form of government was similar to that in neighbouring Estonia and Latvia. Antanas Smetona was a patriarchal figure (the 'leader of the nation') with a hierarchically organised party to support his regime.

The later coups – 1934, Estonian (March) and Latvian (May) – were made possible by the atmosphere of malaise and dissatisfaction that meant there was very little popular protest. This was also partly because political parties were disbanded and the press censored, although there is little doubt that by the early 1930s the democratic regimes had little popular support. Estonia's establishment feared that the insurgent Vaps movement would see its candidate, leading in the signature gathering campaign, likely to be elected president in 1934. At the same time the acting head of state, Konstantin Päts, was struggling to collect the 10,000 signatures needed to stand as a candidate. As a result, Päts invoked his constitutional power to rule by decree for six months (ironically granted through the new Vaps-supported constitution), announced a state of emergency, banned Vaps and arrested 400 of its leaders. Thus began what Estonians call 'the era of silence'. In Latvia, the incumbent, Prime Minister Ulmanis, with the quiet acceptance of President Alberts Kviesis (who was apparently informed of the coup by phone and then carried on with his normal daily routine), suspended parliament, banned parties and ruled by decree. Ulmanis and Päts initially argued that they had acted because of a threatened coup by the extreme right-wing Thundercross and Vaps movements. However, the coups were also a reaction to rapidly falling support for the establishment parties as key elections approached (presidential and then parliamentary in Estonia, parliamentary in Latvia).

The three Baltic authoritarian regimes were broadly similar. Each was governed by just one leader throughout the authoritarian years. Konstantin Päts (Estonia), Kārlis Ulmanis (Latvia) and Antanas Smetona (Lithuania) were all key members of the national awakening movements and had been prominent activists during the battles for autonomy and independence, holding executive posts in the first governments. Päts had even served as a deputy mayor of Tallinn before the 1905 revolution. Their early and long political activism gave their regimes a great deal of legitimacy – having risked their lives and welfare for the aim of independence, they had a broad base of sympathy to draw on, portraying themselves as well-meaning, paternal 'fathers of the state'. Päts and Ulmanis had gone into exile after the 1905 revolution, with the former spending a half decade in Switzerland and Finland, and the latter eight years in the United States, even earning a bachelor's degree at the University of Nebraska. Smetona's time abroad was shorter, coming in 1918 and 1919, when he lobbied in Germany and Scandinavia for an independent Lithuania. Nevertheless, this unique international experience imparted to all three a greater worldliness than many of their peers, and all would have followed the successful progress of authoritarianism in Europe in the inter-war years. The leaders were central to all three authoritarian regimes and created 'Führer cults'. In 1936 Päts replaced the Estonian coat of arms on stamps with his own portrait, while Ulmanis organised a string of extravagant public events to celebrate his regime (Hanovs and Tēraudkalns, 2013).

The era of Baltic authoritarian rule was benign in comparison to other authoritarian regimes in East-Central Europe. In the case of Latvia 'there were no mass killings or settling old political scores through violent action, no mass-long term imprisonment of political opponents, or intimidation through the systematic use of state coercion' (Plakans, 1995, p. 133). However, 300 politicians, primarily communists, social democrats and members of Thundercross were interned in prison camps for up to two-and-a-half years (Pabriks and Purs, 2001, p. 21). Even the wives and children of leading opposition politicians were detained or placed under house arrest (Stranga, 1991).

Political parties were banned. Estonia and Lithuania created ruling parties – the Lithuanian Nationalist Union (*Lietuvių Tautininkų Sąjunga*) and Päts's Patriotic League (*Isamaaliit*) – although they were far less structured than the National Socialists in Germany. Ulmanis ruled by decree without a political party, although he created voluntary associations with which to bind individuals to the state, and he intended to replace political parties with social organisations as the voice of the people. In a 1938 speech he outlined his vision of a parliament that would represent the people directly, without political parties as mediators (Freivalds, 1961, p. 140). A few banned parties moved their operations underground (indeed, the communist parties had been operating underground for many years). However, most simply faded away, revealing underlying weakness in both party organisation and deep-rooted popular support.

The Latvian government was structured along the lines of previous cabinets of ministers, albeit without a parliament to ratify laws. All ministerial appointments were made by Ulmanis himself.[16] He created a series of 'chambers' (*kameras*), each with 90–150 members (with one-third of the membership rotated annually), appointed by the ministry they were affiliated with, beginning with the Economics and Culture ministries. Päts also created 17 similar chambers by 1936. However, in both Estonia and Latvia the ministries were not accountable to the chambers, nor did the chambers fulfill anything more than a strictly formal, procedural function. Indeed, the chambers had neither over-sight functions nor independent powers, and they were manipulated by the authoritarian regimes. In 1937, Päts used a referendum and the constituent assembly to pass a new constitution that came into force on 1 January 1938. The new constitution created a presidential office, elected by a constituent assembly (a post taken up by Päts), and a bicameral legislature. This was more a formalisation of the existing order than the beginning of a loosening of the reins, and there certainly appears to be little evidence supporting Kristian Gerner's and Stefan Hedlund's (1993, p. 58) assertion that all three Baltic states were well on the way to re-democratisation by 1938. Rather, this procedure was intended to give Päts greater legitimacy and authority rather than loosening reins.

Treatment of minorities became more harshly nationalist. Many of the liberal minority laws and regulations of the democratic era were overturned. In Latvia, for example, restrictions on the use of the Russian and German languages were introduced in the private and state sectors, and minority publications censored. All ethnic Latvian children, even those with only one Latvian parent, were forced to attend a Latvian-speaking school. Parts of the economy, which pre-1934 had been under minority ownership, were nationalised because Ulmanis believed that they should be under Latvian ownership (Smith 1996, p. 150). Indeed, this era also saw increased state intervention in the economy. The German presence in the Baltic states all but disappeared in late 1939, when many Baltic Germans followed Hitler's offer to 'return to the Reich'.

However, the roots of later Baltic inaction were unintentionally sown by the authoritarian leaders, who created regimes with little or no internal discussion or debate. In contrast to Finland, when the Soviet Union began to threaten the Baltic states in 1939, there was no energetic public debate on how to react. Of course, the Baltic militaries were far smaller and weaker than the Soviet forces (although the latter proved to be less impressive than expected), and the policies of neutrality ensured that the Balts had no military alliances or partners to turn to and foreign policy consisted 'of hoping against hope' (Plakans, 1995, p. 142). The previously supremely self-confident Päts, Ulmanis and Smetona were seemingly paralysed into inaction and the Baltic states meekly succumbed to Soviet rule.

1.4   War and occupation

The Baltic states were occupied three times between 1940 and 1944, as the Second World War engulfed the eastern littoral of the Baltic Sea. All three occupations were marked by the violent repression of Estonian, Latvian and Lithuanian society.[17] The first Soviet occupation in 1940 saw the deportation of more than 40,000 Balts to *Gulag* hard labour camps between 13–14 June (Plakans, 2011, p. 347). The second saw German occupying forces virtually eradicate the Jewish and Roma minorities in the region. The third saw the Soviet Union carry on from where it left off, with further deportations. These events still resonate today because the German occupation, in which ethnic Balts were not the primary focus of terror, is less grimly remembered, while the first 12 months of Soviet occupation have gone down in Latvian history as 'the terrible year' (*baigais gads*). In contrast, the German occupation, which targeted Jews rather than the titular inhabitants, is simply recalled as the 'German era' in Latvia (*vācu laiks*). The experience of the first year of Soviet occupation saw Russians replace Baltic Germans and Poles as the most feared and disliked minority in the region.

The pattern of takeover was similar in all three states. The first Soviet occupation followed the 23 August 1939 signing of the secret protocols of the Molotov–Ribbentrop pact, which sliced Eastern Europe into two spheres of influence. Estonia, Latvia and eventually Lithuania fell into the Soviet sphere. The Soviet Union then claimed to be threatened by the Baltic states, demanded that 'mutual assistance agreements' be signed, and then moved troops and political advisors into the three states (25,000 each in Estonia and Latvia). This was followed in 1940 by Soviet claims that the terms of the treaties had been broken, leading to more troops crossing the borders, to the forced dismissal of the acting cabinets and to new, hand-picked Soviet governments. As Soviet officials took hold of the region, each Baltic state held visibly falsified elections, followed by the coming to power of Soviet-friendly puppet governments. In August 1940 the newly elected Baltic legislatures sent delegates to Moscow to successfully apply for membership in the Soviet Union. This pattern of takeover was at least partially repeated in early 2014, as modern Russia annexed Crimea, causing understandable apprehension in the Baltic region as politicians reached for their history books. Sovietisation followed as industries were nationalised, personal property over 220 square meters confiscated and larger farms broken up into smaller units. Domestic currencies were replaced by the Soviet rouble at confiscatory rates and any savings over 1,000 roubles were seized. The few remaining parties and NGOs were banned. The last vestiges of independent statehood were the diplomatic corps, which refused to return home. Indeed, all three states maintained legations in the United States until 1991.

Although less violent against the titular populations, the German occupation, which lasted from summer 1941 to autumn 1944, further advanced this destruction. A small number of Baltic Germans returned to the Baltic States in administrative positions, many 'with grudges against the Latvians' and the other titular Baltic nations (Eksteins, 1999, p. 135). The *Reichskommisariat Ostland* – an administrative unit composed of Latvia, Estonia, Lithuania and Belarus – was created to govern the Baltic territories. Private property was not restored nor were savings retrieved. The Jewish population was particularly targeted by the German authorities, with groups of Baltic auxiliary police (often former members of the extremist *Pērkoņkrusts* and Vaps organisations) collaborating with German SS *Einsatzgruppen* and carrying out executions. Almost all Estonia's 1,000 Jews were executed by *Einsatzgruppen A*, which included some Estonians. Far larger numbers of Latvians and Lithuanians participated in the Holocaust (Ezergailis 1996). However, the horrors of the Baltic Holocaust have been more salient to outside observers than to Latvians or Lithuanians who, having been victims of mass Soviet deportations, have found it difficult to summon up sympathy for the victims of the Holocaust.

Germany enlisted over 100,000 Latvians and almost 40,000 Estonians in combat Waffen SS units (only German citizens could join the Wehrmacht, thus the Balts were enlisted into Waffen SS units).

Lithuanians also fought along with the Germans, but resisted the creation of national Waffen SS units. Most Latvians served in the 15th and 19th Latvian Legion divisions, and Estonians in the 20th Legion division, created in 1943 in an attempt to push back the Soviet advance. While some may have been convinced Nazis, the vast majority were fighting against Soviet forces to avoid a repetition of the 1940–1941 'terrible year'. Indeed, many probably hoped to repeat the 1917–1920 trick of artfully switching sides to eventually see the re-emergence of independent Baltic states. This was not to be. Nevertheless, this is now one of the key historical disputes between Balts and Russians. The annual commemorations of these Waffen SS units lead Russians to accuse Balts of fascism while Balts, especially Latvians, remain determined to honour a generation of young men torn between two totalitarian systems.

The decision to annex the Baltic states into the Soviet Union, rather than give them the nominal independence enjoyed by Soviet satellites such as Poland or Czechoslovakia, opened the three states up to large-scale migration (something that the satellites did not experience). It also led to a differing interpretation on the Baltic states' formal status for that half century. To the international community and ethnic Balts this was undoubtedly a period of occupation.[18] Indeed, some scholars describe this period as one of 'colonization' rather than mere occupation (Taagepera, 1993). Epp Annus (2012) pondered this issue in quite some depth in a *Journal of Baltic Studies* article, concluding that while the Soviet era began as an occupation it eventually adopted some of the characteristics of a colonisation, in that land and other resources were exploited by the Soviet Union. However, to the Soviet authorities and the many hundreds of thousands of Russophones who migrated to the region after 1944, it was a voluntary incorporation. The Russian-speaker argument runs something like this: The events of 1940 were not an occupation because the Baltic governments agreed to allow Soviet forces to enter their countries. In contrast, Finland's leaders did not agree and, after bitter fighting in the Winter War (November 1939–March 1940), the Soviets settled for annexing parts of eastern Finland. Thus the Baltic states were annexed and incorporated into the Soviet Union, but not occupied. The Soviets point out that the Estonian, Latvian and Lithuanian governments (elected after Soviet forces had entered the states) signed agreements for the Baltic states to join the Soviet Union. These debates are not purely academic. They form the central cleavage in contemporary Latvian politics. One Latvian newspaper interviewed more than half of the Russophone Harmony Centre's (*Saskaņas Centrs*, SC) parliamentary deputies and found that

none of those interviewed accepted the events of 1940 as an occupation (Ugaine, 2011).

The post–Second World War Russophone migration to the Baltic
states was partly through economic necessity. Estonia lost almost 20 per
cent of its population between 1939 and 1944. In Latvia, estimates as
to the number of refugees who migrated westwards vary from 120,000
to 150,000. The refugees were overwhelmingly 30–50 year-old educated
professionals and their families. Seventy per cent of the teaching staff
of the University of Latvia and the Latvian Agricultural University (the
two leading higher education institutions in inter-war Latvia) emigrated
to the West (Spekke, 1952, p. 87). Between 200,000 and 370,000 Balts
were deported after 1944 (Senn, 1958, p. 124; Misiunas and Taagepera,
1983, p. 73).

For Soviet citizens, the Baltic states were an attractive destination,
being wealthier and more developed than other parts of the Soviet
Union. Between 1945 and 1955 the population of the Latvian republic
increased by some 650,000, of whom only 115,000 were ethnic
Latvians: these were largely sovietised Latvians who had elected to stay
in the Soviet Union after the Russian Revolution of 1917 (Plakans 1995,
p. 154). Migration continued well into the 1960s and 1970s, albeit at
a slower tempo. The authorities justified it at the time by stating that
there was an urgent need for manpower as the Baltic states were industrialised – after all, they had lost some 20 per cent of their population
during and after the war. However, other scholars have argued that the
main aim was subjugation and colonisation of the region (Taagepera,
1993, p. 82). Lithuania escaped this immigration largely because the
country was far less industrialised than its two Baltic neighbours to the
north, and it also had a higher domestic birth rate and a large excess
rural population that could be urbanised, as well as an initially fear-
some 'Forest Brothers' opposition guerrilla movement. Moreover, the
native-born Lithuanian communist leadership was more nationalist
than Estonia's and Latvia's, using its ties with Moscow (including with
the influential soviet ideologist Mikhail Suslov) to attract investment
partly in order to impress the large Lithuanian diaspora living in the
United States (Alexeyeva, 1985).

Cultural Russification entailed marginalisation of the Baltic languages
in state institutions, although the Baltic languages remained in use
at the republic level in radio broadcasts, television and newspapers.
The Soviet period also saw an adjustment of the core territory of the
Baltic states. Estonia lost approximately 2,000 square km (5 per cent
of its territory) as the Estonia-Russia border was moved 12 kilometers

westwards. In the case of Latvia, the district and town of Abrene (about 1,300 square km, or 2 per cent of Latvia's territory, and known in Russia as Pytalovo), which had been on the Latvian side of the border when the Latvian–Russian peace treaty was signed in Riga on 11 August 1920, was annexed to the Pskov district, in the Russian SSR, in November 1944. Lithuania was in a position completely different to the other two Baltic states, in that it regained territory (Vilnius and Klaipeda) following the Soviet occupation, although some land was handed over to the Belarussian SSR. Post-1991 Lithuania did have a minor territorial conflict with Belarus over the small Adutiškis railway station that had been part of inter-war Lithuania but changed hands in the Soviet era. However, this issue was not as serious as that which affected the other two Baltic states, and territory has not been a disputed issue for Lithuania (only the most extreme and marginal fringes of Polish nationalism occasionally call for the return of Vilnius and other pre–Second World War Polish territory). In contrast, the territorial losses remain an open sore in Estonia and Latvia. Although few ethnic Estonians and Latvians remain in these territories, their loss is seen as a humiliation by nationalist politicians who still hope to regain the territory someday. However, this is unlikely. While Balts look to the inter-war states as the defining era of their territorial borders, Russia and Poland look even farther back in history. Nevertheless, this territorial issue is a major mobiliser of the nationalist and radical right political forces in Estonia and Latvia, complicating the signing of Estonian and Latvian border treaties with Russia after 1991.

After the Second World War, the Baltic states were rapidly industrialised, urbanised and collectivised. In the inter-war period the majority of the population had lived in rural areas. This was reversed by the 1950s and, by 1980, 70 per cent of the Latvian population lived in urban areas, leading to housing shortages and another source of conflict between ethnic Latvians and Russian speakers (Lieven, 1994, p. 97). Rapid industrial expansion – based on light industry, the production of consumer goods, food processing, the military-industrial complex and steel-production – led to fast economic growth in the 1950s. Agriculture was collectivised only after the deportations of 1949 eradicated opposition and, by 1951, 98.4 per cent of peasant households had been incorporated into collective farms (Smith, 1996, p. 151). However, this had the effect of further distancing Baltic peasants from supporting Soviet power and also led to a continuing decline in agricultural productivity. A half century later peasants in one rural community in Latvia still associated collectivisation 'with arbitrariness, unreasonableness and injustice' (Skultans, 1997, p. 175).

The Soviet era witnessed varying levels of repression. The Stalin era was the harshest, although the 'thaw' that followed the death of Stalin in 1953 had its limits. In this period, Latvian national communists discovered that there were strict parameters to the reforms that Moscow would allow. Seizing the opportunities that the more liberal environment offered, a number of nationalist Latvian communists had pushed for an end to Russification. This group, led by Eduards Berklavs, the deputy chair of the Soviet Council of Ministers (who was to resurface as a founder in the late 1980s of the Latvian National Independence Movement: *Latvijas Nacionālā Neatkarības Kustība*, or LNNK), sought to increase use of the Latvian language among party and administration functionaries, limit the migration of Russian speakers into Latvia and decrease Latvian industrial dependence on Soviet raw materials (Pabriks and Purs, 2001). However, Khruschev moved against the national communists, and Berklavs and 2,000 other leading Latvian communists were dismissed from their positions. The overwhelmingly Russian composition of the top Communist Party (CP) leadership in Estonia and Latvia (many of whom were ethnic Estonians and Latvians who had settled in Soviet Russia and were regarded as Russians by the local Estonians and Latvians) meant the Baltic communist parties were identified as defending the interests of Russophones rather than Balts, and Latvians never made up a majority in the party (in contrast to Estonia and Lithuania), despite party membership becoming a prerequisite for career development.

Indeed, the Soviet regime never gained legitimacy among the titular Baltic population, and anti-Soviet activities continued throughout the Soviet era. Initially the opposition was armed. Several tens of thousands of partisans hid in the many forests of the Baltic states and attacked Soviet forces and local communists until the mid-1950s. The Forest Brothers (*Metsavennad* in Estonia, *Meža brāļi* in Latvia and *Miško broliai* in Lithuania) numbered some 170,000 partisans in total, with the largest numbers and greatest level of organisation in Lithuania (where partisans published newspapers and even had an officer corps), followed by Latvia (Misiunas and Taagepera, 1983). They received very little support from the West and that which they did obtain was often botched or compromised (Bower, 1993). There were also occasional spontaneous violent demonstrations after major sporting events or rock concerts (as well as counter-demonstrations by Russians against 'fascist' Balts), anti-regime graffiti and a refusal to speak Russian or, in reverse, a Baltic language (Alexeyeva, 1985, p. 92).

Dissident activity, in the form of *samizdat* and occasional demonstrations continued throughout the Soviet era, accelerating in the 1970s when it took the form of cultural renewal. Folklore dance groups and choirs began to mushroom (as in the nineteenth century), and students travelled to the Latvian countryside to renovate old churches and other buildings of national significance. The 1970s also saw an acceleration of appeals to the West and public acts of protest. In 1971, 17 leading Latvian communists sent a letter to communist parties in Western Europe complaining about the Russification of Latvia. In October 1972, a group of Estonian dissidents sent a memorandum to the United Nations requesting the restoration of Estonian statehood and the sending of international election monitors. In the same year a Lithuanian high school student in Kaunas protested Soviet occupation by self-immolation in a central square. In 1979, intellectuals from all three Baltic states called for the nullification of the Molotov–Ribbentrop pact in the Baltic Charter and, in 1980, an Estonian 'Letter of Forty' protested cultural Russification in Estonia. At the same time, in Estonia there were a number of small grassroots clubs, such as *Club Tõru* (Club Acorn, ostensibly a book-lovers' club) and *Noor Tartu* (Young Tartu, aimed at preserving towns) that encouraged discussion and debate of the past, and were eventually the basis for the political plurality of the post-1991 era (Bennich-Björkman, 2007).

Opposition grew as the Soviet Union's economic performance declined in the early 1980s, with the easily accessible natural resources that had driven economic growth since the 1920s becoming scarcer and more expensive to extract. Growth was probably flat in the 1980s, meaning that the standard of living for the majority of the Soviet Union's population was slipping (Rutland, 1994, p. 134). This exacerbated the main elements of the social crisis that had been building since the 1960s: A housing shortage and a decline in the quality of health care, reflected in a rapidly falling average life expectancy as well as in rampant alcoholism. In 1985, the accession to power of Mikhail Gorbachev, who attempted to tackle these challenges, set in motion the chain of events that saw the Baltic states renew their independence by 1991.

1.5 Downfall

The initial impetus for the momentous drive to independence in the late 1980s came from Gorbachev's twin policies of *glasnost* (openness) and *perestroika* (restructuring). The Baltic national movements seized the new openness to protest historical injustices and expose the illegitimacy of Baltic incorporation into the Soviet Union. Political and economic restructuring led to the creation of new republic-level policies and institutions designed to distance the three states from Soviet power. Initially cooperating hand-in-glove, by 1988 Moscow and the Baltics had diverged. The Baltic states, who were at the leading edge of protest in the Soviet Union, encouraging secessionist movements elsewhere in the Soviet Union, first edged towards autarky, then political sovereignty and finally full independence. The parting of the ways was not easy or exclusively peaceful. Latvia and Lithuania, in particular, bore the full force of Soviet economic sanctions and military operations. Ironically, the cultural autonomy they enjoyed as Union SSRs, with Baltic language television and radio stations, newspapers and magazines, publishers and universities, laid the basis for continuing opposition 40 years after incorporation: 'The policies pursued by the Soviet regime in the individual republics, whilst clearly *anti-nationalist*, were far from being *anti-national*' (Smith, 2001, p. xxii).

The émigré communities also played a role, albeit secondary, in the Baltic revolutions. They had proved to be remarkably resilient, creating myriad cultural, political and even financial institutions, and resisting Soviet attempts to destabilise and discredit their activities by disseminating 'vitrolic propaganda against them' (Zake, 2010a, p. vii). Baltic song festivals took place all around the world, and Baltic cultural centres, summer camps and Sunday schools passed the language and traditions down to the next generation. Émigrés took advantage of the Western powers' non-recognition of the Soviet occupation to maintain diplomatic missions in Washington DC and London. An Estonian government-in-exile that claimed legal continuity with the 1940 Päts regime operated in Oslo (although much of the leadership lived in Stockholm) from 1944 until 1992. The sheer size of the several-hundred-thousand strong émigré communities allowed them to publish newspapers and books and to finance an extensive lobbying effort that proved particularly effective in the United States, where they variously portrayed the Soviet regime as colonial, anti-human rights, totalitarian and the initiator of a holocaust against the titular Baltic publics. In the 1980s the exile communities donated ideas, equipment and cash, alongside lobbying efforts in Western capitals, to usher events along.

The Baltic revolution began at the grassroots level with small, brave, illicit organisations mostly led by young people unbowed by the repressions of the Stalin era. These groups initially had little money, few opportunities to publish and almost no access to media. However, they did have popular legitimacy and fast-growing public support. Their primary instrument was public protest. They organised public meetings, demonstrations and rallies and other events that brought together increasing numbers of people. It began in the summer of 1987, when the then-tiny, blue-collar Helsinki-86 organisation led a small nationalist protest on 14 June to commemorate the 1941 deportations. Helsinki-86 had begun life in 1986 attempting to gate-crash a US–Soviet meeting in Jūrmala, Latvia, and later sent handwritten letters to international organisations and statesmen pleading the Baltic case for independence. Further demonstrations followed on 23 August (marking the signing of the Molotov–Ribbentrop pact) and 18 November (Latvia's Independence Day). Mobilisation on dates of historical salience – initially known as the calendar riots (as an historical reference to the reformation in Riga), but later renamed the calendar demonstrations, a better reflection of their intrinsically peaceful nature – set a regular rhythm of opposition and continued right up until the fall of the Soviet Union in August 1991 (Trapans, 1991, p. 28). The early protest leaders were arrested, imprisoned and in many cases sent into exile in the West. But the momentum was set. The culmination for the protests was the August 1989 'Baltic Way' that saw two million Balts link hands to form a more or less continuous human chain across the Baltic states. It was memorable both for its size (two-fifths of the entire Baltic population participated), and for its unmatched demonstration of Baltic unity.

The protests can be arranged into several categories. First, there were groups and individuals motivated by religion, especially in Lithuania, where the Catholic Church had long been a centre of political opposition, publishing the 'Chronicles on the Catholic Church in Lithuania' since the late 1960s. In Latvia, Rebirth and Renewal (*Atdzimšana un Atjaunošanās*) was founded in June 1987 by Lutheran clergymen challenging restrictions on religious freedoms. This 'rebirth' primarily took the form of renovating old churches, but also had an explicit spiritual element that stood in stark contrast to the atheism of the Soviet regime. However, religious organisations were far less influential in Estonia, where the only hint of a religious dimension came from the Heritage Society's restoration of monuments, including rural churches.

Second, other protest groups were driven by a sense of injustice that the titular nations were being marginalised in the Baltic states. The first significant nationalist group was Helsinki-86, which recorded human-rights abuses and later organised the first calendar demonstrations.

These activities were later copied in Estonia where, on 23 August 1987, the Estonian Group for the Publication of the Secret Protocols of the Molotov–Ribbentrop Pact organised the first significant demonstration. A number of the Helsinki-86 activists, as well as Estonia's Tiit Madisson drifted into radical and extreme-right politics after independence. They were brave, unbending critics of the Soviet state but almost equally disillusioned by the open, liberal regimes that took root after independence.

A third group was driven by environmental concerns. In Latvia, the Environmental Protection Club (*Vides Aizsardzības Klubs* – VAK), challenged the authority of the state through opposition to big infrastructure projects that were harmful to the Latvian environment. VAK had many cases to draw on. Latvia had the second-highest level of air pollution in the Soviet Union, and after Leningrad, Riga had the dirtiest drinking water in the Soviet Union, actually experiencing an outbreak of cholera in 1988 (Thompson, 1992, p. 177). VAK began its activities with opposition to the construction of a hydroelectric power station on the river Daugava, and then opposition to the construction of a Riga metro system. The founder of VAK, Dainis Ivāns, went on to be the chairman of the Latvian People's Front (*Latvijas Tautas Fronte* – LTF). In the same way, Estonians mobilised to resist plans to develop phosphorite mining in the country's Rakvere region, including plans for settling 30,000 new Soviet migrants in Estonia. Fears of the fallout from Chernobyl mustered Lithuanians, who shared a border with Belarus.

All these groups placed history at the centre of their dissidence. Indeed, both Juris Dreifelds (1996) and Clare Thompson (1992) argued that history was the central motif of the Baltic independence movements. In the case of Latvia, for example: Rebirth and Renewal was reclaiming the Latvian religious past in the form of old churches; Helsinki-86 marked significant days in Latvian history; and VAK was protecting the land that Latvians had long lived on. This sense of historic injustice was to be a key driving force of the independence movement, temporarily uniting its many different strands.

Another key turning point was the 'revolt of the intellectuals' (Park, 1994). This was the moment that mainstream Soviet organisations, particularly the 'creative' unions and public cultural figures, first distanced themselves, then turned away and against the regime. This undoubtedly gave greater legitimacy to dissident activity and chipped away at the monolithic image of the Soviet state. Indeed, it was the Latvian Writers' Union that called for the creation of a popular front at its June 1988 plenum and, among other things, also called for increased protection for the Latvian language and challenged the legitimacy of Soviet control by publicly stating that Latvia had been occupied in 1940. The media played a crucial role by informing, motivating and mobilising this growing and unprecedented level of public opposition. Indeed, the Estonian Popular Front (*Rahvarinne*) was created as a result of brainstorming on a live television programme. Radio and television broadcast the major political debates in the Baltic and all-Soviet legislatures, and newspapers gradually wriggled away from CP control from early 1987 onwards. In Latvia the *Labvakar!* (*Good Evening!*) television show, first broadcast in Latvia on 31 January 1988, worked in harmony with the independence movement, at one point reaching 84 per cent of its potential audience. At that time there were a limited number of Baltic television channels (just two in Latvia) in the titular languages. But, between 1987 and 1993, 500 new periodicals appeared in Estonia (Ruutsoo, 1996, p. 100). Popular culture is a good indicator of the openness of the Soviet system – revealing what was, and was not, tolerated at certain times. The key year of increased openness was 1989. At this point, Gorbachev's *perestroika* and *demokratizacija* had moved forward enough to tolerate outright calls for Baltic independence. At a cultural level, this was illustrated by the annual Latvian 'Mikrofona' song competition where, on one gala evening, the best Latvian songs of each year were performed before a live audience and simultaneously broadcast on television. In 1988, the 'Mikrofona' concert featured émigré Latvian groups, but by 1989 two of the leading songs were openly calling for independence: 'Freedom for the Baltics' (*'Brīvība Baltijai'*) performed by Opus Pro, and 'Baltics Awake' (*'Atmostās Baltija'*) sung by Viktors Zemgalis.

However, even as momentum was building towards independence by the late 1980s, the Baltic independence movements did not have a grand strategy for achieving that independence 'in the way that professional military planners and communist revolutionaries had studied possible paths to success' (Clemens, 1991, p. 119). Indeed, there were many disputes among Baltic activists on how independence could best be achieved. In Estonia and Latvia in 1988 this crystallised into two sides with two strategies: radical nationalists and moderate popular fronts. Lithuania, with its small minority, Russian speakers and Poles, population, did not see a separate nationalist movement emerge. Rather, nationalists were a part of the popular front movement.

Radical nationalists in Latvia were represented by LNNK, which was almost exclusively ethnic Latvian. LNNK was the first large Baltic movement to convene a founding congress (June 1988), and the movement claimed a fee-paying membership of over 10,000 by 1989 (Trapans, 1991,

p. 29). A second even more radical group were the Citizens' Committees in Estonia and Latvia, which were initiated by the most nationalist wing of the dissident movement. The first Citizens Committee was founded in Estonia in February 1989. The Latvian Citizens' Committee aimed to gather 800,000 signatures (a majority of the ethnic Latvian population) in order to call a 'Citizens' Congress' with the aim of declaring an independent Latvia. By 1990, it had collected half a million signatures (Hiden and Salmon, 1994, p. 159). The congresses identified themselves as the direct successors to the inter-war parliaments and refused to recognise the legitimacy of Soviet institutions, arguing that they were tools of the occupying forces.

The three Baltic popular fronts were all founded in October 1988 and loosely cooperated in the following years, most significantly in the May 1989 Baltic Assembly held in Tallinn. The Latvian People's Front (LTF) initially claimed a membership of 120,000, one-third of whom were also CP members. By the end of the year its membership had shot up to 250,000 (Smith, 1996, p. 158). The popular fronts provided a broad tent for opponents of the Soviet Union and Latvia's contained communists and dissidents, nationalists and human rights campaigners, environmentalists and religious groups. The toleration by the LTF of this diversity of opinion stood in stark contrast to the more radical, exclusive and nationalist Citizens' Congress organisations in Estonia and Latvia. However, in some cases their memberships did overlap, and all three drifted towards the nationalist right in subsequent years. The Lithuanian Front, better known as *Sajūdis*, also began as a moderate organisation but pivoted to the nationalist right far quicker than did its Estonian and Latvian counterparts as the Kaunas nationalists replaced the Vilnius moderates.

The battle between the popular fronts and the congresses can also be conceptualised as a battle between rival institutions. The Citizens' Congresses believed they had a moral monopoly on representing Estonia and Latvia internationally, while the republic-level Supreme Soviet legislatures, which were dominated by the popular fronts after the 1990 elections, would deal with Moscow (Hiden and Salmon, 1994, p. 162). The result was that the 'Supreme Soviet won the battle of the institutions [as the basis for future parliaments], but the [popular fronts] gradually adopted most of the policies of the Congresses, and hence of the radical groups' (Norgaard and Johannsen, 1999, p. 24).

This blizzard of nationalist activity and the drive to independence left many Russian speakers in the Baltic states 'surprised, confused and antagonised' (Trapans, 1991, p. 6). They began organising into anti-reform groups led by 'Intermovements' (known as the Intermovement in Estonia, Interfront in Latvia and *Yedinstvo* (Unity) in Lithuania). They were an amalgamation of pro-Soviet forces primarily composed of ethnic Russian communist party members as well as retired Soviet military officers. In many ways they were umbrella organisations similar to the popular fronts. In Latvia, their first meeting took place at the Riga Aviation Institute, where over 99 per cent of students were Russophones. Indeed, the overwhelming majority of its claimed 300,000 membership in Latvia came from the 800,000 plus Russian-speaking minority (Smith, 1996, p. 161). Estonia's Intermovement was founded in March 1989 and, within weeks, was capable of organising a demonstration of 30–40,000 people against the January 1989 language laws that had made Estonian the official language of the republic.

In contrast to the popular fronts, the Intermovements did not have political programmes. Rather, they opposed all liberalisation and favoured reactionary retrenchment. Thus the March 1989 founding congress of the Estonian Intermovement saw it railing against the recent Estonian legislation that had legalised Estonian as the official language of the republic and authorised the Estonian tricolour flag. Radicals even called for north-eastern parts of Estonia, including Tallinn, to be annexed by the Leningrad Oblast of the Russian Soviet Federative Socialist Republic (RSFSR) while other fringe elements called for the restart of deportations of Estonians. With this kind of inflammatory language, any common ground was difficult to find and the two sides polarised.

The communist parties were torn apart by different loyalties to these movements. They were initially ordered to work together with the popular fronts, to harness their energy and power in pursuit of Gorbachev's restructuring goals. However, they were too weak to do so, and were led by events, rather than themselves leading events. As Kęstutis Girnius (1991, p. 59) wrote of the Lithuanian Communist Party: '[E]ven its most daring plans are always too little too late – faint echoes of more imaginative *Sąjūdis* proposals'.

A momentous turning point in the struggle for independence was the gradual defection of first a minority, but then the majority, of Communist Party members to the pro-independence side. The Estonian and Latvian CPs splintered into pro- and anti-reform groups in 1990, during their annual congress, with the split largely along ethnic lines. Even the Communist Youth (*Komsomol*) organisations broke from the party. This meant that real ground-level communist power in the Baltic states was unravelling and, just as importantly, meant that the independence movements gained access to valuable resources – particularly media – that could be used in their battle. In short, the outsiders became insiders with all the benefits this change brought. Reform communists, who would go on to play significant roles in the post-1991 states, emerged at this time. Edgar Savisaar and Marju Lauristin in Estonia, Anatolijs Gorbunovs in Latvia and Algirdas Brazauskas in Lithuania (although the latter two held far more senior positions in the CP than their Estonian counterparts). They were to retain huge popularity in the new states, to the distress of the dissidents that they had at one stage confronted and who felt that the public's support of these former communists was a betrayal of the revolutions.

The remaining hard-line communist deputies doubled down on their harsh, pro-Soviet policies. They began by voting in one of their own as the new First Secretary, such as the hard-line Alfreds Rubiks, mayor of Riga, in Latvia. Up until that point the Latvian CP had cooperated closely with the LTF. However, the communist parties were rapidly shedding members. By 1989, they were no longer even the largest political organisations in the Baltic states. In Latvia, the CP had just 184,000 members to the 250,000 in the LTF. This is the point at which the pro- and anti-independence cleavage gradually started morphing into an ethnic divide. An opinion poll carried out in late 1988 found that 74 per cent of Latvians and 10 per cent of Russians supported the LTF, while 48 per cent of Russians and 6 per cent of Latvians supported Interfront (Clemens, 1991, p. 170).

By 1989, parties began to reappear on the political scene, many claiming to be the heirs of the political parties of the inter-war era. For example, the LSDSP held its twentieth congress (and first since 1934), in Jūrmala, from 2–3 December 1989. New parties also appeared, such as the Latvian National Rebirth Party in April 1989, and the Republican Party in October 1989. Independent organisations also developed, although in the late 1980s these were primarily reformed inter-war organisations, such as the Scout Movement and the Red Cross. However, there were also some new organisations, such as the League of Women, formed to protect young Latvian soldiers who were serving in the Red Army.

Thus, by 1989 there were a multiplicity of NGOs, frequent anti-regime demonstrations and a number of fledgling parties. Song festivals in Estonia and Latvia mobilised huge numbers of people and created a visible momentum for action. Everything was set for the next stage: elections. First, the spring 1989 elections to the All Union Congress of People's Deputies in Moscow, followed by elections to the Republic-level Estonian, Latvian and Lithuanian SSR Supreme Councils. The All Union elections saw the pro-reform groups claim their first electoral successes and the emergence of a new political class. The elections revealed the extensive public base of the popular fronts and gave them their first taste of electoral success.

This electoral success continued into the Supreme Council elections, which saw reformists take control of the republic-level legislatures. As with the Constitutional Assemblies of the inter-war era, the Supreme Councils were rather more than mere transitional legislative institutions. The Latvian legislature passed a number of important pieces of legislation kick-starting the privatisation process and renewing the independent mandate of the Bank of Latvia. Lithuania's *Sąjūdis* used its election victory to declare the restoration of full independence on 11 March 1990. Moscow responded with an economic blockade so severe that it tempered later Estonian and Latvian declarations. The Soviet constitution allowed the constituent republics to conduct their own foreign relations, a technicality that the Baltic states fully utilised, sending their 'foreign ministers' to as many multilateral and bilateral meetings as would have them. However, at this point the Baltic states had achieved political independence but continued to live under 'military and economic occupation' (Taagepera, 1993, p. 169).

Events moved ahead rapidly in 1991. Between February and March all three states held independence referendums, having rejected cooperation with Gorbachev's referendum on a new union treaty for Soviet states. The referendums saw a majority of the Baltic populations support a break with the Soviet Union, leading to a further deterioration of relations with Moscow. The failed August coup in Moscow opened a window of opportunity for the Estonian and Latvian governments to follow Lithuania and declare independence. Following the collapse of the coup in Moscow, these declarations were recognised, first by Iceland (22 August), and then by a number of major states until US recognition on 1 September and the Soviet Union on 6 September. The three Baltic states joined the United Nations in September 1991, and by the end of the year were tied into the international community through a multiplicity of organisations.

Following independence the broad political umbrella of the popular fronts collapsed into three parts: (a) national liberals; (b) reform communists; and (c) national radicals (Dellenbrant, 1994, p. 106). With only a few exceptions (such as Edgar Savisaar, Mart Laar and Lennart Meri in Estonia, or Anatolijs Gorbunovs in Latvia and Algirdas Brazauskas in Lithuania), very few of the leading Baltic politicians of the 1980s and dissidents of the earlier age would play significant roles in the democratic politics of the following era. Indeed, *Sąjūdis* lost the 1992 parliamentary election to the ex-communist Lithuanian Liberal Democratic Labour Party (LDDP), and the Latvian Popular Front did not win a single seat in the 1993 parliamentary election. Office holders were punished by voters as the painful economic and social transition bit hard.

Conclusions

History remains salient in the contemporary Baltic states for three major reasons. First, the contemporary states had very little experience of democratic politics to draw upon in 1991. In contrast to Western Europe, the inter-war authoritarian governments and extreme-right movements were not discredited. Indeed, the authoritarian eras were remembered with greater affection than was the preceding era of competitive politics. Political parties in particular were remembered as corrupt and self-serving. The Baltic communist parties, with their nomenclature system of rewarding party members with better apartments and access to imported consumer goods, reinforced this image. This implied *cultural* challenges to the creation of the new democratic system. Second, just as the tsarist era was reflected in the key policies of the inter-war era – the need for land reform, finding new foreign trade partners, and minority policy – the Soviet era left its mark on the modern Baltic states with the need for a triple transition: in the political, economic and social spheres. If they were to reconstruct themselves in the image of Western Europe, especially the neighbouring Nordic states, then almost every part of the Baltic states' public and private life had to be redrawn and reformed. Finally, parts of the Baltic historical experience remain disputed at both the domestic and international levels. The issue of occupation versus voluntary annexation still divides Balts and Russophones in Estonia and Latvia and continues to cast a long shadow over bilateral relations with modern Russia.

2
Elected and Unelected Institutions

Having broken away from the Soviet Union, the Baltic states rapidly moved towards new constitutional orders more in line with the demands of the new democratic and market-economy framework that they were committed to building. The aim was to construct the major elected and unelected political institutions that would allow them to join the principal European organisations and usher in an era of boring normality. From what was a similar starting point, the Baltic states chose very different constitutional frameworks (although the demands of integration with the Western world has led to some institutional convergence). Nevertheless all three have largely achieved their ambition of making politics more boring.

This chapter deals with the key political institutions that shape and enforce the political order of the Baltic states. Thus, the first part of the chapter considers the 'elected' institutions that shape the political systems. It begins with an overview of the three constitutions and then moves on to look at the legislatures, executives, heads of state and local politics. The second part focuses on the major unelected institutions that implement and enforce the rules of the game shaping political competition: the bureaucracy and the courts as well as the police, armed forces and clandestine agencies.

2.1 Constitutions

Constitutions frame the legal basis for a democratic political system by setting the limits of state power as well as guarding individual rights and freedoms through basic laws and rules that stand above day-to-day political conflicts. Constitution writing is the critical and necessary first stage of democratisation. In late August 1991 the three Baltic states were faced with a number of constitutional options. For one, they could choose to readopt the inter-war constitutions abandoned after Soviet occupation in 1940. The illegitimacy of the Soviet occupation was the driving factor behind the independence movements and thus a return to the pre-1940 status quo would have a certain logical validity. On the flip side, however, in all three states the inter-war constitutional arrangements had been unable to prevent a slide into authoritarianism, and the 1938 Estonian constitution was actually written during the authoritarian era. The opposite approach would have entailed maintaining the Soviet era constitutions as the basic law (as Hungary had done post-1989), and then progressively delete, construct and amend the document as time went forward. This approach would have the advantage of gradually constructing the new democratic institutions and adapting them to changes in the situation. However, this idea was deeply unpopular because it seemingly granted the Soviet-era documents a legitimacy that they did not deserve. It also risked anti-democratic forces capturing the constitution-writing process later down the line. A third option was to write an entirely new constitutional document, although this raised a number of additional complicated issues: Who would write the document (the legislatures or a specially elected body? If the latter, how would it be elected?) and how would it be approved (by a vote in the body that wrote it? In a referendum? And who would be allowed to vote?). These issues proved particularly contentious and polarising in Latvia, which chose to reintroduce its 1922 constitution. Estonia and Lithuania, however, chose to write new constitutions.

Indeed, on 4 July 1992 Estonia was the first former Soviet republic to enact a new constitution. It convened a special 60-member constituent assembly to write a new constitution, as the Soviet Union fell apart already in August 1991. To ensure popular legitimacy, 30 members of the assembly came from the Estonian Supreme Council and another 30 from the more radically nationalist Estonian Congress. After detailed and fractious debate, much of which hinged around the extent to which the 1938 authoritarian-era constitution could be readopted (with its balance between presidential and legislative powers), the authors of the new constitution agreed on a greatly modified version of the 1938 document, with a weaker presidency. The greatest proponent of a strong presidency had been Arnold Rüütel, then chairman of the Supreme Council (effectively, an executive president), who was popular for his prudent management of Estonia's escape from the Soviet Union and thus was a leading candidate to win any presidential election. However, in the

Estonian Congress movement his Soviet *nomenklatura* background was anathema to the nationalists, who strongly supported the creation of a powerful legislature (Smith, 2001, p. 71). The constitution was thus a compromise between acknowledging the legal continuity of the 1940 state, but without the unacceptable parts of the 1938 authoritarian constitution. It was briefly, and unsuccessfully, opposed by the radical 'Restitution' movement that campaigned for the uncorrected reintroduction of the authoritarian 1938 constitution. There was also some public support for the creation of a stronger presidency. However, only minor, mostly terminological, changes were made by the constituent assembly and the new constitution was approved by an overwhelming 91.2 per cent of Estonian voters on 28 June 1992. In 1993 the newly elected Latvian parliament readopted the 1922 constitution. This gave a legal basis for initially limiting citizenship to those people, and their children, who had held citizenship in 1940, and for denying it to the Russian speakers who had settled in Latvia after that time. As a document designed in the aftermath of the First World War, it has inevitably been significantly amended and augmented.

While the Estonian and Latvian constitutional orders were clearly parliamentarian, Lithuania adopted a semi-presidential model. A popularly elected president has charge of certain foreign policy and security functions, with domestic politics controlled by a prime minister and cabinet of ministers. This was the result of a compromise between *Sajūdis*, which favoured a strong presidency (believing that it had the public support for its candidate to be elected) and the communist successor, Lithuanian Democratic Labour Party (LDLP), which had stronger grassroots, organisation and campaigning skills and was likely to be the winner in a parliamentary election. Thus, the adoption of Lithuania's constitution proved to be far more fractious than in Estonia and Latvia, even though Lithuania had actually moved first, re-establishing the 1938 authoritarian-era constitution after the 1990 legislative elections and then rapidly adopting an interim provisional basic law until a new constitution could be adopted. Then, however, Lithuania's politicians became bogged down in a fractious battle over the extent of presidential powers. *Sajūdis'* leader, Vytautas Landsbergis, pushed for greater presidential powers in defence and foreign affairs, creating the impression that 'the constitution was being created for him personally' (Ashbourne, 1999, p. 44). In spring 1992 a referendum was held on the powers of the presidency. While more than two-thirds of voters (69.5 per cent) supported a strong presidency, those voting in favour were less than the 50 per cent plus one needed for adopting a constitutional amendment and, thus, it did not pass. Half a year later a compromise constitution was put forward to a referendum vote together with the first post-communist era parliamentary elections. On 25 October 1992, 75 per cent of voters supported this draft, which had significantly watered down the powers of the president.

All three constitutions, particularly the Latvian, have since been amended in order to adjust for changes in the international and domestic situation. The Estonian constitution has been modified the least, with no amendments made in the first decade after its ratification in 1992. In contrast, the Latvian constitution has been amended most frequently (eight times), largely because it was written in 1922 and lacked many of the clauses expected of contemporary constitutions (such as human rights legislation) and in other cases had to be updated to fit in with modern democratic norms (such as lowering the voting age). These amendments can be placed into four categories (Pettai, Auers and Ramonaite, 2011, p. 146). First, all three constitutions have been adapted to the changing demands of the electoral system. In the case of Estonia and Lithuania, the terms of office for local governments were extended, while the Latvian constitution was amended to extend both presidential and parliamentary terms of office and to lower the voting age from the pre-war 21 to the European norm of 18. Second, the Baltic states were forced to amend their constitutions to allow for accession into the European Union and, in the case of Latvia, to allow for EU citizens to vote in local and European elections and, in the Lithuanian case, to allow foreign entities to purchase land. The third group of amendments dealt with strengthening national identity. Estonia and Latvia responded to the perceived threat of large national minorities by reinforcing the position of the titular languages in the constitution. Latvia also added an oath that parliamentary deputies make upon taking up office, aimed at the large bloc of Russian-speaking deputies whose loyalty to Latvia was often questioned by ethnic Latvian deputies. The threat that some nationalists felt from integration with the West is reflected in a 2006 Latvian amendment that defined marriage as being between a man and a woman. The fourth group of amendments has tackled institutional developments. In the case of Estonia and Lithuania this has dealt with changing the institution that has the power to appoint the commander of the armed forces (Estonia) and the prosecutor-general (Lithuania). Latvia has seen a great deal more institutional change, including the establishment of a constitutional court, limits to prime ministerial law-making powers and changes to citizens' initiative and referendum arrangements.

Perhaps because of its readoption of the 1922 constitution with no popular referendum to legitimise this move, the core constitutional order in Latvia has been frequently challenged. Parts of the political elite and the public still support the creation of a more presidential system. In March 2002 the Latvian Social Democratic Workers Party initiated a signature-gathering drive to force a referendum on a new constitution which, among other substantial reforms, envisaged a popularly elected president. However, the party's low popular support (it won just 4 per cent of the vote in the 2002 parliamentary election) meant that it failed to mobilise enough signatories for the initiative to clear the first hurdle. More recently, Latvian president Valdis Zatlers called for the creation of a presidential system. In an echo of the 1930s, Zatlers believed that a president would be able to rise above the fractious and volatile political party system, unite the country, and overcome corruption in the political system. Later in 2011, Zatlers used his constitutional powers to (successfully) call for a referendum on the recall of parliament.

In 2012 a group of prominent lawyers and politicians, spearheaded by Egils Levits, Latvia's judge at the Court of Justice of the European Union in Luxembourg, began debating a preamble for the Latvian constitution. While the Estonian and Lithuanian constitutions have preambles soaked in symbolism that lay out the aims and reason for the existence of the state (Estonia's constitution begins: 'With unwavering faith and a steadfast will to strengthen and develop the state, which is established on the inextinguishable right of the people of Estonia to national self-determination ... '), the Latvian constitution dryly begins: 'The people of Latvia, in freely elected Constitutional Assembly, have adopted the following State Constitution'. As with many other political discussions, the debate quickly polarised into a discussion about Russians and Latvians, with Russian-speaker politicians claiming that the preamble would define Latvia as a state defined by ethnicity. Latvian politicians countered that it would simply enshrine Latvian culture and language as central to the Latvian state. In the final session of parliament before the 2014 summer break, the Latvian parliament accepted the amendments to the Latvian constitution that created the new preamble.[1]

2.2   Legislatures

As small, centralised countries, all three Baltic states opted for unicameral legislatures. An important decision had to be taken on where to locate the parliaments. After all, the buildings and architectural designs of contemporary legislatures serve as symbols and calling cards of the states that they represent. There was little discussion that the restored Estonian and Latvian legislatures would return to their pre-war buildings as highly visible and physical links to the pre-occupation independent states. Thus the Estonian parliament (*Riigikogu*) is based in the courtyard of the Toompea Palace in the centre of Tallinn in a building, completed in 1922, that has since been restored and modernised and specifically designed to house the legislature. The Latvian parliament (*Saeima*) also returned to its pre-occupation building in the Old Town part of central Riga. The main building of the legislature was completed in 1867 for the Baltic German Livonian Knights, who disbanded in 1917. The building was designed by the first academically trained ethnic Latvian architect, giving it some symbolic importance. The building was subsequently used by the People's Council and the short-lived Latvian SSR before being taken over by the Constitutional Assembly in 1920. A 1997 renovation saw the plenary hall restored to the inter-war semi-circular amphitheatre style, replacing the 'school-boy' rows of seats favoured by Soviet-era legislatures (and still in use in Tallinn). In contrast to its northern neighbours, Lithuania's parliament (*Seimas*) is located in a new series of buildings in the centre of Vilnius (in any case, the inter-war legislature had been located in Kaunas). The first post-independence Seimas met in a Soviet-era building constructed in 1980 to house the Supreme Council of the Lithuanian Soviet Socialist Republic. However, in 2007 the plenary hall was moved to a modern purpose-built structure. As such, it is far more spacious, modern, light and airy (reflecting openness and transparency) and better suited to the demands of a modern legislature than the cramped Estonian and Latvian structures. However, as is the case with the overcrowded House of Commons in the United Kingdom, tradition trumps comfort and efficiency in Estonia and Latvia.

Deputies are organised into parliamentary groups (also known as fractions in the *Saeima* and factions in the *Seimas* and *Riigikogu*). In an attempt to limit the fragmentation of political groups and the defection of individual deputies between parliamentary groups, the Estonian and Latvian legislatures only allow parliamentary deputies to join one parliamentary group over the life of a parliament, and that must be composed of members elected from the same list of candidates. If a deputy leaves a group, then that person becomes an unaffiliated deputy (although unaffiliated Latvian deputies can then band together in a political block that has less access to economic and administrative benefits than does a group). These efforts to limit fragmentation have been only partially successful. At the end of 2013, the Estonian parliament had

Table 2.1   Comparison of Baltic legislatures

	Estonia	Latvia	Lithuania
Name	*Riigikogu*	*Saeima*	*Seimas*
Structure	Unicameral	Unicameral	Unicameral
Size	101	100	141
Minimum number of deputies in parliamentary group	5	5	7
Term of election (years)	4	4	4
Sessions	Jan.–June Sept.–Dec.	Autumn, Winter, Spring	Spring (March–June) Autumn (Sept.–Dec.)
Plenary days	Monday–Thursday	Thursday	Tuesday & Thursday
Average deputy monthly salary (2012)	€3,374	€2,476	€2,380
Permanent committees	11	15	15

Source: Baltic constitutions and Preisvergleich (2013).

six unaffiliated deputies, the Latvian parliament ten and the Lithuanian Seimas five. Indeed, six of the ten independent Latvian deputies had broken from the party with which they had been elected – the Zatlers Reform Party (*Zatlera Reformu Partija*, ZRP) – before the first plenary session of the 2011 parliament had even been convened. However, with a broader historical perspective it is clear that the Baltic parliamentary groups are no longer as volatile or fractured as they were in the 1990s.

Participation in a political group gives deputies access to additional resources. While deputies in all three states receive office space and allowances to employ assistants, the comparatively low level of assistant salaries generally tends to attract relatively young and untried early career professionals who offer much enthusiasm but little expertise, experience or policy advice. As a result, additional personnel employed by party groups or the committees deputies sit on can be a valuable resource. Another source of assistance are the researchers connected to the legislature's library. The Lithuanian *Seimas* employs 25 researchers for the

141 deputies while the Estonian *Riigikogu* also has a research branch. In contrast, the Latvian parliament has no research department or specialised researchers. This means that the Latvian legislature typically has to rely on data and analysis prepared by the executive. Latvian deputies can often be poorly briefed. In December 2012 the Latvian branch of Transparency International, Delna, organised a one-day seminar on the role of research in the Latvian parliament. Participating parliamentary deputies made clear that they largely understood that the parliament needed more expert advice and, indeed, that Latvia was the only state in the Nordic-Baltic region that did not give research assistance to its parliamentarians. However, they stated that the biggest obstacle to increasing research funding, and opening a dedicated department, was the Latvian publics opposition to increasing the parliament's budget. Saeima officials are wary of increasing spending and personnel in the legislature, even if this comes at the cost of qualitative decision-making.

The detailed work of writing and debating legislation as well as finding political compromise between different interests is done within the parliamentary committees that are at the heart of law-making in contemporary legislatures. The standing committees typically mirror government ministries and shadow their work, regularly calling ministers, officials and experts to testify before the committees. The Baltic parliaments also have the possibility of creating ad hoc investigating committees that can address political emergencies. These committees have occasionally been hijacked for political point scoring. One extreme example occurred in Latvia in the late 1990s. The 'pedophilia incident' began in the Latvian parliament in February 2000 when Jānis Ādamsons (a deputy in the opposition Latvian Social Democrat Workers Party), chair of a parliamentary investigating committee looking at links between a pedophilia case and Latvia's political and economic elite, used his parliamentary immunity during a plenary session to accuse Prime Minister Andris Šķēle, Justice Minister Valdis Birkavs (who went on a short-lived hunger strike after the accusation) and head of the Tax Authority, Andrejs Sončiks, of involvement in the pedophile ring. While the prosecutor's office found them innocent of all accusations by that August, the allegations had contributed to the loss of confidence and subsequent collapse of the government in April that year. Ādamsons was subsequently investigated by prosecutors after losing his parliamentary immunity and fined €14,800 (130 minimum monthly salaries) by a local Riga court, a fine that was later upheld by Latvia's supreme court.

How influential are the three Baltic parliaments? In terms of Philip Norton's (1998) binary typology of *policymaking* and *policy-influencing* legislatures, the Baltic parliaments clearly fall into the latter grouping, as do almost all other European legislatures. While the Baltic legislatures can and do hold governments to account, scrutinise officials and influence policy, the bulk of legislation is largely shaped outside parliament by the executive. Jose M. Magone (2011, p. 203) categorises the three Baltic states' parliaments as 'weak reactive' institutions. This is largely attributed to the weaker resources available to parliamentarians, as well as the lower levels of specialisation and experience caused by higher electoral volatility than in the older European democracies. The international parliamentary powers index (Fish and Kroenig, 2009) – a global survey of parliaments that attempts to gauge and compare formal powers over the executive, institutional autonomy, authority in specific areas and institutional capacity – saw Latvia and Lithuania score 0.78, and Estonia 0.75 (with the range from 1.00 being most powerful and 0.00 least powerful). The score of 0.78 placed Latvia and Lithuania on a par with the UK, Dutch and Danish parliaments and was actually higher than the US score. This indicates that the Baltic constitutional order is genuinely parliamentary and that the formal powers allocated to the institutions are significant. However, the lack of resources outlined above, as well as a high turnover of deputies (Polsby, 1968), tilts power away from the Baltic states' legislatures and towards the executive.

2.3   Executives

Executive power in the Baltic states lies with prime ministers and cabinets of ministers usually elected to office by multi-party parliamentary coalitions. Only the Lithuanian Democratic Labour Party has won a plurality of seats – in the 1992 Seimas election, 73/141 – and subsequently formed a single-party government. Moreover, the semi-presidentialism of Lithuania, where the popularly elected president has certain foreign and security powers, is only a partial exception (see the following section on Baltic presidents). Prior to 2007, Latvia had the strongest executive, which was largely due to Article 81 of the constitution granting cabinet the power to issue regulations with the force of law between sessions of parliament, although the regulations did need to be later approved by parliament (Pettai and Madise, 2006, p. 294). However, in 2007 parliament amended the constitution by striking Article 81 following a campaign by President Vaira Vīķe-Freiberga, who had claimed incompatibility between modern democracy and the clause. The Latvian executive is now more in line with Estonia and Lithuania.

Presidents play the key role in nominating prime ministers in all three Baltic states. Presidents typically consult with all the parties represented in parliament in order to identify a candidate supported by a parliamentary majority. In addition, parties and parliamentary groups also negotiate between themselves, particularly in the allocation of ministerial offices. Nevertheless, the final choice of candidate lies with the president, who can attempt to exert his will on the legislature. In late 2013 the Latvian president, Andris Bērziņš, rejected the candidacy of Artis Pabriks (Unity), an experienced defence minister (and a former foreign minister) as successor to Valdis Dombrovskis, who had submitted his resignation that November after the collapse of a supermarket roof took more than 50 lives. While Pabriks had the support of both his party and a parliamentary majority, Bērziņš' personal animosity towards Pabriks led to rejection out of hand. In other cases, however, parties have held the upper hand and forced the president to accede to their will. After the October 2012 parliamentary elections, Lithuanian president, Dalia Grybauskaitė, was forced to nominate a centre-left government that contained the Labour Party and its leader, Viktor Uspaskich, who was still facing tax fraud charges at that time. The president had initially urged the left-wing parties that won the election to reject collaboration with the Labour Party. Nevertheless, with no other options she was eventually forced to relent and nominate a new government coalition that included the Labour Party. Grybauskaitė even broke with protocol and refused to personally attend the opening of parliament, sending written greetings instead. In the mid-1990s an exceptionally fragmented parliament led the Latvian president to nominate a non-party candidate, Andris Šķēle, as prime minister.

Political elites in the Baltic states have favoured minority or minimum-winning coalitions over surplus majorities.[2] Indeed, Estonia has never had a surplus majority government, while Lithuania and Latvia have enjoyed only brief eras of surplus majorities: in the second half of the 1990s, and Latvia twice more in the 2000s (Parliament and Government Composition Database, 2014). However, in December 2012 the Lithuanian parliament approved a new four-party surplus majority government that could both override potential presidential vetoes from President Grybauskaitė, who had only grudgingly nominated the centre-left government coalition, and change the Lithuanian constitution.

A key issue in executive performance is the length of time the executive stays in office. The longer a cabinet stays in power, the more it can effectively lead, govern and shape policy. Conversely, a high turnover of coalitions can be indicative of weak government. Pettai, Auers and Ramonaite (2012, pp. 146–147) discussed and calculated three different measures of government duration. The first, legal investiture, counts the number of days a government is in power from the date it takes office to the day it leaves office. The second party government method considers a new government to have been formed when the substance of the governing coalition fundamentally changes: typically after one or more of the coalition partners leaves, but the government continues to function with a different, usually reduced, basis of support. The final effective government approach considers only the number of days that governments effectively govern. In other words, lame-duck executives who are in office simply because a new alternative executive has not yet been elected to office, and thus have little mandate to govern, are not counted from the day that they announce their intention to step down.

Table 2.2 reveals the differences in government duration that these alternate methods produce. Latvia clearly is different to Estonia and Lithuania regardless of the measure used. It has seen far more government change and fragmentation leading to far shorter terms of office. Nevertheless, while government duration in Estonia and Lithuania, according to the effective government measure, is above the average for the post-communist states of East-Central Europe, it still lags behind Western Europe, although governments in the Baltic states have proved increasingly stable over time (Ryans, Conrad and Golder, 2010). The governments elected after the 2007 Estonian and 2008 Lithuanian parliamentary elections served full terms, despite the strains caused by the economic recessions of 2008–2010. At the same time, Latvian prime

Table 2.2   Government duration in the Baltic states, 1992–2012[3]

	Legal investiture		Party government		Effective government	
	N.	Avg. days	N.	Avg. days	N.	Avg. days
Estonia	10	672	12	559	11	575
Latvia	15	446	18	369	18	344
Lithuania	11	655	12	601	11	630

Source: Pettai, Auers and Ramonaite (2012, p. 147) and updated with author's own calculations.

minister Valdis Dombrovskis led three consecutive governments between 2009 and 2013, becoming Latvia's longest-serving prime minister. This also helps to explain why governments have been able to execute policy despite relatively frequent changes in government: There has been a great deal of continuity in personnel in the key ministries. In the 1990s the Latvia's Way political party dominated the foreign ministry, ensuring a consistent pro-Western foreign policy of integration with the EU and NATO. In the same way, Mārtiņš Roze served as minister of agriculture in five different government coalitions between 2002 and 2009, ensuring remarkable policy continuity even as governments came and went (Pettai, Auers and Ramonaitė, 2012). However, this also indicates the weakness of Baltic prime ministers who have certainly been partially 'presidentialised' in all three states, becoming both the electoral and party face. However, they have failed to concentrate executive power in their hands (Poguntke and Webb, 2005). Rather, all three Baltic states have a form of fragmented cabinet government in which parties assume responsibility for groups of ministries, and prime ministers have relatively weak oversight over what happens in these ministries. The preference for minority or minimum-winning coalitions also means that parties and ministers have greater opportunity to threaten their coalition partners with exit (and thus likely collapse of the coalition) if they are not allowed to fully control their ministries.

As could be expected, the three executives have generally dominated the legislatures. A growing majority of legislation originates from the executive. In the 1990s, between half and two-thirds of final legislative acts originated from the executive, but as political parties institutionalised and party leaders gained experience and exerted increasing control over members, the executive initiated an increasing quantity of legislation, culminating at over 80 per cent of all Estonian and Latvian legislation in the middle of the first decade of the twenty-first century (Pettai, Auers and Ramonaitė, 2011, p. 147). The percentage remained much lower in Lithuania (falling to just 39 per cent between 2004 and 2008) as a result of the country's semi-presidential order creating a stronger parliamentary identity. Lithuania's single-mandate districts, as well as committees lacking the right of legislative initiative (in contrast to Estonia and Latvia where committees do have this right), have seen more individual bills in the *Seimas* (Pettai and Madise, 2006, p. 301). In Latvia, parliamentarians are additionally burdened by the need to band together in order to initiate legislation (five deputies are needed to initiate legislation) while in Estonia and Lithuania individual deputies can initiate the process.

2.4   Presidents

All three states adopted presidential offices with differing electoral procedures but similar powers. Lithuania opted for a semi-presidential system
with a popularly elected president. Latvia's president is appointed in
a parliamentary vote. Estonia combines a parliamentary vote with a
special electoral college if parliament cannot decide (although Estonia's
first post-communist presidential election saw a transitional compromise of a popular vote, followed by the electoral college).

The role of the president caused most discussion and debate in the
1991–1992 Estonian Constitutional Assembly and in the Lithuanian
legislature's debates on the new constitution. Debates polarised around
the need for a popularly elected versus parliament-elected president.
The Estonian Constitutional Assembly debated the costs and benefits
of five different constitutional models before ultimately settling on a
parliamentary model with an indirectly elected presidency. Ultimately,
a compromise foresaw the popular election of Estonia's first post-1991
president in a first round of voting, with following presidents elected
in a procedure that has up to five rounds. In the first stage, presidential candidates, who must be 40 years old and Estonian-born, need to
be nominated by one-fifth of the members of the *Riigikogu* and garner
two-thirds of the votes of all deputies in order to be elected to office.
If no candidate is chosen in three rounds of voting, then the next
round is held within a month by an electoral assembly composed of
both deputies from the legislature as well as representatives from local
governments. At the fourth round a candidate needs to be elected
with a majority, but in the fifth and final round a plurality of votes
suffices.

In Lithuania *Sąjūdis'* leader Vytautas Landsbergis strongly favoured
a presidential system (not least because Landsbergis pictured himself
winning it). However, other political leaders, including prominent
members of *Sąjūdis*, had little appetite for granting extensive executive powers to one of their peers and preferred to concentrate political power in the legislature. A May 1992 referendum also saw the
Lithuanian public reject the restoration of the office of a president. The
eventual constitutional compromise approved by the public at the end
of the year was a semi-presidential system heavily weighted in favour
of the legislature.

There were few such debates in early post-1991 Latvia, when the logic
of the legal continuity of the state meant the readoption of the inter-war

parliamentary system with a president elected by parliament. However, debates on the reintroduction of a popularly elected president regularly flare up in Latvia. Towards the end of his term in office, President Valdis Zatlers (2007–2011) pushed for a public debate on reforms to the office, arguing that a stronger presidency, including a popularly elected president, was needed in order to counterbalance the powers of a parliament that he increasingly considered to be some sort of rogue institution. His predecessor, Vaira Vīķe-Freiberga, had also expressed sympathy for a directly elected president with enhanced executive powers. A number of political parties have also proposed revamping the presidential office to make it popularly elected. The Latvian Social Democratic Worker's Party (*Latvijas Sociāldemokrātiskā Strādnieku Partija*, LSDSP) wrote a largely ignored new constitution in 2001 that centred around the idea of an elected presidency, and a few years later started collecting signatures in a failed attempt to hold a referendum on the issue in 2007. In 2011, the National Alliance submitted a set of revisions to the constitution that included a directly elected president (although these plans were shelved when, a few months later that year, President Zatlers successfully called for a referendum to recall parliament). However, the majority of parliamentary parties, as well as Latvia's most influential legal thinker and judge at the European Court of Justice, Egils Levits, are opposed to a popularly elected president. The issue regularly appears on the political agenda because there is a tremendous amount of public support for it. Annual opinion polls on the issue find that between 1999 and 2014, 74–86 per cent of the public agree with the statement that 'the Latvian public, not parliamentary deputies, should elect the president' (Kaktins, 2014).

Jose Magone (2011, p. 170) claimed that 'normally the head of state is a prestigious elderly statesman or stateswoman who commands respect from all sectors of society'. Only a small minority of post-1991 Baltic presidents could, at the time of their election, truthfully be described as a statesman (defined here as a capable, experienced, knowledgeable and respected national political figure), although a great number left office having achieved that level of respect and public popularity.

Estonia's Lennart Meri is a case in point. With hindsight he is viewed as one of the post-communist world's greatest and most respected statesmen, having overseen Estonia's transformation from the Soviet Union to the cusp of the European Union when he left office in 2001. However, in Estonia's 1992 presidential election he actually finished a distant second to Arnold Rüütel in the popular vote.[4] Meri was a more

Table 2.3   Post-1991 Baltic presidents, 1992–2014

Estonia	Latvia	Lithuania
Lennart Meri 1992–1996 1996–2001	Guntis Ulmanis 1993–1996 1996–1999	Algirdas Brazauskas 1993–1998
Arnold Rüütel 2001–2006	Vaira Vīke-Freiberga 1999–2003 2003–2007	Valdas Adamkus 1998–2003
Toomas Hendrik Ilves 2006–2011 2011–	Valdis Zatlers 2007–2011	Rolandas Paksas 2003–2004
	Andris Bērziņš 2011–	Artūras Paulauskas (acting president) April–July 2004 Valdas Adamkus 2004–2009
		Dalia Grybauskaitė 2009–2014 2014–

popular figure in the legislature and collected 59 votes to Rüütel's 31 in the later *Riigikogu* vote. The parliamentary vote appeared to disregard the earlier public poll, although the other two losing candidates would likely have urged their supporters to side with Meri in the case of a public second-round runoff vote.[5] At that time the public may have regarded Meri as possibly too erratic and impulsive to hold the president's post. Later, however, this unpredictability was a central part of Meri's colourful and unorthodox character, and stories of his charming informality are legion. A former British ambassador to Estonia recounted how:

On a state visit to Lithuania in the late 1990s, he [Meri] stopped his official convoy, asked a girl in the street if he could borrow her bike and cycled off to find a much-loved bookshop. On another occasion, he found the coffee served at a City lunch in London so unpleasant that he stopped the convoy again, this time for an espresso at Pret A Manger. (Craddock, 2006)

The first decade and a half of presidential politics in Estonia was dominated by the clash between Meri and Rüütel. The two again contested the 1996 presidential election. After three inconclusive rounds of voting in the *Riigikogu*, the 374-member electoral body was convened and elected Meri president (196–126 votes) over Rüütel (who was eventually elected president in 2001, although five years later he became the only Estonian president to not be re-elected to the post, when he lost out to Toomas Hendrik Ilves). Both Rüütel and Ilves, although very different personalities, are presidents who already fit the 'statesman' description when coming into office. Rüütel had been a leading communist figure in the late years of the Soviet Union, serving as the last chairman of the Presidium of the Supreme Soviet of the Estonian SSR from 1983 to 1990, and then from 1990 to 1992 as chairman of the Supreme Soviet of the Estonian SSR (later the Supreme Council of Estonia). As such, he was a national figure and symbol of the political transition. Ilves, in contrast, had been born to an Estonian émigré family in Sweden and raised in the United States before returning to Estonia after independence. Similar to Meri, he had served as an outspoken and deep-thinking Estonian foreign minister and was a serving member of the European Parliament for the Moderate Party when elected president in 2006.

The calibre and 'statesmanship' of Latvia's presidents when taking up office is very different. Indeed, the trend of weak, compromise candidates is far more pronounced in Latvia, where the first three presidents entered office as controversial, politically appointed unknowns, but left as respected statesmen. This difference is largely explained by the contrasting methods of election. In Estonia, parliamentary parties are not forced to compromise with each other, because after three rounds of voting the task of electing the president is switched to a broader electoral body. This is not the case in Latvia, where only parliament can elect a president, and some form of compromise is inevitable. There is a clear pattern in the appointment of Latvian presidents that was only partially broken with the election of Andris Bērziņš in 2011. The major political parties initially nominate their candidates for president, but do not expect these first nominations to win. In 1993 Latvia's Way (*Latvijas Ceļš*, LC), which had won the biggest share of the seats in the previous month's parliamentary election, had nominated Gunārs Meierovics, the son of Latvia's most famous inter-war foreign minister Zigfrīds Anna Meierovics, who had been a senior figure in the Latvian émigré community, but died young in a car accident in 1925. Meierovics's defeat by Guntis Ulmanis, a nondescript former public utilities manager, was a major shock. Ulmanis, who had only resigned from the Latvian Communist Party in 1989, was elected to the post largely on the strength of his surname (his uncle was Latvia's inter-war dictator, Kārlis Ulmanis) and the symbolic link to the inter-war era that this provided. Indeed, he bears a striking physical resemblance to the old dictator, not least because of a shared flat-top haircut. At that time Ulmanis was a member of the renewed Latvia's Farmers Union party (*Latvijas Zemnieku Savienība*, LZS), which his uncle had dominated in the inter-war era. He renounced his party membership, establishing Latvia's tradition of non-party presidents. Ulmanis was much mocked for his weak English-language knowledge and Soviet *nomenklatura* aura, but his discreet political manoeuvering guided Latvia through some potentially rocky waters, not least when he returned the controversial first version of the 1994 citizenship law, which contained strict numerical annual citizenship quotas, to parliament. By 1996 he was a popular president and was re-elected in the first round of voting.

Ulmanis was succeeded by Vaira Vīķe-Freiberga, a recently retired Canadian–Latvian professor of psychology, who had returned to Latvia in 1998 to become the first head of the Latvian Institute (and with one eye on the 1999 vote for the presidency). She became the first female president in Baltic history. Although she had been mentioned as a potential candidate as early as December 1998, she was the candidate of Latvia's intelligentsia and was largely unknown in Latvia (Egle, 1999). Vīķe-Freiberga entered the race very late and was only introduced as a formal candidate in the *sixth* round of voting, after the previous, much better-known candidates (such as composer Raimonds Pauls and Anatolijs Gorbunovs, Latvia's version of Arnold Rüütel) had failed to rustle up the 51-plus votes needed to elect a president (indeed, no candidate garnered more than 33 votes). Nevertheless, after being elected Vīķe-Freiberga quickly became a popular figure and was re-elected unopposed to a second term in 2003.

Vīķe-Freiberga was followed by Valdis Zatlers, another unknown candidate, who was a surgeon and head of a Latvian hospital. His candidacy was famously discussed during a political meeting at the Riga Zoo, away from the prying eyes of the media. Three major political figures (former foreign ministers Sandra Kalniete and Māris Riekstiņš and former culture minister Karina Pētersone) had been nominated in the run-up to the vote before the leaders of the governing parties agreed to unite around Zatlers. After he was elected, he was immediately plunged into a vociferous debate on bribery and corruption, having previously admitted to taking 'envelopes' (containing petty bribes) from his clients in return for surgery work that had already been ostensibly financed by the state. Moreover, he was seen as the symbol of the backroom deals between political 'oligarchs' that had long scarred Latvian politics. However, as with his predecessors, over the course of his four-year presidency, Zatlers rose like a phoenix from the ashes to eventually call and lead a campaign to recall a parliament that he claimed had fallen under the illicit control of a small group of oligarchs that were threatening Latvia's very fabric of democracy. Several days after calling the referendum, Zatlers was not re-elected to the presidency, beaten by retired banker Andris Bērziņš, who had been elected to the parliament on the Green-Farmer's party list in the 2010 election and had replaced Zatlers as the political establishment's favoured candidate.

These secondary (or compromise) candidates were elected as a result of the polarisation of the Latvian political system. When parties fail to have their preferred candidates elected, they are forced to seek compromise. Not wishing to give any party sway over the presidency, they opt for a compromise (although the parties may secretly hope that they will have some influence over the candidate that they agree on). This compromise candidate, not being affiliated to any party, is not constrained by party influence and has greater room for manoeuver, including criticism of political parties (which always goes down well with Latvia's jaded electorate) and, eventually, the unpopular presidents become the candidates of the people, lauded for their prudent use of a president's domestic powers (Ulmanis and Zatlers) or for their foreign policy nous (Vīķe-Freiberga).

Lithuania's experience is different again. First, Lithuania's semi-presidential regime type is typically categorised as premier–presidential (Shugart and Carey, 1992).[6] The office holders' presidential powers are actually relatively weak and comparable to those of Estonian and Latvian heads of state (see Table 2.4). Algis Krupavičius (2014, p. 214) argued that 'the parliamentary element is very strong in the Lithuanian premier–presidential regime. Almost all presidential powers are matched by countervailing powers vested in the *Seimas*.' Lithuania's first elected president, Algirdas Brazauskas, was content to fulfil a largely ceremonial role as president (perhaps because his Democratic Labour Party also dominated the legislature and government), setting relatively narrow public expectations and parameters for his successors in the presidential office. The major difference between the Lithuanian presidency and its Baltic counterparts is the nature of their election. Presidents in Lithuania, just like political parties, are more subject to the vagaries of the political pendulum – in contrast to Estonian and Latvian presidents, who tend to be less partisan and thus typically get more popular the longer they are in office. Even popular presidents face the risk of not being re-elected to the post (in May 2014, Dalia Grybauskaitė became the first Lithuanian president to be returned to the post in consecutive elections).

Lithuania has been the only post-communist state to experience the impeachment of a president. Rolandas Paksas was famous as a prize-winning stunt pilot long before he entered politics. After building a successful construction company, Paksas was first elected mayor of Vilnius (in 1997) and then as Lithuania's prime minister (in 1999) for five fiery months before stepping down after a spat over the sale of *Mažeikių Nafta* oil refinery to an American oil company.[7] His seemingly principled resignation gave him the political capital to launch a successful bid for the presidency in 2002 (Norkus, 2008). However, less than two years later Paksas was impeached by the Lithuanian parliament following an investigation by the Constitutional Court that indicted him on three charges (illegally granting Lithuanian citizenship to a campaign sponsor, leaking confidential wire-tapping information and applying pressure on business owners to sell out to his friends). He was temporarily replaced by Arturas Paulauskas, the chair of Parliament. In the following early presidential election the public supported the re-election of the steady hand of Valdas Adamkus to rebuild the presidency.

While some Baltic presidents are elected as the result of the congruence of a set of unique political circumstances, two types of individuals have been elected to the presidency in all three Baltic states. First, there is the popular ex-Soviet official who seems to represent the path from tacitly supporting communism to independence, a path taken by so many individuals (Rüütel, Ulmanis and Brazauskas). Second, in the mid-2000s all three Baltic states had former émigré presidents who had spent the majority of their lives in North America (Ilves, Vīķe-Freiberga and

Table 2.4   Comparison of key presidential powers

	Estonia	Latvia	Lithuania
Call early elections	Yes (partial)[8]	Yes (partial)[9]	Yes (partial)[10]
Nominate prime minister	Yes[11]	Yes	Yes[12]
Initiate legislation	No	Yes	Yes
Suspensive veto	Yes	Yes[13]	Yes[14]
Appoint commander-in-chief	No	No[15]	No[16]
Nominate chief justice of the supreme court	Yes	No	Yes

Source: Constitutions of Estonia, Latvia and Lithuania.

Adamkus). Émigrés had already been prominent presidential candidates in the first 'founding' presidential vote in 1992/1993 (Rein Taagepera in Estonia, Gunārs Meierovics in Latvia and Stasys Lozoraitis in Lithuania) and have had far more influence over the Baltic presidencies than over any other political institutions in the Baltic states. This is at least partly because of the international role that Baltic presidents played in the 25 years of post-1991 independence. President Ilves specifically stated that his native knowledge of English allowed him to better hear and react to any Western condescension (Greeley, 2012). Thus, émigré presidents were more rigorous in their defence of the Baltic states than were presidents less capable in the English language (although the multilingual first post-1991 Estonian president, Lennart Meri, is an exception here). For example, below is the archived twitter feed from Estonian president Ilves' defence of Estonia's economic austerity measures to a critique on Paul Krugman's *New York Times* blog (later turned into a short 16 minute opera – *Nostra Culpa* – that debuted in Tallinn in 2013):

> *8:57 p.m.* Let's write about something we know nothing about & be smug, overbearing & patronising: after all, they're just wogs.
>
> *9:06 p.m.* Guess a Nobel in trade means you can pontificate on fiscal matters & declare my country a "wasteland." Must be a Princeton vs Columbia thing.
>
> *9:15 p.m.* But yes, what do we know? We're just dumb & silly East Europeans. Unenlightened. Someday we too will understand. Nostra culpa.
>
> *9:32 p.m.* Let's sh*t on East Europeans: their English is bad, won't respond & actually do what they've agreed to & reelect govts that are responsible.
>
> *10:10 p.m.* Chill. Just because my country's policy runs against the Received Wisdom & I object doesn't mean y'all gotta follow me. (Greeley, 2012)

In addition to knowledge of English, there are two possible explanations for the mid-1990s trend for émigré presidential politicians in the Baltic states. First, they may be seen as more worldly and experienced in democratic politics (and the market system) than are local politicians and thus better able to consolidate Baltic democratisation. A second advantage may be their lack of domestic networks, which implies a lower risk of corruption and graft (Skulte, 2005, p. 180). In this sense their long émigré-era separation from domestic politics is the great advantage.

The presidents enjoy a variety of constitutional powers and influence over domestic and international politics. Perhaps the most significant is the power of suspensive veto – to reject and return laws to parliament – which has been used most often in Lithuania, where presidents rejected 175 laws between 1992 and 2010, compared to 59 times in the same time period in Estonia and just 35 times in Latvia between 1993 and 2010 (Koker, 2013). Presidents were particularly active in the early years of the transformation, when parliaments were by necessity preparing a great number of laws, and presidents frequently had to temper the legislation. Lennart Meri vetoed 41 pieces of legislation, double the number rejected by his successors.

The president is a moderating force in all three states. Presidential institutions have proved strong, rigorous and capable of opposing parliament when needed. Lithuania's impeachment of Paksas indicated that oversight of presidential institutions is also effective. In terms of categorisation, both Estonia's and Latvia's presidents are technically amongst the weakest heads of states in Europe (Toomla, 2014). However, Estonian presidents, particularly Meri and Ilves, have been major political players thanks to their moral authority, while Latvian presidents gain influence over the course of their presidencies through their distance from feuding party politics. In confrontations between parliament and president, Latvian presidents have won (Auers, 2014). Lithuania's popularly elected president has more popular legitimacy but similar legislative and appointment powers. However, the greater legitimacy has led to more active use of the presidential veto and a greater legislative role.

2.5   Decentralisation and local government

This section considers politics at the local level. The centralising tendencies of the Soviet system of governance had no place for elected local governments, and the first local government elections since the inter-war era were only held in 1989 as the Soviet Union unravelled. Regular elections have taken place since then (see Chapter 3) although, as we would expect, there is a significant gap between electoral turnout in national and local elections. Latvia has restricted participation in local elections to citizens (although since 2004 resident registered EU citizens can also take part in the elections), while both Estonia and Lithuania have allowed permanent residents to participate in the polls.

Vanags and Vilka (2008, pp. 83–84) point out a number of similarities between the local-government models of the Baltic states. For a start, all three states have gradually moved to decentralise government and give local authorities more independence in their decision-making. The small average size of local governments in Estonia and Latvia has encouraged pooling of resources and greater cooperation in delivering services to inhabitants. Moreover, local governments also perform functions delegated to them by central government.

The Baltic national governments have moved towards reducing the number of local authorities in order to create larger, more financially sustainable local authorities. Estonia has a two-tier local government system with 15 counties (*Maakonad*) that are essentially administrative units of the Ministry of the Interior and overseen by a government-appointed governor (with a five-year term of office). However, almost all functions are delegated to the municipal level (of which in 2014 there were 215 – 30 urban and 185 rural). The counties play a coordinating role, encouraging cooperation between municipalities. Following a major overhaul of local government in 2008, Latvia's single-tier system now has 118 municipalities (9 urban and 109 rural. Prior to 1 July 2009 there were 548 municipalities). Lithuania, in contrast, moved fastest and furthest in reforming the number of local authorities, and now has the fewest municipalities in the region – just 60 – which means that Lithuania actually has the largest municipalities in the European Union (with an average size between 30–50,000 people). As is the case with Estonia, Lithuania also has a two-tier system with ten counties (*Apskritys*) and governors (appointed by the central government), who act as a link between the municipalities and the central government.

Decentralisation of powers has been a major policy aim of all three states. This entails three key dimensions: (a) Political decentralisation transfers political authority from central to locally elected actors and institutions; (b) fiscal decentralisation grants local government tax-and-spend powers; and (c) administrative de-concentrates, delegates and devolves authority, responsibility and resources for public services (Aristovnik, 2012). Lithuania's quick move to reform local government resulted in greater fiscal decentralisation; 36 per cent of total national government expenditure in 2012 was at the municipal level, while in Latvia the figure was 28 per cent and, in Estonia, 25 per cent (Davulis, 2013, p. 21). Although this is well below the wealthy-country OECD average, it is above the norm for post-communist states (Aristovnik, 2012). Local authorities have but limited financial independence in generating funds, with the overwhelming majority of resources being generated by state subsidies and redistributed national taxes rather than revenues raised at the local level. In the same way, both key policymaking powers and public services are yet to be significantly devolved in Estonia and Latvia, where the small size of most municipalities makes it difficult to maintain these services. In contrast, the large municipalities have both the finances and the will to increase their autonomy from central government. In recent years the mayors of the richest Baltic cities have started to question the way in which funds are redistributed between municipalities – in Estonia and Latvia in particular. They have started granting certain rights to residents of Tallinn and Riga, which serve to both build regional support for their administrations (mayors Nils Ušakovs in Riga and Edgar Savisaar in Tallinn – are both identified with Russian voters and interests and use these policies to reach across ethnic groups to reward and enhance their constituencies) as well as increase potential revenues by getting people to 'declare' themselves as living in the municipality. A common argument used by both mayors has been that residents of the capital cities subsidise both visitors and those who work in the capital city but live elsewhere. In 2013 Tallinn introduced free public transport for registered residents, although tourists and those resident elsewhere in Estonia still had to pay €1.60 per ride (Vedler, 2014). Riga attempted to adopt the same system in 2014, but was thwarted by parliament, which argued that Riga was the capital city of Latvia and should not be made inaccessible to other Latvian residents.

Mayors in the Baltic states tend to serve far longer in office than do national leaders. Figure 2.1 shows that Latvian mayors in Ventspils, Liepaja and Jelgava have served particularly long terms in office. This is primarily explained by enduring weaknesses in political party organisation in Latvia (see Chapter 3). National political parties in Latvia have rarely focused on building large membership organisations or establishing regional offices. This has allowed regional and municipal parties, typically set up as vehicles for local political and economic elites, to seize control of local institutions and build up local electoral 'machines'. The Ventspils municipality is an extreme example of this trend. Aivars Lembergs has held the mayor's office of the small, wealthy oil transit port city since the late 1980s. He has long been suspected of playing a central role in the spontaneous privatisation of the many cash-generating, transit-related businesses in the city, although his trial on extorting bribes, money laundering and conflicts of interest, initiated in 2005 when he was arrested and charged by Latvian prosecutors, had still not ended in 2014. These charges have not dented his popularity and his political vehicle: For Ventspils and Latvia (*Ventspilij un Latvijai*,

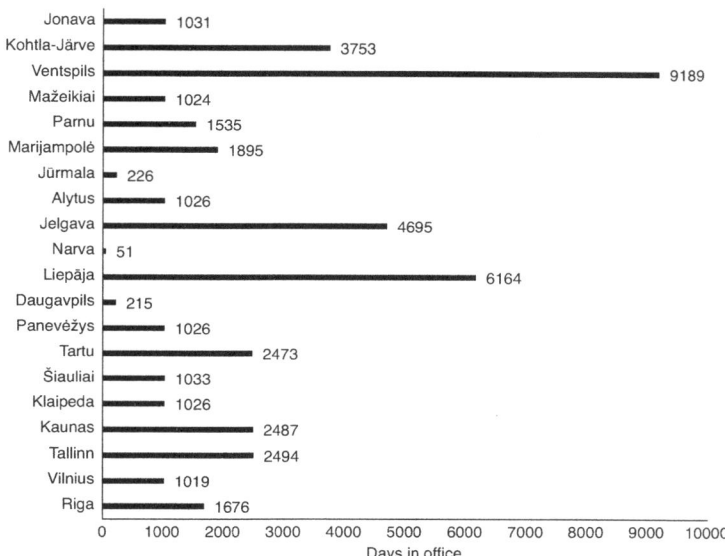

Figure 2.1 Incumbent mayors in the 20 largest municipalities in the Baltic states. Consecutive days in office (From first election to 31 January 2014)

Source: Municipality homepages. Author's calculations.

VuL) collected 69.4 per cent of the vote in 2013, an increase on its 2009 share of 60 per cent. Moreover, Lembergs has used his influence at the national level, with his small regional party, forging an alliance with the Green/Farmers Union that has given him influence in most government coalitions since the early 2000s.

However, Ventspils, as well as the large municipalities, are exceptions. Most local authorities in the Baltic states are small, relatively poor and reliant on funds from the central government. As a result, the Baltic states remain comparatively centralised, unitary states.

2.6   The bureaucracy

While the political executives and legislatures were either created anew or resurrected from the inter-war era, many of the key unelected institutions of the new democracies were inherited from the Soviet system and, as such, have proved to be much harder to construct or reform. This part of the chapter focuses on three particularly important institutions – the bureaucracies, courts and state security services.

The Baltic public administrations have been *developed* rather than *reformed*. The inherited communist bureaucratic structures had focused on implementation, the suppression of citizens and direct control of the economy. This made them so 'irrelevant and inadequate' for the double demands of democracy and the market economy that they effectively had to be built from scratch (Verheijen, 2003, p. 312). The three Baltic states initially had relatively small civil services. Many critical functions had been carried out by the central bureaucracy in Moscow during the Soviet era. Thus the early post-1991 years saw an influx of young people into the Baltic bureaucracies while Estonia and Latvia saw a simultaneous exit of personnel lacking the titular language skills or necessary citizenship. Another group to exit the public sector in all three states was made up of those with Western language or commercial skills that could be monetised in the private sector. The dominant neo-liberal and new public management paradigms at the start of the 1990s (particularly in the then-influential World Bank and IMF) meant that international advisers did not urge reformers to focus on public administration as a necessary and central part of the new state. As a result, much of the bureaucratic construction that did take place was ad hoc, piecemeal and lacked the strategy, coordination or detailed planning that could be found in other branches of the reform process, not least because decision-makers often lacked a deeper understanding of the rationale of the West–East policy transfers undertaken (Agh, 2003; Randmaa-Liiv, Nakrošis and Gyorgy, 2010, p. 162).

The Baltic states quickly established institutions to coordinate the changes in the public sector. For example, Lithuania established the Ministry of Public Administration Reform and Local Authorities (MPARLA), and Latvia the Ministry of State Reform. Training centres such as the Lithuanian Institute of Public Administration (LIVADIS) were also established in the 1990s. New civil service and public administration laws were written. Key external experts, such as Sir Robin Mountfield, a former permanent secretary of the UK Cabinet Office, helped with the restructuring of the civil service. Estonia quickly embraced new public management (NPM) ideas and concepts, while Latvia and Lithuania came to these much later and with less enthusiasm, but still enacted many NPM reforms. Estonia's enthusiasm is largely explained by the youthful Isamaa-led government of 1992, which was elected on a platform of 'A clean break with the past', and had a number of youthful government ministers who aimed to put this motto into practice. The neo-liberal paradigm was dominant in the restructuring of the public administration, as it was in economic developments. The size of the public sector shrank as a number of services were privatised. One clear tendency has been for the steady reduction and consolidation of government ministries, while the number of public agencies flowered. However, this was largely done in an uncoordinated way.

A clearer focus only came at the end of the 1990s, when EU accession prioritised the salience of bureaucratic structures for the transition to EU membership. From the late 1990s onwards the annual reports on accession to the EU contained specific directions on reform and advocated the further creation of agencies leading to a wave of new institutions focusing on regulation and the management of EU funds (Randmaa-Liiv, Nakrosis and Gyorgy, 2010, p. 167) In the long term, this resulted in the decentralisation and fragmentation of the public administration into overly specialised bureaucrats and agencies that lacked coordination mechanisms (Randmaa-Liiv, 2008, pp. 9–10). The primary driver for reform and modernisation of the Baltic bureaucracies was the priority of gaining accession to the European Union. This has also affected the policy level. For example, the medium-term planning and development budgets of the Baltic states have been adjusted to fit in with the seven-year European Union budgets in order to reflect the importance of the regional and agricultural funds in planning regional development in the Baltic states.

Public-sector reforms have generally been judged to be a great success. A 2009 Organisation for Economic Cooperation and Development 'Support for Improvement in Governance and Management' (OECD SIGMA) paper on post-EU accession developments in public administration stressed that the three Baltic states were front-runners in continuous development of their civil services:

> Lithuania, Latvia, and to a lesser extent Estonia stand out in that they have continued pre-accession reforms and upgraded their civil service systems. In all three countries, the civil service system has reached a relatively high degree of fit with European principles of administration, but the achievements remain vulnerable and unconsolidated. At the time of writing, Lithuania was the regional frontrunner in the area of civil service professionalisation. (Meyer-Sahling, 2009, p. 7)

The professionalisation of the administration is visible in a number of areas. Open competition for job opportunities is now a central feature of the Baltic public administrations, although only Lithuania has an examination system.[17] Estonia and Latvia use exams only on an ad hoc basis. Various tools of new public management, such as performance-related pay and the subcontracting of services has been widespread. A remaining problem was with the relatively small salaries in the public sector. This was overcome in Latvia through the creation of secret 'management contracts' and a culture of bonuses that augmented the basic salaries of top civil servants. This, in turn, led to the rather strange situation of ministries having a number of civil servants earning significantly more than their ministers.

The 2008–2010 financial crisis led to a hurried reassessment, rationalisation and reorganisation of the public sector, and the number of agencies was rapidly cut (although the process had begun in 2004 in Estonia). At the same time, the agencies with functions related to the EU have been largely immune to these changes. The decline of external influence and the increased relevance of domestic effects means that we see increased variation in the national public administrations. The economic crisis principally changed the way in which public-sector salaries were structured in the Baltic states. This was particularly the case in Latvia, which formerly had a system of loosely regulated 'management contracts' that allowed the minister and his top civil servants to boost the regular salary of officials with a secret, allegedly performance-related, management contract. These contracts allowed ministries to pay salaries comparable to the private sector. The crisis also resulted in increased transparency of salaries, and all ministries in the Baltic states are now obliged to publish the monthly salaries of their employees (in addition to annual financial declarations that are also publically available).

The higher levels of the Baltic public administrations now rank among the least politicised administrations in the post-communist region. Top civil servants in Estonia and Latvia are appointed for a five-year fixed term and are relatively difficult to remove from office. Leading civil servants in Lithuania are appointed for an indeterminate period. All three states have introduced evaluation and performance systems, and merit-based promotion is far more likely than that based on political connections or party membership (Meyer-Sahling, 2009). A new index of politicisation of the highest ranks of the civil service in post-communist states found the following:

The data show that the senior civil service of the three Baltic states is largely de-politicised. Even for the top level, the politicisation scores are rather low, especially for Estonia and Lithuania. This picture is largely confirmed by the interviews. In all three countries, the top level is subject to open competition. Vacancies are advertised and selection is done by selection commissions that consist of public officials and/or independent external experts. This does not mean that ministers have no say over the appointment to the highest non-political post in the ministries. They can refuse the proposals that are made to them (all three countries). (Meyer-Sahling and Veen, 2012, p. 10)[18]

Estonia led the way and had the lowest level of politicisation with a score of 14, while Latvia (24) and Lithuania (28) were also well below the mean score of 44 for the 8 post-communist states surveyed. However, while the development of public administration systems can be broadly deemed to be a success, the judiciary and courts have proved to be more immune to change.

2.7   Courts and judges

Legal systems uphold both democracy and the market economy. Courts and judges sustain the core rules of the state and resolve conflicts between different private and public actors. Naturally, the legal systems of the Baltic states have undergone root and branch change since 1991. However, the fundamental restructuring of courts and the justice system were not addressed at the earliest stage of the transformation, when the focus was on building the market and writing the new constitutions and laws. In the medium term this proved to be rather problematic. In the communist system the courts were not independent arbiters of laws but a tool of government that did little more than legitimise decisions taken at a higher level. Moreover, courts played virtually no role in arbitrating economic conflicts, but instead focused on social engineering. At the most fundamental level, the legal system needed to be depoliticised and made independent. Formal independence was achieved relatively quickly, albeit at the cost of decision-making capacity. By the mid-1990s the reform process was driven by the importance attached to joining the EU, once again strengthening the adoption of law – the infamous *acquis communautaire* – at the cost of strengthening and building legal institutions. Only later was there a realisation that the core legal *institutions* needed to be strengthened:

As a result of weak capacity and rapid and nontransparent lawmaking processes, existing institutions – including courts, lawyers, regulatory bodies, and others charged with implementation – often had difficulty understanding, applying, and enforcing the new laws being passed by Parliaments. This led to significant 'implementation gaps' – that is, gaps between what legislation required and what happened in practice, which in turn led to growing public mistrust in courts. (Anderson, Bernstein and Gray, 2005, p. xii)

These weaknesses in the legal system were exploited by unscrupulous actors, as discussed in greater depth in Chapter 4 of this volume. In terms of the political system, the major legal political actors in modern European democracies are the constitutional courts. The Baltic states all adopted varying models of this court in the 1990s. Estonia opted for a system in which the powers of a constitutional court are combined with those of a supreme court, while Latvia and Lithuania established independent constitutional courts primarily staffed with legal scholars. Estonia also has a legal chancellor who performs constitutional review functions in terms of both reviewing draft laws before they are passed by the legislature, interpreting the constitutionality of existing laws and referring cases to the Constitutional Review Chamber of the Supreme Court for particularly contentious issues.

The appointment system in all three states spreads responsibility for staffing the constitutional courts among several institutions. The president of Estonia nominates the chief justice, who is then voted on by the legislature. The chief justice then nominates other supreme court judges for a legislative vote. They have no term limits. In contrast, Latvia's seven constitutional court judges are elected for ten-year terms. In an attempt to ensure a politically independent court, candidates for judges are nominated from three different sources. Three judges are nominated by the parliament (with at least 10 per cent of deputies needed to support the initial nomination), two by the Cabinet of Ministers and two others by the Latvian supreme court. All seven have to be confirmed by an absolute parliamentary majority (51 votes). Lithuania's nine supreme court justices serve for nine non-renewable years and, similar to Latvia, are elected by the legislature after being nominated by a combination of the president (three), the speaker of the Seimas (three) and the chief justice of the supreme court (three). The constitutional courts have steadily gained in influence and made an increasing number of rulings. As Pettai, Auers and Ramonaitė (2011, p. 146) pointed out, this has been a result of the courts acquiring more powers as Estonian and Latvian individuals gained the right to file claims at the courts, as well as an increase in public 'awareness of the power and relevance of these courts'.

2.8   State security: police, military and clandestine services

All three Baltic states quickly needed to re-establish control over the internal and, as far as possible, external security of their states. The first step in this process was to either take over existing Soviet institutions or to work from a *tabula rasa* and establish entirely new organisations (in this case re-establishing institutions from the inter-war era effectively amounted to the same thing). This was no easy task. The security services had been enormously unpopular among the general public, and there was little initial appetite to establish security agencies, especially domestic or clandestine services. The security apparatus in the Soviet era protected the state not the citizens. This core function now had to be flipped around. There have been two clear trends. While domestic police forces were gradually reformed, the national militaries and clandestine services were created anew.

The police forces in the Soviet era were known as the militia. They were deeply politicised, centralised and secretive institutions and structured in a military fashion. Innovations that emerged in the West, such as community policing and local actions against local crimes were unheard of in the Soviet context. Many of these Soviet traditions, such as the use of military ranks, have been maintained, although other core dimensions of the police have been reformed. Indeed, restructuring of the police was started even before the Baltic states had split from the Soviet Union. Estonia's new police law was passed in 1990 (and eventually replaced in 1998), Lithuania's in 1990 (updated in 2000 with a new law) while Latvia passed a new law on the police in June 1991, a few months before the

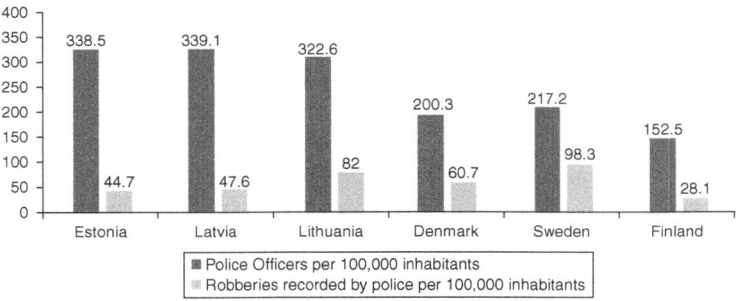

Figure 2.2   Police officers and recorded robberies in Nordic/Baltic region, 2010
Source: Eurostat (2014) and UNODC (2014).

collapse of the Soviet Union. Latvia's law created three levels of police forces: the state and security police that both operated throughout the country, and local police forces based in municipalities. Estonia's system has a state police that is divided into 17 regions. Lithuania's police also has separate national and municipal levels. The ethnic composition of the police in Estonia and Latvia has changed over the course of the last quarter century, with the Russophones who once dominated the police force leaving because of a lack of language skills. Titular Balts were encouraged to enrol in the police academies, while Russophones were discouraged – again largely because of language barriers. In 1991 about two-thirds of the Estonian police were Russophones. By 1996, the last year in which the Estonian police published ethnic statistics on its composition, the situation had been reversed, and 70 per cent of the police force was ethnic Estonian (Saar, 1999, p. 29). Another major change is the introduction of women into the police forces, and Estonia and Latvia (which needed to replace the Russophones who exited the police) are now among the European Union countries with the greatest share of women in the police force.[19]

The police forces were initially overwhelmed by the simultaneous changes in management and oversight as well as by the rise in crime that accompanied independence. Police salaries were low, and officers often had to decide between using the power of their authority for illicit gain (accept or extort bribes) or exiting the profession. Another way to increase the salary was to moonlight as security guards, something that was possible due to the shift structure of the working day. At the same time as policemen were facing up to these hard choices, there was a huge rise in crime and criminality in the Baltic states. The police forces were overcome and found it especially hard to keep up with criminal gangs that had at their disposal huge resources, often greater than the financially stretched police. For example, all three states experienced a surge in trafficking of women, caused by the rapid appearance of sex and entertainment industries, often illicit, in the region. The economic crisis meant that there were few economic opportunities for young women. Relatively open borders with both the East and the West led to the states becoming source, transit and destination countries for human trafficking, with several thousand young Baltic women being trafficked to Western Europe every year (Trofimovienė, 2008, p. 156). In the early 1990s all three Baltic states experienced vicious battles between home-grown and Russian criminal gangs seeking to take control of the local markets. The Estonian 'bloody autumn' of 1994 alone saw 100 murders related to organised crime (Kastrand, 2006, p. 7). In the second half of the 1990s the organised crime gangs became less visible as they consolidated their gains, and the long economic boom of the 2000s saw an accompanying fall in crime levels. Figure 2.2. shows that the Baltic states now have lower recorded levels of certain crimes, such as robberies, than do their Nordic neighbours (although this also has a lot to do with how often crimes are reported and how they are logged). At the same time, the figure also shows that the three states have far higher numbers of employed police officers. This can be explained by the continuing reliance on the shift system – police officers work 24 hours and then have several days off (often spent as security guards for private companies) before returning to work. This shift system requires a higher number of officers than do shorter shifts.

Prison services have been largely neglected and little money has been invested into constructing or modernising Baltic prisons. The only new prison construction in the region is Estonia's Viru prison. Baltic prisons have been much criticised by non-governmental organisations for their generally run-down appearance and crowded environment. This was particularly the case in the early 1990s when stretched financing and rising crime rates led to chaos and brief losses of control. There were 23 murders in Estonian prisons in 1993, although this was down to one by 1998 (Saar, 1999, p. 36). In comparative European terms the three Baltic states have the highest prison population rates in the EU, with judges still clearly favouring incarceration over other forms of punishment.[20]

Another pressing concern in 1991 was the establishment of independent, civilly controlled national militaries. Just as the reform of courts and judges was driven by the external demands of accession to the EU, the organisation of the Baltic militaries was driven by the needs of NATO accession (discussed in greater detail in Chapter 6). However, there were a number of immediate constraints. First, the continued presence of ex-Soviet (now Russian) military meant that there were few suitable bases in which to locate the new armed forces. And when the Russian troops did leave, the military bases were typically ransacked and unsuited for immediate use. Moreover, the cash-strapped Baltic states simply did not have the financial resources necessary to purchase the modern equipment needed to build up the armed forces. The expense of military equipment meant that the forces were initially reliant on foreign assistance. As a result, although there were discussions and planning of the new military in the early years of independence the reality was that 'Latvia was incapable of organising a single infantry battalion' (Rajevs, 2004). The demands of quickly building military forces from scratch meant that the backbone of the newly created military forces were both former Soviet and Western officers. Parliamentary oversight could be achieved quite quickly because the armed forces were built up from scratch. However, three factors hampered the effective implementation of this oversight (Jonušaitė, 2004). First, parliament lacked an institutional and individual knowledge of the military. This led to those deputies with some sort of military experience being given outsized influence. Second, the core secretive nature of military organisations meant that wider debates on the activities of the military were difficult. The organisations themselves only passed on information with great reluctance. Finally, the Baltic states had few independent sources of information on what was happening in the military – journalists in this field were inexperienced, and think-tanks had yet to appear. This placed even greater power in the hands of the armed forces.

The Baltic has long been a region in which rival spy agencies battle for control and influence (Lucas, 2012, p. 18).[21] The Russian ex-KGB defector, Oleg Gordievsky, outlined the reasons for enhanced Russian interest in the Baltic states:

> From a psychological point of view, the Baltic states are regarded as the former Soviet Union. The fact that they have turned so completely away from Russia and exercised fully independent policies clearly provokes Moscow's anger. There is a belief in Moscow that the Balts are somehow against Russia. ... Moreover, Balts have been speaking about integration into Europe and also about joining NATO. For Russian chauvinists, this is a blow below the belt. Moscow certainly sees all this as a strategic threat. ... The enlargement of NATO hurts their pride. Last but not least, Russian services are convinced the Baltic states are a launching pad for Western intelligence in their secret war against Moscow. ... I'd say this: the Baltic states are as interesting for Russia from an intelligence point of view as any other nation in Europe – even more so. Since St. Petersburg, Moscow and Pskov are nearby, they take the Baltics very seriously, indeed. For Moscow, I believe that the Baltic states are now certainly a higher priority than, say, Finland. (Sildam and Mattson, 2001)

In 1992 Vasili Mitrokhin met a British diplomat at the freshly opened British embassy in Riga and gave him a sample of the KGB documents he had in his possession – a cache that would eventually be known as the famous Mitrokhin KGB archive. In 2008 Estonian security forces arrested Herman Simm, a civil servant in Estonia's Ministry of Defence, who was found to be responsible for one of the biggest security breaches in NATO history. In the same year, Latvia expelled three Russian diplomats for attempting to buy NATO secrets. Then, in 2012, Estonia arrested Aleksei and Viktoria Dressen, an Estonian couple eventually convicted of treason for spying for Russia. That same year Belarus arrested a number of its citizens and accused them of spying for Lithuania. In 2013 Vladimir Veitman confessed to spying for Russia. These events outline the importance of the Baltic states as a playground for Russian and Western spies. These events also point towards the success of Estonia's spy agencies. As President Ilves pointed out: 'We caught four moles in the last five years. That means one of two things. Either we're the only country in the EU with a mole problem, or we're the only country in the EU doing anything about it' (Weiss, 2014).

Despite the great initial external intelligence service interest, there was little haste in constructing new intelligence services to replace the KGB. Larry L. Watts (2007) pointed out that 'transition populations tend to favor the destruction of intelligence apparatuses, not their reform', and the initial Baltic reaction was to dismantle the oppressive security agencies rather than replace them. Moreover, while economic and constitutional advisors flooded the post-communist region, intelligence agents from both friendly and hostile states did their job – collect information – rather than advise the new states on the construction of modern intelligence agencies. This began to change in the mid-1990s as the Baltic states began to edge towards membership in the European Union and NATO.

The construction of the agencies took place with broadly unfavourable background conditions. The economic decline outlined in Chapter 5 as well as the growth of corruption, allowed illicit groups and networks to use the chaos and confusion of the transition to further their own aims and compromise law and order institutions in the new states. Nevertheless, clandestine agencies were formed. Lithuania's State Security Department was set up in March 1990. In March 1991 the Estonian government re-established the Estonian Internal Security Service (known as the KaPo).[22] For the next decade it functioned as a part of the police until being reclassified in 2001 as a security service. Latvia's Constitution Protection Bureau (*Satversmes Aizsardzības Birojs*, SAB) was set up in 1995 and is one of the country's three security services (together with the Security Police and Military Counter-Intelligence). SAB has the broadest responsibilities, being responsible for security vetting of public officials, as well as being the intelligence and counterintelligence agency. The core structures of the three agencies are very similar. They are all overseen by a combination of civilian legislative and executive institutions, depoliticised and part of a broader network of collaborating Western agencies. NATO accession played a very important role in the restructuring of these services, not least because NATO authorities were concerned by possible leaks of classified documents to Russia and thus insisted on certain reforms to the way in which the Baltic agencies worked.

There has been a degree of steadiness in terms of the leadership of these organisations. Both Estonia and Latvia have had only three service chiefs since the organisations were set up, although the Lithuanian agency has been far more unstable with 11 heads between 1990 and 2014. The heads of these services are well known to the public, often appearing on television and giving interviews to newspapers and other media. Politicisation of the clandestine agencies had been one of the initial fears that needed to be tackled. The first head of Latvia's clandestine agency was Lainis Kamaldiņš, a member of the Latvia's Way party. There was some concern that he used the instruments of the service to favour his party colleagues and further their interests. As a result, both his successors have been politically neutral. Indeed, they are individuals who were seen as being above the cut and thrust of everyday politics. Kamaldiņš' immediate successor, Jānis Kažociņš a British–Latvian, was a retired brigadier general from the British Army who had previously served as the UK's military attaché in the Baltic states. He was a figure whom Latvia's future NATO allies fully trusted, a crucial thing at that time as Latvia struggled to fulfill the NATO accession criteria. However, the Lithuanian State Security Department has been more politicised. In 2006 and 2007 the whole clandestine establishment was thrown into disarray as a parliamentary committee investigated illicit links between the security department, government officials and pro-Russian businesses. The security chief, Arvydas Pocius, was forced from office and a new head appointed. Senior politicians feared that the whole department had been compromised.

All three security agencies publish annual reports outlining the major threats and challenges they deal with. The most detailed reports are prepared by the KaPo, while Lithuania's State Security Department only publishes its accounts and other quantitative data on its activities (such as how many people have been vetted). Latvia's account is more substantive than Lithuania's but lacks the detail of Estonia's. Nevertheless, the reports show the landscape of internal (and partly external) threats that contemporary Baltic states face. KaPo's 2013 annual report makes clear that the major security challenges are posed by Russian influence in the region – spying as well as soft power – and corruption within the state (Estonian Internal Security Service, 2014). Although there are also sections on international terrorism and descriptions of the Muslim community in Estonia, these appear to be sops to Estonia's international partners rather than seen as potential threats to law and order. The Latvian Constitution Defence Bureau's report for the same year entirely focused on Russia's clandestine activities within Latvia, as well as cyber attacks launched from Russia. Lithuania's State Security Department's report for 2013 also focused on Russia, even identifying and accusing a Russian diplomat of attempting to obtain classified documents during Lithuania's presidency of the European Union as well as stating that Russia uses both electronic and human resources to regularly spy on Lithuania (Reuters, 2014).

Conclusions

The core democratic institutions have been functioning in the Baltic states for a quarter century. The three constitutions balance powers between legislatures, executives and the courts and the unelected bureaucracies and security services fulfil the functions that they are given. These institutions are constantly developing and changing, as is the case with comparable institutions elsewhere in Europe. They have faced unexpected and unprecedented challenges, such as the impeachment of Rolandas Paksas or the recall of the Latvian parliament in 2011, which tested their institutional and democratic rigour. There can be little doubt that the Baltic states' democratic institutions are consolidated.

Western actors and conditionality were crucial in advising, financing and pushing for reforms and institutional development. The Western orientation of Baltic elites meant that the states were open to this advice and guidance (even to the appointment of a high-ranking ex-British military officer as Latvia's spy chief). Moreover, as the following chapter will show, while the Baltic states were initially accused of having weak, fragmented parties and fickle voters, the parliaments (and especially the governments of all three states) showed remarkable policy consistency and support for core democratic institutions, which gave them the breathing space to develop and mature.

3
Elections, Referendums and Parties

By the end of 2014, the Baltic states had held a total of 19 parliamentary, 19 municipal and 3 cycles of European Parliament elections. Lithuania, which elects its president via a national popular vote, had additionally held six presidential polls. Another 23 referendums have been held since August 1991. The rigidity of the Lithuanian and Latvian electoral and judicial institutions have been tested by the 2004 impeachment of Lithuanian president, Rolandas Paksas, and the subsequent early presidential election, as well as a referendum on the recall of Latvia's parliament in the summer of 2011 and the following early election. Estonia is recognised as an electoral innovator, being the first state in the world to regularly use Internet voting in municipal and national elections. Elections are now a normal, even occasionally boring, part of the Baltic political system. Indeed, trends from older Western democracies – declining turnout, disenchanted voters – have taken hold in the post-communist Baltic and East-Central European regions.

Referendum and citizens' initiative mechanisms have been used increasingly frequently in Latvia and Lithuania, although they remain rare in Estonia. While referendums have been used by dominant elites in Lithuania to legitimise their actions, in Latvia they have been used as an opposition tool to control government actions as well as a form of electoral campaigning and attention-seeking by fringe groups.

Consolidating and institutionalising the party systems has proven to be more challenging and far less linear than the strengthening of electoral institutions. Only a few of the parties that competed in the 1992/1993 founding elections still exist in their previous name or form, although many parties in each country can, at a pinch, trace their origins back to these first elections. Almost all parties can trace their origins, either directly or spiritually, back to one of the three major political blocs that dominated Estonian and Latvian politics in the late 1980s – the radical nationalist Congress movements, the moderate popular fronts and the reactionary Russophone Inter movements. In the initial post-Soviet decade the Lithuanian party system appeared to be the first to mature into a stable competition between two large left and right parties (based on the Lithuanian popular front and former communist parties). However, the 2000 parliamentary election shattered the old order and saw newer, fuzzier lines of political division emerge as several new parties were elected to parliament. In contrast, the 1990s saw the Estonian and, particularly, the Latvian party systems marked by fission, fusion and volatility. While the Estonian party system settled down to more regular patterns of competition in the twenty-first century – indeed, the 2011 parliamentary election saw Estonia become the first post-communist state in Europe to have no newly formed political parties compete in a national election – the Latvian party system has been slower to consolidate.

This chapter considers elections, referendums, parties and party systems in the Baltic states. It begins with a discussion of the electoral rules structuring party competition in the Baltic states, and then moves on to analyse electoral outcomes, covering national, municipal and European elections. The next section considers the increasing frequency and political role of referendums in the political system. The final part begins with a discussion of the three party systems, from their origins in the late 1980s up to the main contemporary cleavages and lines of competition, and then focuses on the institutional setting of the party system and the organisational structures of the political parties themselves.

3.1 Elections

The latter years of Soviet rule provided both established and fledgling Baltic elites with valuable experience in conducting large-scale democratic elections. The first free elections of the modern era were held during the last years of the Soviet Union as Mikhail Gorbachev liberalised the Soviet political system. The first multi-candidate election came in March 1989, when voters turned out to elect representatives to the newly created USSR Congress of People's Deputies, which replaced the Supreme Soviet of the Soviet Union. Winning candidates had to receive an absolute majority of votes in single-seat districts with a run-off between the top two candidates if there was no absolute majority in the first round. The popular fronts won at least three-quarters of the seats in every Baltic state. This was then followed in 1990 by elections to new Supreme Councils (sometimes also referred to as the Supreme Soviets), where reform candidates garnered a two-thirds majority in all three legislatures. Thus despite the financial, media and organisational dominance of the local communist parties, voters in the Baltic states overwhelmingly supported pro-independence candidates. While Latvia and Lithuania again used the established Soviet electoral rules of single-member constituencies, Estonia experimented with a proportional representation by single transferable vote system (Taagepera, 1990).[1] The Estonian political leadership was likely encouraged to innovate by Estonian-American political scientist Rein Taagepera, a world-renowned expert on electoral systems (Kask, 1996, p. 197). All permanent residents and Soviet military personnel over 18 years of age based in the Baltic states were allowed to vote in both these elections (ballot papers were printed in both Russian and the titular Baltic languages). The next, post-Soviet era, elections would have a very different electorate in Estonia and Latvia.

Several core electoral issues needed to be addressed after August 1991. The radical nationalist Congress movements in Estonia and Latvia, as well as the increasingly assertive nationalism of *Sajūdis* in Lithuania, placed the issue of *who* exactly would be allowed to vote at the top of the political agenda. Second came the multiplicity of issues addressing *how* people should vote. Third, the Baltic states needed to settle on legitimate and acceptable formulas for counting and distributing the votes. In other words, a mechanism that would turn votes into seats. While the issue of granting electoral rights dogged Estonian and Latvian politics throughout the 1990s, the latter two issues were addressed quickly and with little controversy.

While there was initially no great haste to hold new elections following independence in 1991, growing public dissatisfaction with the political leadership's handling of economic reforms and rising social and economic distress caused by the systemic transition meant that pressure for new elections appeared by the end of the year. Estonia and Lithuania held founding elections in 1992, although domestic bickering over the composition of the demos delayed Latvia's elections until spring 1993. While organisation and planning of the technical details of the elections were eased by both the democratic electoral experience of the late Soviet era and the assistance of a multiplicity of international actors, the final say in the shape of the ballots was very much in the hands of Baltic leaders.

The most ticklish issue in Estonia and Latvia related to the handling of voting rights for the Russophone community. Lithuania, with its small share of Russian-speakers, passed a citizenship law in 1989 and then updated it in 1991 (adding language and constitutional knowledge requirements to the naturalisation process). The law granted automatic citizenship to individuals, and their direct descendants, who could prove citizenship at the time of the 1940 Soviet annexation, as well as those meeting ten-year residency criteria. This meant that the overwhelming majority of Lithuania's resident population, as well as a large number of émigrés, were able to vote in the 1992 founding elections.

Estonia and Latvia, with their large Russophone minorities, rejected the Lithuanian 'zero-option' citizenship model. Lawmakers were pushed and prodded to ever more radical and exclusionary positions by their Citizen's Congresses. In 1992 Estonia reinstated an amended version of the 1938 citizenship law that essentially meant that Soviet-era immigrants would have to fulfil a two-year residency requirement in addition to a test of their Estonian language skills. As a temporary measure, Latvia also reinstated its 1919 citizenship law, but the Supreme Council then announced that it did not have a mandate to write a new citizenship law because it was a legislature elected during the illegal Soviet occupation. It left this task to the first post-Soviet legislature that would be elected in late spring 1993 by the direct descendants of pre-1940 Latvian citizens. These laws ensured that the first elections would have overwhelmingly ethnic Estonian and Latvian electorates.

The newly elected Latvian parliament finally adopted a citizenship law that came into force in July 1994. It initially contained quotas, later replaced with windows that allowed only certain categories of people to apply for citizenship in any given year, after the president had returned the earlier law. It was only liberalised after a national referendum in 1998 following severe international pressure. The effect of this legislation is that Estonia and especially Latvia, maintained large communities of non-citizens well into the twenty-first century (nationality, minority and citizenship issues are further elaborated in Chapter 4). One resulting feature of the Latvian electoral landscape has been the gradual increase in the share of the vote for Russophone parties, as increasing numbers of Russophones become citizens.

All three states made substantial changes to their electoral legislation prior to the first post-Soviet elections and have continued making tweaks ever since. New electoral laws were passed in 1992. Latvia's 1992

Law on Elections was largely based on the inter-war 1922 electoral legislation which, as Jānis Peniķis (2010/2011, p. 46) points out, was itself
based on the 1919 law on the election of the Constitutional Assembly.
As is the case with Lithuania, it has been heavily amended but still forms
the basis for Latvia's elections.[2] Estonia's current electoral law was most
recently adopted in 2002.[3] Table 3.1 lays out the basic electoral rules in
the Baltic states.

The three electoral systems share many similarities. All have a 5 per
cent threshold, and the term of all three legislatures has at various points
been extended to 4 years. Universal suffrage is from 18, and 21-year-
olds can stand for parliament in Estonia and Latvia, although 25 is
the minimum age in Lithuania. All three states also allow for different
forms of preference voting. The Estonian system has obligatory voting
for candidates within its open-list proportional system (a party's total
constituency vote is the sum of individual candidates' votes). Party lists
are available at polling stations, and voters write the individual code
number of their preferred candidate onto their ballot paper. The Latvian

Table 3.1   Basic electoral rules in the Baltic states

	Estonia	Latvia	Lithuania
Seats	101	100	141
Election Month	March	October	October
Parliamentary term in years	4 (since 1995)	4 (since 1998)	4 (since 1992)
Possibility for early election	Yes	Yes	Yes
Electoral system	Proportional representation	Proportional representation	Mixed (70 seats proportional representation and 71 single-member districts)
Number of multi-member districts	12[4]	5	1 (national)
Threshold	5%	5%	5% (party's) 7% (party alliances)
Divisors	D'Hondt	Sainte Laguë	Hare quota

Source: Central Election Commissions.

ballot is also quite distinct, with an open party list system that allows voters to support individual candidates by drawing a cross next to their names, or to reject them by striking out the name. This option was used by almost one-third of voters in the 2010 election. This affects the final order of candidates elected to parliament and gives voters greater power: 'all voters determine how many seats a party gains, but only preference voters determine who is elected to those seats' (Millard, 2011, p. 311–312). This led to a practice by which Latvia's parties would place their most popular candidates (known as 'locomotives' for their ability to pull other candidates into the legislature) on the ballot in all five constituencies in order to maximise their attraction across the country (and the party would then calculate which district the 'locomotive' would represent). This practice was banned in 2010 following intense lobbying by the Latvian Electoral Reform Society. Lithuania's preferential vote is a closed list system. In all three Baltic states this inevitably leads to intra-party competition between candidates from the same party who campaign individually, as much as for the party that they represent, in an attempt to leapfrog their party colleagues in the list.

However, there are also notable differences. Since 1995 only registered political parties and party alliances can put forward candidate lists in Latvia. Lithuania has similar legislation. In contrast, the Estonian electoral law allows political parties to put forward candidate lists (electoral alliances were banned in 1997) and citizens to nominate independent candidates in an electoral district. Estonia has a population register and voters have to cast their ballots in the districts where they are resident. Latvia has no electoral register, which allows voters to cast their ballots in any constituency. Voters produce a passport that is then stamped to avoid multiple-voting. The exception is overseas voters whose votes are added to the Riga electoral district. Lithuania has a mixed ballot for parliamentary elections (and also directly elects its president), but Latvia and Lithuania have proportional representation models, albeit with differing vote-counting systems. Estonia has a three-step system for turning votes into seats. First, the personal mandates are distributed between the candidates who reached the simple quota (the number of valid votes divided by number of mandates) in their district. Second, the votes cast for candidates of a political party that received at least 5 per cent of the national vote are counted, and parties get seats according to the number of times their votes in the electoral district exceed the simple quota (and parties receive an extra mandate if the remaining number of votes is at least 75 per cent of the simple quota). Third, the remaining seats are distributed at national level using a modified version of the

D'Hondt method. Latvia uses an unmodified Sainte Laguë formula to allocate seats between parties within the electoral districts and Lithuania uses the Hare quota to distribute the 70 proportional representation seats in the legislature – dividing the total of valid votes by the number of seats to be allocated and then distributing the remaining seats to parties whose remainder is closest to the divisor.

Estonia's electoral experimentation has not been limited to simply trying out the single transferable vote system in the 1990 poll. It has gained international attention (and substantiated its 'E-stonia' sobriquet) by becoming the first state in the world to allow Internet voting in parliamentary elections. Estonia began developing the technology in 2002, tested it in the October 2005 municipal election, and has since utilised it in the 2007 and 2011 parliamentary elections, as well as in the 2009 and 2014 European Parliament vote and the 2009 and 2013 municipal elections. This radical innovation was possible because Estonia created the necessary legal and technological infrastructure and, it has been claimed, also has a political culture supportive of experimentation and innovation (Trechsel, Alvarez and Hall, 2008).[5] The key advance was the introduction of identification cards for online transactions in 2002. These cards are used in daily online interactions with the state (paying taxes or ordering passports, for example) and the private sector (online banking, purchasing insurance) which familiarised individuals with online transactions and has made them more comfortable with Internet voting. As Figure 3.1 indicates, a growing number of voters have utilised the Internet option. Although an international team of cyber security experts claimed that there were fundamental safety flaws and vulnerabilities in the Estonian Internet voting system (based on their observation of the October 2013 municipal vote), the Estonian central election commission has declared its intention to continue utilising the system.[6] The Estonian example has inevitably prompted frequent debate on introducing Internet voting in Latvia and Lithuania. However, the Latvian and Lithuanian election commissions have not supported these initiatives, citing fears that Internet voting might introduce a shadow of doubt over electoral outcomes and thus delegitimise the elections in the eyes of the public.

Similarly to other European democracies, elections in the Baltic states have been marked by a downward trend in electoral participation. Figure 3.2 traces turnout from the 1990 Supreme Council elections to the 2012 Lithuanian parliamentary poll. Turnout in the Supreme Council and the founding elections was, unsurprisingly, extremely high as the Baltic publics seized the opportunity to participate in real elections for

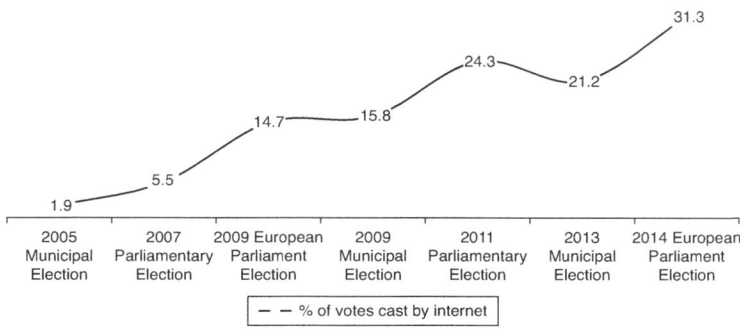

Figure 3.1 Percentage of votes cast by Internet. Elections in Estonia, 2005–2013
Source: Estonian National Election Commission (2014).

the first time in more than half a decade and defy the Soviet regime by voting for pro-independence candidates. However, turnout began falling in the mid-to-late 1990s as the novelty of democratic elections wore off and increasing disenchantment with the political system, prompted by sharp falls in the standard of living as well as a string of political corruption scandals, began to take hold. The biggest fall in turnout has been in Lithuania, where a number of parliamentary elections have seen a lower than 50 per cent turnout, possibly because the electorate includes almost the entire population. Even the 2011 early parliamentary election in Latvia – called by then-president Valdis Zatlers in a dramatic late-night television address after the Latvian parliament had rejected a request from the Latvian prosecutors' office to remove the parliamentary immunity of Ainārs Šlesers, whom Zatlers had accused of being one of a triumvirate of 'oligarchs' undermining the Latvian democratic system – attracted the lowest turnout of any Latvian parliamentary election (Auers, 2012).[7]

Falling turnout can also be seen in Lithuania's presidential elections, the only other first-order elections in the Baltic states. While the first presidential elections in 1993 attracted 78.62 per cent of voters in the first round, 52.17 per cent voted in the first round in 2014, a figure that has remained remarkably stable since the 2003 poll.[8]

European Parliament elections in the Baltic states certainly fit the standard 'second-order elections' model in that they receive far less public and media attention, and mainstream political parties are less concerned with the result than with national (or municipal) elections (Reif and Shmitt, 1980). Turnout is also much lower, although there

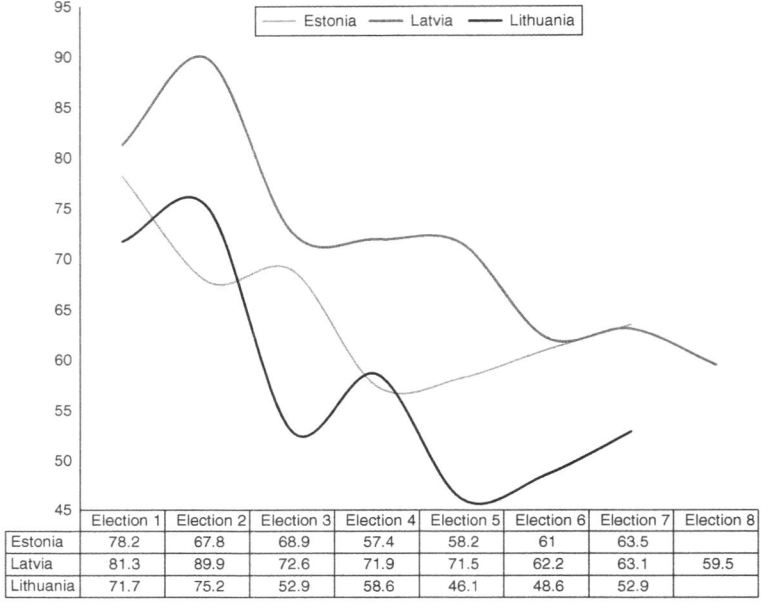

	Election 1	Election 2	Election 3	Election 4	Election 5	Election 6	Election 7	Election 8
Estonia	78.2	67.8	68.9	57.4	58.2	61	63.5	
Latvia	81.3	89.9	72.6	71.9	71.5	62.2	63.1	59.5
Lithuania	71.7	75.2	52.9	58.6	46.1	48.6	52.9	

Figure 3.2   Turnout in Estonian, Latvian and Lithuanian parliamentary elections, 1990–2012

Source: Sikk (2014).

is a less pronounced tendency to punish the government parties and vote for fringe parties than the traditional model would suggest. This is because the discourse in the Baltic states is often about representing the *states* and *nations* at the European level, rather than ideological or political interests. At the same time the most experienced statesmen are typically found in the governing mainstream parties. These politicians, in turn, have been ready to defect from national politics to Brussels and Strasbourg because of the far higher salaries and benefits on offer as well as the career boost that the European Union gives domestic politicians. Both Estonia (Toomas Hendrik Ilves, an MEP) and Lithuania (Dalia Grybauskaitė, a European commissioner) have elected presidents straight from the European institutions, while Latvia's longest-serving prime minister, Valdis Dombrovskis, was an MEP before taking up the prime minister's post.[9] Dombrovskis was re-elected to the European Parliament in 2014 and then appointed a Vice-President of the European Commission where he was joined by former Estonian prime minister

Andrus Ansip. Jumping from domestic to European office (and back) has become a normal part of the Baltic political system.

All three states have adapted their electoral systems to the peculiarities of the European Parliament. Estonia (6 MEPs), Latvia (8 MEPs) and Lithuania (13 MEPs in 2004, 12 in 2009 and 11 in 2014) all created single, national constituencies. Latvia uses an open-list system similar to that utilised in parliamentary elections (dividing seats with the Saint-Laguë method) while Estonia vacillated from an open list in 2004 to a closed list in 2009 and then back to an open list in 2014 (and divides seats with the d'Hondt method). Lithuania also uses an open list (albeit with the Hagenbach-Bischoff variant of the d'Hondt method). As is the case with national elections, Estonia also allows individual candidates to run. Estonia's lists are strongly personalised, with 'locomotives' often heading up the candidate lists although they have no intention of taking up their place in the European Parliament (Edgar Savisaar has led the Centre Party list in all three elections, but always announced that he will not take up an MEP post if elected). Latvia's and Lithuania's lists have no need for locomotives, because leading party politicians are ready to take up office in Brussels for both financial and personal prestige reasons.

As Figure 3.3 indicates, there have been wide fluctuations in turnout for all three European Parliament elections. The biggest swing has been in Lithuania, which saw turnout above the EU average in 2004 and

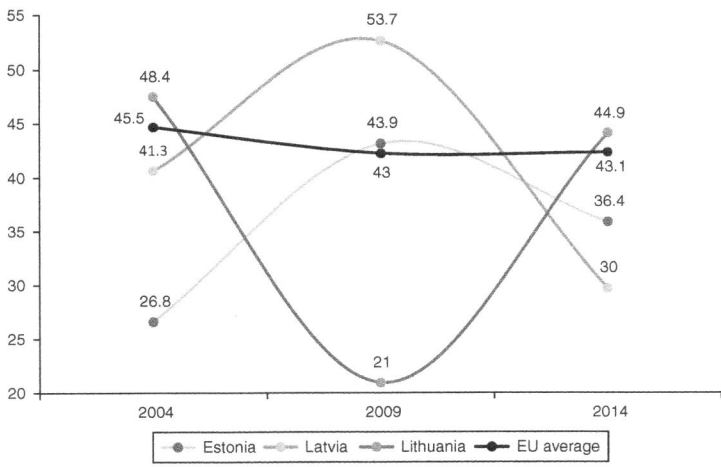

Figure 3.3 Turnout in European Parliament elections, 2004–2014
Source: Central Election Commissions.

2014, but a huge slump to 21 per cent in 2009. However, this deviation can be easily explained by the fact that in 2004 and 2014 the European election was held on the same day as national presidential elections. Similarly, Latvia's high turnout in 2009 was the result of parallel municipal elections attracting voters while Estonia's 2009 European Parliament campaign had been electrified by Indrek Tarand's individual crusade.

Although the first, 2004, European elections saw campaigning and debate revolve around European issues in Estonia, 2009 and 2014 saw a reversion to increased focus on domestic debates (Sikk, 2006, 2009). In contrast, Latvian and Lithuanian European elections have always been dominated by domestic issues (not least because the 2004 and 2014 Lithuanian and 2009 Latvian polls were held concurrently with domestic elections) and there is relatively little substantial discussion of *Europe* in the European elections. Discussion typically revolves around who is best placed to defend national interests in Brussels, hence the dominant 'fight for Lithuania in Brussels' slogan in Lithuania's first European Parliament election (Mazylis and Unikaite, 2004, p. 1). European Parliament campaigns in Latvia have a strong ethnic dimension and have revolved around opposing historical narratives of occupation versus annexation as well as debates about who is best placed to represent Latvian interests in Brussels (Auers, 2011).

The Baltic states have elected a number of high profile, experienced politicians to the European Parliament. Nevertheless, the European Parliament elections have also thrown up surprises. In 2009 Indrek Tarand, an independent candidate, came second in the European Parliament election in Estonia, winning a quarter of the votes. Although his vote share fell to 13.2 per cent in 2014, he was re-elected for a second European Parliament term. The 2014 election also saw the unexpected fragmentation of the Russophone vote in Latvia, with Harmony Centre finishing third (having won the biggest share of the vote in the 2010 and 2011 parliamentary elections) and Unity winning 46.2 per cent of the votes, the biggest share won by any party in a national or European poll in Latvia's history.

Estonia was the first Baltic state to hold municipal elections after 1991, passing local government election laws in 1993 (and again in 1996 and 2002 with many amendments since). The legislation revised the two-tier Soviet-era model of local government, effectively eradicating the upper county level, leaving only cities and rural municipalities. Consolidation of local government has been slow, from 254 units in 1993 to 215 in the 2013 local election. There remains a huge diversity in the size of the municipalities, ranging from over 400,000 residents in Tallinn to just a

Table 3.2 Municipal elections in the Baltic states

	Estonia	Latvia	Lithuania
Number of municipalities (First election)	254 (1993)	594 (1994)	56 (1995)
Number of municipalities (Most recent election)	215 (2013)	119 (2013)	60 (2011)
Term of office (years)	4 (since 2005)	4 (since 1997)	4 (since 2007)
Electoral system	Proportional representation multi-member districts	Proportional representation multi-member districts	Proportional representation multi-member districts
Threshold	5%	5%	4% (party's) 6% (party alliances)
Divisors	D'Hondt	Sainte Laguë	Hare quota
Average mean turnout (number of elections)	53.3% (7)	55% (6)	55.7% (6)
Gap between mean turnout in municipal and national elections	–9.5%	–15.1%	–10.9%

Source: Central Election Commissions.

few hundred in the smaller municipalities (Estonian National Election Committee, 2012). Latvia initially had an even larger number of munici-palities (594 in 1994) and the political battle to consolidate them into bigger units proved to be fraught and drawn out, concluding in 2009 when local government was restructured into 119 administrative units. In contrast, Lithuania increased the number of municipalities from 56 to 60 in 2000. One feature common to all three states has been the growing strength of political parties as organisations, as they have begun to take up an ever greater share of seats in municipalities, although many of the larger municipalities, especially in Latvia, remain controlled by small, local parties.

The evidence for municipal elections as second order elections is rather more muddled. Turnout is well below the average for parliamen-tary elections. However, the elections in the capital cities of Tallinn and

Riga often bear many similarities to national elections. The capital cities are disproportionately large and wealthy in both Estonia and (especially) Latvia, meaning that for political parties the battle to control the municipality is almost as essential as that to control the state. Moreover, both Tallinn and Riga have a high concentration of Russophones, often turning the election into a battle between the titular and Russophone ethnic groups. Interest in Estonia can be especially high because Estonia's non-citizens also vote in municipal elections. In 2014 both capital cities were controlled by political parties that had been re-elected to office and are supportive of the Russophone communities (Mayor Edgar Savisaar's party in Tallinn and Mayor Nil Ušakovs' renamed Harmony Social Democratic party in Riga). Thus the 2013 municipal election in Latvia saw overall mean average turnout of 46 per cent, but the turnout in Riga was 55.5 per cent (Latvian Central Election Commission, 2014). In the same year the municipal elections in Estonia saw a national turnout of 58 per cent but a higher turnout of 64.1 per cent in Tallinn (Estonian National Election Commission, 2014). The salient issues in the elections in the capital cities are typically ethnicity based or extensions of national political issues. However, local issues predominate in smaller municipalities.

3.2 Referendums and initiatives

Referendums were one of the main political instruments used in the Baltic states in the early 1990s. All three states held consultative independence referendums in 1991 in order to legitimise the popular fronts' campaign to break away from the Soviet Union. In the following years Estonia and Lithuania used the referendum mechanism to legitimate major political decisions, particularly the adoption of new constitutions. However, since 1992 Estonia has only had one referendum – on accession to the EU – while Lithuania had a surge of referendums in the mid-1990s, at one point leading post-communist states in the number of referendums (Krupavicius and Zvaliauskas, 2001, p. 119). Latvia has taken the lead since the late 1990s, holding seven referendums between 2003 and 2012.

Estonia's June 1992 poll on its draft constitution was supported by 91.3 per cent of voters. An additional question asked if Russophones who had applied for Estonian citizenship should be allowed to vote in the election. This was rejected by 53 per cent of voters. Two Russophone regions of Estonia (Narva and Sillamäe) subsequently held referendums on regional independence which were supported by 90 per cent of voters in both cases. However, the Estonian Supreme Court struck down both referendums. The rarity of referendums in Estonia is largely because the Estonian constitution grants parliament great authority on when and how to allow a referendum and has no mechanisms for citizens' initiatives.

In contrast, the re-adopted 1922 Latvian constitution – drafted by, among others, representatives from the Latvian Social Democratic Workers Party who had spent many contented years of exile in Switzerland and been converted to its long-standing tradition of referendums and initiatives (Šilde, 1976, p. 355) – contains five clauses providing for popular initiatives and referendums that have been used with increasing frequency.[10] The first post-Soviet referendum was held concurrently with the October 1998 parliamentary election and concerned the repeal of the law on amendments to the citizenship law called by the nationalist For Fatherland and Freedom/Latvian National Independence Movement party, which had gathered the one-third of parliamentary deputies needed to call a referendum that was seen as a crucial moment in Latvia's democratisation, with the amendments needing to be adopted if Latvia were to join the European Union and NATO. A 1999 referendum on a new pension law failed after a low turnout fell below the minimum quorum – the government parties had urged the public to not participate. The turnout of 72.5 per cent for the 2003 referendum on European Union accession actually exceeded the turnout at the previous parliamentary election, and the 'yes' vote of 67 per cent was far higher than pollsters had predicted. The years 2007 and 2008 saw an increase in the use of referendums. First, then president, Vaira Vīķe-Freiberga, opposed changes to two national security laws and triggered a referendum that was ultimately unnecessary as the government coalition caved in to her demands and dropped the changes to the law (although for legal reasons the referendums went ahead anyway and as a result failed to gather the necessary turnout). Two separate 2008 initiatives – one a constitutional amendment that would give the public the power to dissolve a sitting parliament through a referendum, and one raising the size of the state pension – managed to attract the 10 per cent of signatures needed to trigger a referendum, but failed to garner the minimum turnout for the laws to go onto the statute book.

Latvia has particularly generous provisions for citizens' initiatives. This has led to initiatives becoming political tools used by opposition or extra-parliamentary parties, groups and movements and thus often being an electoral strategy rather than a tool of popular democracy (Auers, 2012). In 2012 Latvia saw an extremely emotionally charged and polarising referendum on introducing Russian as a second state language. It attracted a turnout of 71.1 per cent, the highest for an election or referendum in Latvia since 2003. Voters divided along ethnic lines, with three to one voting against the initiative. The initiative was coordinated by the Russophone Native Language NGO that claimed it was a fight for political rights after two decades of political discrimination and drew parallels with Martin Luther King's civil rights movement. In contrast, Latvians viewed the initiative as a traitorous attack on the very foundations of the Latvian state and turned out in unprecedented numbers. Even before this referendum the Latvian parliament had started debating changes in the legislation on citizens' initiatives with the aims of increasing the number of signatures that have to be collected in order to trigger a referendum, as well as of creating a vetting procedure that ensures that initiatives do not contravene Latvia's core constitutional arrangements. These new laws were later used to deny a referendum on introducing the euro into Latvia (arguing that Latvians had already voted on this issue in 2003 when participating in the referendum on membership of the European Union).

Latvia also has one other innovative grassroots enterprise that provides a link between citizens' initiatives and the legislature. The *Mana Balss* (My Voice) Internet platform was created by a group of enthusiastic young social entrepreneurs and allows anyone to post an initiative (that is vetted by the organisation's volunteer lawyers once it has gathered 100 signatures) in an attempt to attract the 10,000 electronic signatures needed to submit the legislation to parliament. Two laws have already been passed through this system (Mana Balss, 2014).

Lithuania passed a law on referendums in 1989 that was subsequently much amended until a new referendum law was passed by the Lithuanian parliament in June 2002. Between 1991 and 2014 Lithuania saw 13 referendums and 1 plebiscite. The majority (nine) dealt with constitutional issues and the others with economic issues, the latter two addressing Lithuania's nuclear power policy. However, only 4 passed, largely because 50 per cent of the electorate is needed to turnout to provide a quorum. The first post-1991 referendums were used by the political elite to rubber-stamp decisions that had already been made by the governing elite (restoring the presidency, withdrawing Russian troops, adopting a new constitution and the 1996 constitutional amendments, compensating bank savers and selling agricultural land). Thus, because of the organisational and administrative challenges in putting together a citizens' initiative (for instance, requiring 300,000 signatures to trigger a referendum), the referendum mechanisms have been used as

Table 3.3   Referendums and citizen initiatives in the Baltic states, 1990–2014

Year	Purpose	Turnout (%)	For	Against
Estonia				
1991	Independence	1,144,309 (82.9%)	77.8%	21.4%
1992	Adoption of new constitution	669,080 (66.8%)	91.3%	33.1%
2003	EU membership	867,714 (64.0%)	66.8%	33.1%
Latvia				
1991	Independence	1,666,128 (87.6%)	73.7%	24.79%
1998	Citizenship	928,040 (69.2%)	45.0%	52.5%
1999	Pensions Law	339,879 (24.1%)	94.2%	5.3%
2003	EU membership	1,010,467 (72.5%)	67.0%	32.3%
2007	National Security Law A	338,764 (23%)	96.5%	3.0%
2007	National Security Law B	338,747 (23%)	96.4%	3.1%
2008	Constitutional amendments	629,119 (42%)	96.8%	3.0%
2008	Pensions Law	347,182 (22.9%)	96.4%	3.3%
2011	Recall of parliament	689,988 (44.7%)	94.3%	5.5%
2012	State language	1,098,921 (71.1%)	24.9%	74.8%
Lithuania				
1991	Independence	2,247,810 (84.7%)	90.2%	6.5%
1992	Restoration of president's office	1,525,985 (59.2%)	69.3%	25.6%
1992	Withdrawal of Russian troops	1,931,278 (76.1%)	90.7%	7.26%
1992	Adoption of new constitution	1,919,073 (75.3%)	75.4%	21.0%
1994	Privatisation, banking savings and distorted justice	895,778 (36.9%)	83.6%	10.3%
1996	Constitutional amendment I: Composition of parliament	1,353,448 (52.1%)	65.0%	17.6%
1996	Constitutional amendment II: Date of elections to parliament	1,353,448 (52.1%)	74.3%	19.1%
1996	Constitutional amendment III: Budget expenditures	1,353,448 (52.1%)	43.4%	40.0%
1996	Compensation of banking savings	1,362,573 (52.5%)	89.9%	8.2%
1996	Sale of agricultural land	1,031,623 (39.7%)	90.2%	6.5%
2003	EU membership	1,672,317 (63.4%)	69.3%	25.6%
2008	Ignalina Nuclear Power Plant	1,305,825 (48.4%)	88.6%	8.3%
2012	Visaginas Nuclear Power Plant	1,361,082 (52.6%)	35.2%	64.8%
2014	Sale of agricultural land to foreigners	379,915 (15%)	70.8%	26.4%

Source: Central Election Commissions.

a political tool by major Lithuanian political parties rather than as an opposition instrument, which is the case in Latvia. (Auers, Krupavicius and Ruus, 2009).

3.3   Political parties

Political parties have been perhaps the most important actors in the post-independence development of the Baltic states. They have shaped the constitutional order, largely kept to the rules of the game, provided the political elite to staff public office and consolidated democracy as the only legitimate system of governance. However, political parties in the region are also distrusted and disliked. This is because the Baltic party systems have experienced the same developmental problems as other post-communist party systems: fragmentation, blurry cleavages and fuzzy ideologies, fragile links between voters and parties leading to volatility, weak party organisations and low levels of party institutionalisation (Evans and Whitefield, 1998; Lewis, 2000, 2006; Mair and van Biezen, 2001; Tavits, 2008).

The Baltic states' party systems were already partially formed in August 1991 when the countries emerged from Soviet occupation as independent sovereign states. Several years of vibrant political activity between 1988 and 1991 had laid the basis for new parties and party systems to emerge. Indeed, the broad, sweeping movement to break away from the Soviet Union saw social divisions emerge and political entrepreneurs gain valuable organisational experience. After 1991 new rules and laws governing political party activity were gradually adopted and began to shape the underlying nature of the political systems. At the same time, it quickly became clear that there would be no far-reaching purge of the Baltic polities. There were no sweeping Nuremberg-type de-Sovietisation trials (despite demands from the Citizens' Committees in Estonia and Latvia and from the more radical nationalists in *Sajūdis*[11]). Only a few political figures from the communist era were lustrated and barred from participating in the new democracy.[12] Indeed, the post-communist Lithuanian Democratic Labour Party was arguably the most influential political party in Lithuania in the 1990s.

A fast-growing number of political parties appeared after 1991 as the three large political blocs of the late Soviet era – nationalist congress movements, mainstream popular fronts and reactionary Inter movements – disintegrated into a multiplicity of competing political parties. What followed was a decade of political party fission, fusion, fragmentation and creation in Estonia and Latvia, although the Lithuanian party system initially seemed consolidated into a stable left–right cleavage. However, these positions were at least partially reversed in the first part of the twenty-first century as the momentous 2000 parliamentary election in Lithuania saw the decade-old party system disintegrate and a number of new political forces enter the system. Over the next decade and a half the Lithuanian and Latvian party systems continued to be unpredictably volatile while the Estonian system consolidated.

The Pedersen Index – 'the net change within the electoral party system resulting from individual vote transfers' (Pedersen, 1979, p. 3) – has traditionally been used to measure and compare electoral volatility. When applied to the three Baltic states it reveals significantly higher volatility in Latvia and Lithuania than in Estonia, where there has been a steady consolidation of voters and parties (see Figure 3.4). Indeed, Estonia's 2011 volatility index, when just four established parties were returned to parliament, was comparable to that of established West European party systems. However, scholars have pointed out that this measure is far too simplistic to be applied to the post-communist states because it fails to differentiate among individuals switching votes between established parties and those who cast their vote for a new party (Sikk, 2005, Tavits, 2008). More refined research that explicitly splits volatility into two separate components – Type A, caused by new party entry and old party exit (which indicates *weak* party institutionalisation), and Type B,

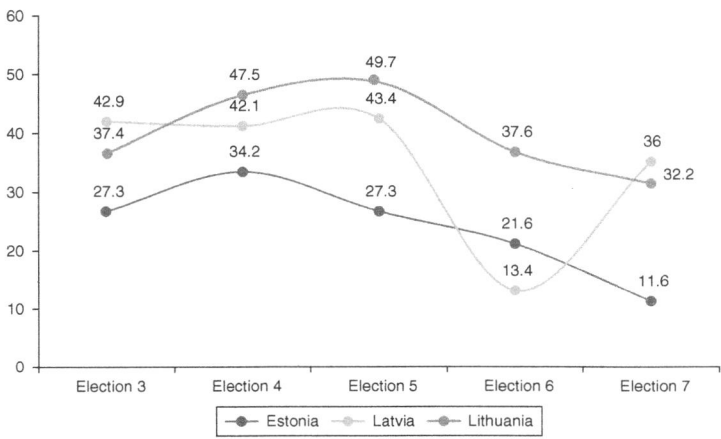

Figure 3.4 Electoral volatility in the Baltic states, 1992–2012 (Pedersen Index)
Source: Caramani and van Biezen (2007); Saarts (2011) and author's calculations.[13]

caused by vote switching between existing parties (and is a *necessary* part of democratic party competition) – finds that while the level of vote-switching is very similar in all three Baltic states, new party entry is far more pronounced in Latvia and Lithuania (Powell and Tucker, 2013).[14] An alternative way of measuring the stability of established parties was proposed by Tõnis Saarts (2011) based on earlier work by Paul Lewis (2006) and Pettai, Auers and Ramonaite (2011). Saarts argued that a measure of 'more established parties' (defined as those represented in the legislature on one or more occasions) brings increased clarity to the Baltic party systems. Table 3.4. applies this indicator to all the elections in the contemporary Baltic states (barring the 1990 Supreme Soviet and 1992/1993 elections when parties were either not formed or were participating in elections for the first time). It clearly shows that a far greater proportion of votes go to established parties in Estonia (100% in the 2011 election) while, apart from the 2006 election, the Latvian electorate is more likely to switch to new political parties. The trend in Lithuania was for consolidation at the start of the period and then fragmentation in Election 4 (the 2000 parliamentary poll) before a gradual increase in votes for more established parties with every election.

These trends are also reflected in the data for the effective number of electoral and parliamentary parties in the Baltic states (see Figures 3.5 and 3.6). Using the Laakso and Taagepera (1979) measure to count and weight parties by their share of the vote in parliamentary elections (effective number of electoral parties) and share of seats in the legislature (effective number of parliamentary parties) it is possible to identify clear, but differing, trends in the three states. In both measures it is clear that the effective number of parties in Lithuania has increased from an initially low base. In contrast, Estonia and Latvia have witnessed a gradual, albeit non-linear, reduction in the number of effective electoral and parliamentary parties.[15]

This phenomenon can be explained by a number of factors. First, Estonia and Latvia saw a supply of new parties as a response to changes

Table 3.4   Proportion of votes taken by 'more established parties'

	Election 3	Election 4	Election 5	Election 6	Election 7	Election 8	Average
Estonia	61%	100%	75%	93%	100%	–	86%
Latvia	37%	47%	50%	100%	54%	73%	60%
Lithuania	91%	40%	45%	60%	83%	–	64%

Source: Saarts (2011) and authors' own calculations.

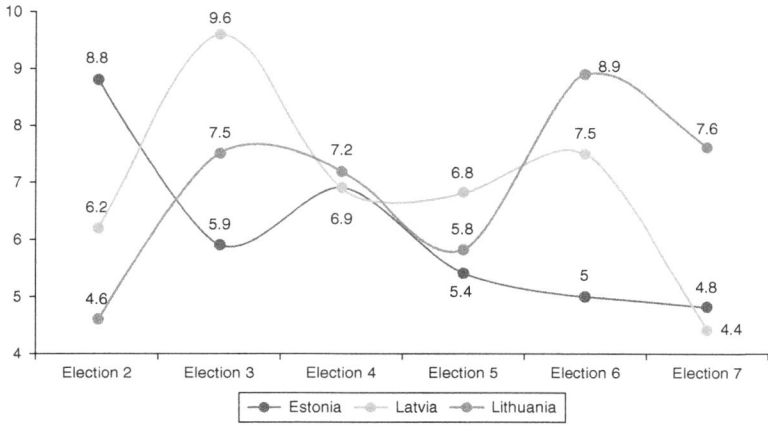

Figure 3.5 Effective number of electoral parties (ENEP) in the Baltic states, 1992–2012

Source: Gallagher (2014).

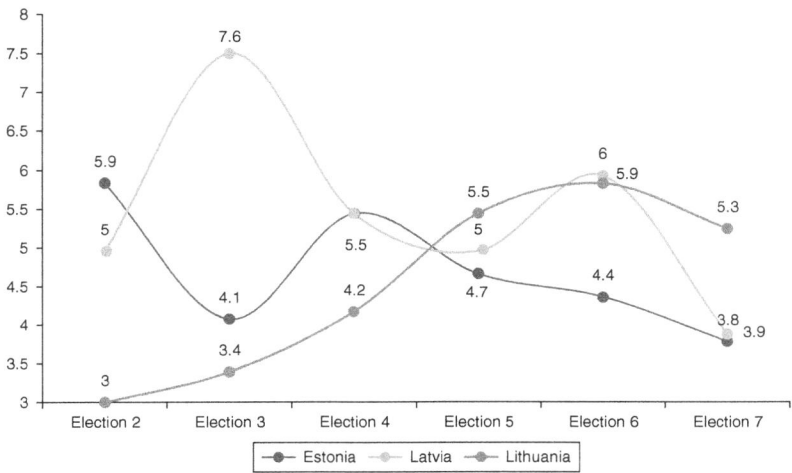

Figure 3.6 Effective number of parliamentary parties (ENPP) in the Baltic states, 1992–2012

Source: Gallagher (2014).

in the composition of the electorate in the 1990s, with an increasing number of Russophones gaining the right to vote. The Estonian system then began to consolidate as the costs and barriers of new party entry increased (a higher minimum membership and state funding for existing parties based on their share of the vote), while those parties already in the system benefitted from increasing flows of public funds and public recognition. Meanwhile, the barriers of entry to the Latvian and Lithuanian systems remained low, encouraging a constant flow of political entrepreneurs to try their luck. Radical changes in campaigning laws (limiting advertising opportunities and spending totals) and the introduction of public financing for parties in the 2000s gradually cut off opportunities for new parties in Latvia.

Although there is a clear trend for consolidation, the unpredictability, fragmentation and volatility of the first two decades of party politics has left its mark on Baltic voters. The Baltic political landscape has long been marked by the publics' disregard for political parties. Trust in political parties, as measured in the biannual Eurobarometer reports, reveals that between 2004 and 2013, less than 10 per cent of Latvians and Lithuanians tended to trust their political parties, while Estonians hovered between 14 and 22 per cent, typically just a few points above the average for the European Union (Standard Eurobarometer, 2004–2013). Much of the public initially mourned the unique sense of national unity that had shaped the anti-Soviet movements and found the political competition and inevitable feuds that divided former friends and colleagues to be particularly jarring. This distrust has also contributed to the volatility of the party systems in Latvia and Lithuania, especially. The Baltic publics have found it hard to identify with concrete political parties and have shifted their political support from party to party at election time. The turn against parties also partially explains the decreasing turnout in elections.

However, it is an interesting feature of the Baltic states that while political parties and party systems have been more volatile and unstable than those of their Western counterparts, there has been a great deal of policy continuity. This is partly because certain key aspects of the transition – particularly political integration with Western international organisations such as NATO and the European Union – have rarely been disputed. But also because political elites have often abandoned their political ships rather than gone down with them. Thus, while party names, symbols and some aspects of their political platforms or ideologies may have changed, their core policies, and often the people who man the executive to turn these ideas into policy, have remained the same.

This section further considers the post-1991 development of political parties and party systems in the Baltic states. It begins with a brief review of the broad umbrella movements of the late 1980s and then tracks their fragmentation into political parties as they began to prepare for the 1992/1993 founding elections, as well as sketches out the contours of the party system since then. It then moves on to consider the cleavages and political divisions and the resulting ideological spectrum that has structured party competition in Estonia, Latvia and Lithuania. It then discusses the different institutional frameworks of laws and regulations that govern party activity, including party financing regulations and the ease with which parties can be created. The final part focuses on parties as political organisations, considering the extent to which parties are oligarchic, their openness to the recruitment of new members, where they source policy innovations, and their links to domestic and international think tanks and core political ideologies.

3.3.1 The starting point

The origins of the contemporary party systems of the three Baltic states can be traced back to the mid-1980s. Mikhail Gorbachev's accession to power in Moscow unleashed first a trickle and then a flood of democratisation that led to the formation of a growing number of different political organisations. These early years of political activity were marked by an intense learning curve for political activists who discovered, often unaided, how to address, attract and mobilise the public. In 1989 and 1990 these parties and activists gained the experience of participating in elections. Lessons were also learnt by the cadres of the three Baltic communist parties, who also had to adapt to the changing political conditions and compete for votes. This era is remembered with great popular affection – a time when Estonians, Latvians and Lithuanians were largely unified in purpose, and the prickly divisions of the democratic competitive era were yet to emerge. However, the divisions were beginning to be framed.

The first dominant political actors were the three popular fronts, formed in late 1988 and victorious in the 1989 and 1990 legislative elections. However, this was an era of extraordinary politics, as political leaders and public united in a single ambition – sovereignty for the Baltic states. The popular fronts were umbrella organisations that were hugely successful in uniting sharply differing, even opposing, political actors. Within the fronts there was constant debate and discussion on the future economic, welfare and citizenships models that the independent states should adopt. However, these debates were sidelined in the public sphere as activists enthusiastically, and increasingly successfully, tackled the Soviet monolith. The Estonian and Latvian popular fronts were particularly broad, and they united moderate communists and nationalists as well as Greens, Social Democrats and even small numbers of émigrés, who were beginning to take advantage of the Soviet Union's increasingly open borders to relocate to the Baltic states. The Lithuanian Popular Front, *Sajūdis*, was somewhat different in that it was more radically nationalist and far more ethnically homogenous than its two Baltic counterparts (Norgaard, 1995, p. 92).

The popular fronts were opposed by the reactionary Russophone-dominated Inter movements that supported the Baltic communist parties and favoured keeping the Soviet Union together. However, even the Inter movements were more diverse than they might have initially appeared, containing a mix of retired and active Soviet military personnel, unbending communists, enterprise managers and recent Russophone immigrants as well as those who had been living in the Baltic republics for multiple generations. At the same time, however, the Inter movements did not have an absolute monopoly over the affections of Russophones, many of whom supported the market and democratic reforms put forward by the popular fronts. The Inter movement was far weaker in Lithuania, with its much smaller share of Russophones in the population.

The third part of the political equation in Estonia and Latvia were the radical nationalist Congress movements (in Lithuania radicals were generally to be found within *Sajūdis*). Indeed, the first major non-communist *parties* in the Baltic states were already active in these movements in the 1980s. The Estonian National Independence Party (*Eesti Rahvusliku Sõltumatuse Partei*, ERSP) was the first registered independent political party in the Soviet Union. In contrast to the Estonian Popular Front, it strived for Estonian independence by purposefully disengaging from the Soviet political institutions that it considered to be illegitimate, and instead collected data on pre-1940 citizens and their families in order to eventually organise elections in which only Estonians who could trace their ethnic heritage to the inter-war era could participate. The Congress intended to use the electoral and legislative rules set out in the pre-Soviet occupation Estonian constitution. The Latvian equivalent to ERSP was the Latvian National Independence Movement (*Latvijas Nacionālās Neatkarības Kustība*, LNNK), which supported the

Latvian Citizens' Congress, and mirrored the broad aims and tactics of the Estonian Congress, although it ultimately failed to match its political success.

These three large blocs fragmented after 1991 as political actors began to organise in preparation for the first parliamentary elections, although the major parties that dominated politics in the 1990s all emerged from these movements. Indeed, all three contemporary party systems are still at least partly shaped by these three large blocs.

The bulk of new parties emerged from the popular fronts. In the case of Estonia this included the Moderate Party (*Rahvaerakond Mõõdukad*, an alliance of Social Democrats and the Estonian Rural Centre Party) the Estonian Coalition Party (*Eesti Koonderakond*) which contained the moderate reform communists and the less nationalist members of the Popular Front of Estonia and also the Estonian Centre Party (*Eesti Keskerakond*), which was far friendlier to the Russophone community and pushed for the 'zero' citizenship option. Latvia's direct successor to its Popular Front was Latvia's Way (*Latvijas Ceļš*, LC), a political party formed in the run-up to the spring 1993 parliamentary poll, when it became increasingly clear that the governing Popular Front of Latvia (which had re-registered itself as a political party) was unlikely to be elected to the legislature. LC was actually very similar to the popular front in that it was a 'political bouillabaisse' bringing together the moderate communists who had supported the Popular Front of Latvia, émigré Latvians (who had spent much of the communist era criticising the Latvian communists), and members of a shadowy organisation known as Club 21 (*Klubs 21*), which united the post-communist political and economic elite. The People's Harmony Party (*Tautas Saskaņa Partija*, TSP) – led by Jānis Jurkāns, a former Latvian foreign minister who in 1992 was fired by Latvian prime minister Ivars Godmanis for being too friendly with Russia – also descended from the popular front. Similarly to Edgar Savisaar's Estonian Centre Party, the People's Harmony Party claimed to be the true successor to the popular front in that it favoured granting citizenship to all permanent residents in Latvia, something that was originally supported by the popular front in 1989 and 1990. Sąjūdis in Lithuania initially competed in the 1992 election under its own name and was only rebranded the Homeland Union (*Tėvynės Sąjunga*) in 1993. It was still represented in the 2012 parliament as the Homeland Union-Lithuanian Christian Democrats (*Tėvynės Sąjunga- Lietuvos Krikščionys Demokratai*, TS-LKD).

Successor parties to the Inter movements have proven to be particularly strong in Latvia, but of little or no contemporary strength in Estonia and Lithuania. The Latvian Socialist Party (*Latvijas Sociālistiskā Partija*, LSP) and For Human Rights in a United Latvia (*Par Cilvēka Tiesībām Vienotā Latvijā*, PCTVL, which renamed itself Latvia's Russian Party in 2013) both of which later merged with TSP and formed the Harmony Centre Party (*Saskaņas Centrs*, SC), only to later break-up again, emerged as the champion of Latvia's Russophone community and are direct heirs to the Latvian Interfront. However, it is a broad grouping and struggles to keep all its competing factions together.

Both Estonia and Latvia also have successors to their radical nationalist Congress movements. The Fatherland National Coalition Party (Pro Patria), which formed the first post-Soviet era government with ERSP after the 1992 elections, sprang from the Estonian Citizen's Congress. The radical right of the Congress movement in Latvia can still be found in the National Alliance, which is an alliance of the established For Fatherland and Freedom/Latvian National Independence Movement (*Tēvzemei un Brīvībai/Latvijas Nacionālās Neatkarības Kustība*, TB/LNNK), where the LNNK still plays an important role. However, the most radical elements of the Congress movements, those that fail to accept any compromise with the contemporary liberal democratic norms of Europe, have been pushed to the political fringes, which is a source of deep irritation to them. Several Latvian radicals, who were exiled from the Soviet Union after the first opposition movements, chose to remain in exile and constantly criticise the democratic regime. The Internet gave them a new lease on life and allowed them to create sites such as the Latvian People's Tribunal (*Latvijas Tautas Tribunāls*) – run by former Helsinki-86 activist Linards Grantiņš – which holds virtual trials and then invariably imposes harsh sentences on the various politicians, academics and businessmen whom they perceive to have betrayed the interests of the Latvian nation.[16]

A fourth source for new parties was the inter-war era of party democracy in the Baltic states. However, these successor parties largely proved to be short-lived in all three states. The exception is Latvia's Farmer's Union (*Latvijas Zemnieku Savienība*, LZS) which is still in the Latvian parliament, and often in government, two decades after independence. It has had an ideologically unusual but successful electoral alliance with Latvia's Green Party (*Latvijas Zaļā Partija*, LZP) and the regional For Latvia and Ventspils (*Latvijai un Ventspilij*, LuV). Other successor parties faltered as they discovered that their voter constituencies no longer existed. This was particularly felt by Latvia's Christian Democratic, Centre, and even Social Democratic parties as they struggled for votes in

Table 3.5 Political parties elected to the Estonian parliament, 1992–2011

Name of Party	1992 Vote %	1992 Seats	1995 Vote %	1995 Seats	1999 Vote %	1999 Seats	2003 Vote %	2003 Seats	2007 Vote %	2007 Seats	2011 Vote %	2011 Seats
Pro Patria (& ERSP in 1995, union with Res Publica from 2006)	22	29	7.9	8	16.1	18	7.3	7	17.9	19	20.5	23
Secure Home	13.6	17										
Popular Front (Centre Party from 1995)	12.2	15	14.2	16	23.4	28	25.4	28	26.1	29	23.3	26
Moderates (Social Democrats from 2004)	9.7	12	6.0	6	15.2	17	7.0	6	10.6	10	17.1	19
Estonian National Independence Party	8.8	10										
Estonian Royalist Party	7.1	8										
Estonian Citizen	6.9	8										
Coalition Party & Rural Union			32.2	41								
Coalition Party					7.6	7						
Rural Union					7.3	7	13.0	13	7.1	6		
Estonian Reform Party			16.2	19	15.9	18	17.7	19	27.8	31	28.6	33
Our Home is Estonia			5.9	6								
The Right Wing			5.0	5								
Estonian United People's Party					6.1	6						
Res Publica (with Pro Patria from 2006)							24.6	28				
Greens									7.1	6		
Independents		2										

Source: Estonian National Election Committee, Sikk, 2014.

Table 3.6 Political parties elected to the Latvian parliament, 1993–2011

Name of Party	1993 Vote %	Seats	1995 Vote %	Seats	1998 Vote %	Seats	2002 Vote %	Seats	2006 Vote %	Seats	2010 Vote %	Seats	2011 Vote %	Seats
Latvia's Way	32.4	36	14.6	17	18.0	21								
LNNK	13.6	15	6.3	8										
LNNK/TB (1998)					14.7	17	5.4	7	6.9	8				
National Alliance (2010)											7.8	8	13.9	14
TSP/PCTVL	12.0	13	5.6	6	14.1	16	19.0	25	6.0	6	26.6	29	28.4	31
Harmony (2006)									14.4	17				
LZS (with Greens from 2002)	10.7	12					9.4	12	16.7	18	20.1	22	12.2	13
Equal Rights	5.8	7												
Fatherland & Freedom	5.4	6	11.9	14										
Christian democratic Union	5.0	6	6.3	8										
Democratic Centre Party	4.8	5												
Democratic Party Master			15.2	18										
TKL			14.9	16										
Latvian Unity Party			7.1	8										
Latvian Socialist Party			5.6	5										
People's Party					21.2	24	16.6	20	19.6	23				
LSDSP					12.8	14								
New era							23.9	26	16.4	18				
Unity (2010)											31.2	33	18.8	20
New Party (2002)					7.3	8								
LPP (2002)							9.5	10						
LPP/LC (2006)									8.6	10				
PLL (2010)											7.7	8		
Zatlers' Reform Party													20.8	22

Source: Latvian Central Election Commission, 2014.

Table 3.7 Political parties elected to the Lithuanian parliament (Percentage of PR votes), 1992–2012

Name of Party	1992 Vote %	Seats	1996 Vote %	Seats	2000 Vote %	Seats	2004 Vote %	Seats	2008 Vote %	Seats	2012 Vote %	Seats
Democratic Labour Party (LDLP)	44.0	73	10.0	12								
Social Democratic Party (SDP) (with LDLP from 2000)	6.0	8	6.9	12	31.1	49	20.7	20	11.8	26	19.2	38
Homeland Union	21.2	30	31.3	70	8.6	9	14.8	25	19.6	44	15.7	33
Christian Democratic Party	12.6	18	10.4	16	3.1	2						
Centre Union	2.5	2	8.7	13	2.9	2						
Liberal Union (with Centre Union from 2004)			1.9	1	17.3	34	9.2	18	5.3	8		
Pole's Electoral Action	2.1	4	3.1	1	1.9	2	3.8	2	4.8	3	6.1	8
New Democracy/Women's Party (Peasant and Green Union from 2012)			3.9	1	*	2	6.6	10	3.7	3	4.1	1
New Union (Social Liberals)					19.6	29	*	11	3.7	1		
Labour Party							28.6	39	9.0	10	20.7	29
Order and Justice							11.4	11	12.7	15	7.6	12
National Revival Party									15.1	16		
Liberal Movement									5.7	11	9.0	10
The Way of Courage											8.3	7
Others & independent candidates	8.2	6	20.0	15	10.7	12	3.6	5	8.6	4	7.2	3

Source: Sikk, 2014, Lithuanian Central Election Committee, Lithuania, 2014.
*In electoral coalition with the Social Democrats

the 1990s. Ironically, these parties had survived in émigré communities in Europe and North America, but now disappeared.

Public dissatisfaction with the jolting economic and social transition led to new parties being formed in advance of the second post-1991 parliamentary elections. At this point it is important to emphasise a difference between 'new' and 'genuinely new' political parties. The former type of party was typically a splinter group broken away from an existing party, a merger of two or more established parties, a simple re-naming/re-branding of a political force that had lost public support or also the creation of a political vehicle for an established 'independent' minister or prime minister who is already part of the political elite. In contrast, genuinely new parties 'are not successors of any previous parliamentary parties, have a novel name as well as structure, and do not have any important figures from past democratic politics among its major members' (Sikk, 2005, p. 399).

The majority of the new parties that appeared in the 1990s and early 2000s were not 'genuinely new'. Rather, they were reconfigured political vehicles for established elites that attempted to tap into the public's desire for a new political class to sort out the economic crises of the post-Soviet period. The Latvian party system was particularly volatile at this time, with a great number of new parties entering the party system. Thus the nationalist-populist People's Movement for Latvia–Siegerists' Party (*Tautas kustība Latvijai-Zīgerista Partija*, TKL) that won 16 seats in the 1995 Latvian parliamentary election was a party formed by Joahim Siegerist, a radical right-wing populist German who had mysteriously wangled Latvian citizenship in the early 1990s. Siegerist largely funded the election campaign of the nationalist LNNK in the 1993 election, for which he was rewarded with a seat in parliament (Dreifelds, 1996). However, six months later Siegerist was forced to resign, having become a frequent embarrassment to the party with his populist comments and (for a nationalist party) an embarrassing inability to speak Latvian. A short time later he was also expelled from parliament for non-attendance. Siegerist simply formed his own political party, funded an expensive populist advertising campaign (including the distribution of free bananas at political rallies) that appealed directly to the traditional 'losers' of the transition – the elderly, rural dwellers, manual and state workers – and threatened to imprison corrupt officials and businessmen while also promising universally high levels of welfare.

The 1990s and first decade of the twenty-first century saw the creation of a number of political parties structured around previously independent, charismatic political leaders. Siim Kallas, the then president of the Bank of Estonia, broke with *Pro Patria* in 1994 and formed the Reform Party, which has been a constant in the Estonian Parliament since 1995. In Latvia the two-time prime minister, Andris Šķēle, formed the People's Party (*Tautas Partija*, TP) in May 1998, five months before the parliamentary election. The party instantly had a small parliamentary group of five deputies after defections from three other parties. TP won the 1998 election with 24 seats and finished third in 2002 with 20 seats. Similarly, Artūras Paulauskas, a former prosecutor-general, formed the New Union (Social Liberals) (*Naujoji sąjunga [socialliberalai]*) party in 1998 after he had lost the presidential election to Valdas Adamkus by less than 1 per cent of the vote. The party finished second in the 2000 election with 19.6 per cent of the vote. Then, in 2002, two-time Lithuanian prime minister (and former mayor of Vilnius) Rolandas Paksas broke with the Liberal Union Party and created the Liberal Democratic Party with which he was elected to the presidency in 2002 (although he was subsequently impeached and removed from office for violating his oath and the Lithuanian constitution by collaborating with a Lithuanian-Russian businessman accused of having links with the Russian underworld).

The 2002 and 2003 parliamentary elections saw a number of 'genuinely new' parties break into the Baltic states' party system in Latvia and Estonia. In 2002 New Era (*Jaunais Laiks*, JL) won more than a quarter of the seats in the parliamentary elections, and its leader, Einars Repše (who had left the post of president of the Bank of Latvia to create the party) became prime minister. The following year Rally for the Republic – *Res Publica* (*Ühendus Vabariigi Eest* – *Res Publica*) won a share of the vote similar to New Era (24.6% to New Era's 24%) in finishing second in Estonia's parliamentary election. Both these parties had almost no links to the established parties. New Era actively attempted to recruit people who had never before operated in Latvian politics, while *Res Publica*, initially led by the professor of political science, Rein Taagepera, then former state auditor Juhan Parts, relied on the members of its grassroots organisation, which had been set up as an NGO since 1989. Although both parties have since fused with other parties (*Res Publica* with *Pro Patria* and New Era with a number of other centrist parties and political independents to form the Unity, *Vienotība*, party), they remain major players in the Estonian and Latvian party systems.

The type, frequency and regularity with which these new parties have appeared has led scholars to challenge established theories on new party formation. In an influential article, Paul Lucardie (2000) identified three types of new parties to have emerged in Western Europe over the previous decades: *prophetic* parties that express a new ideology;

purifiers that cleanse an ideology soiled by prevailing parties; and *proloc-utors* that articulate new interests without reference to any particular ideology. However, none of these explanations is useful for the case of New Era or *Res Publica* (Sikk, 2004). Rather, these parties focused on 'the need to change *how* politics are made, rather than having any radically different views on *what* substantially needed to be done' (Bagenholm and Johansson Heino, 2008, p. 2). In other words, at their very core was the fuzzy concept of *newness* rather than an ideology or some newly articulated political interests (Sikk, 2012). However, this is not to say that there are no political cleavages in the Baltic states. Indeed, clear cleavages and political divisions can be identified in all three.

3.3.2   Cleavages and divisions

The sociological approach to the study of political parties is underpinned by the understanding that parties form as a result of the institutionalisa-tion of social conflict, and are anchored in society at ascriptive, attitu-dinal and behavioural levels (Lipset and Rokkan, 1967; Rae and Taylor, 1970). In the inter-war era, the Baltic states had clearly articulated social cleavages and had organised parties that represented these interests (see Chapter 1 in this volume). However, post-Second World War modernisa-tion in Western Europe saw the barriers between different social groups gradually worn down and the emergence of 'value cleavages that iden-tify only communities of like-minded individuals' (Dalton, Flanagan and Beck, 1984, p. 474). The collapse of communism led to a further questioning of the value of cleavage-based approaches to party politics. Soviet occupation brought the collectivisation of agriculture, secularisa-tion of society, rapid industrialisation and significant changes in Estonia's and Latvia's ethnic composition, leading to a situation in which many of the traditional cleavages no longer existed in post-communist states. Thus the communist era is usually seen as having distorted or destroyed the traditional bases of society through the uprooting and dislocation of both urban and rural populations as well as of the church and other social bases. In the 1990s, post-communist party systems were inevitably open, fluid, volatile and inherently unstable. Moreover, the creation of cleavage-based parties in East-Central Europe was hampered by the fast pace and complexity of the transition, by the differences in the model of party ('charismatic and clientelistic' rather than programmatic), and by a 'mediatised' type of campaigning (Rommele, 1999, p. 12). Thus, while with the introduction of competitive elections parties representing the major cleavages of the inter-war period did emerge, their success was rather short-lived. They found that 'their constituencies [had] changed almost beyond recognition by more than half a century of dictatorship' (Berglund and Dellenbrant, 1994, p. 249). The established cleavages of Western Europe were clearly unlikely to suddenly appear in the Baltic states, particularly at a time when these cleavages were losing salience in the older democracies. Moreover, the cleavages to take hold in the post-communist states would inevitably reflect both the scars of 50 years of externally imposed communism as well as the strains of the economic, social and political transition.

This section identifies and compares the salient cleavages and political divides that have emerged in the Baltic states over the last two decades of party competition. A salient cleavage has three dimensions: It reflects a major division in society with which individuals identify and is expressed through an organised political party (Gallagher et al., 1992). In contrast, a political divide is a partial division in society that lacks the depth of the traditional Lipset- and Rokkan-type cleavages, but is nevertheless representative of a split between sections of society. A political divide is operationalised as having two of the three dimensions of a full cleavage (Deegan-Krause, 2004).

The three large political blocks of the anti-communist era were certainly rooted in different social constituencies – pro- and anti-independence, titular nationalists and Russian nationalists, pro- and anti-communists. However, this was not the case for the vast majority of new parties created after 1991. The inter-war era successor parties discovered that their social bases – liberal professionals, industrial workers, rural smallholders and so on – either no longer existed or, in the case of industrial workers, were no longer prepared to support what was to them a discredited political ideology. Moreover, many of the existing social groups were in a state of flux, rapidly shrinking, growing and morphing as post-communist economic reforms kicked in. The successors to the big three movements, as well as the new and genuinely new parties, were typically created by opportunist political entrepreneurs with the assistance of new political and public relations specialists. Other parties were constructed by intellectuals with little contact or knowledge of the constituencies they aimed to represent (Schopflin, 1993). The most successful parties in post-communist Europe have been entirely new creations that adapted to the domestic situation and found new political constituencies that represented cleavages and divides often unique to that state (van Biezen, 2005, p. 154).

Estonia's large Russophone minority makes an ethnic cleavage all but inevitable. However, the cleavage is not as visible as Latvia's ethnic cleavage, largely because the Centre Party, which has attracted the majority of Russophone votes in the twenty-first century, is less explicitly pro-Russian (and pro-Russia) than the Latvian parties, not least because it is led by an ethnic Estonian, Edgar Savisaar, and is the direct successor of the Popular Front of Estonia. However, the issue of citizenship in the early 1990s, followed by debates on language instruction in secondary schools with a high density of Russophones, and then the night of the Bronze Soldier riots in Tallinn in April 2007, have all ensured that ethnic issues remain at the top of the political agenda. Russia's annexation of Crimea in early 2014 was recognised by Edgar Savisaar as leading to more friction between the 'Estonian' and the Russophone parties. There is also a left–right cleavage. The social democrats have been represented in parliament since 1992 (as the 'Moderates' until 2004), and the Centre party also often adopts left-wing socio-economic positions. However, they have both often served in government coalitions, executing explicitly liberal economic policies (Mikkel, 2006).

Scholars have argued that the two key cleavages that emerged in post-independence Latvia were socio-economic (focusing 'around the pace and extent of market reforms') and ethnic/nationalist (Pettai and Kreuzer 1999, p. 166). Indeed, at one point in the early 2000s it was even argued that Latvia had moved to a primary socio-economic cleavage because globalisation and the integration of Latvia into the international political, economic and commercial world had accelerated the creation of a new middle class that had superceded the ethnic issue (Bottolfs 2000; Zake 2002). Hermann Smith-Sivertsen (2004) also suggested that Latvia had urban/rural and independence cleavages. However, these are simply two dimensions of the ethnic cleavage that has remained salient in Latvia, while the socio-economic dimension has declined in relevance (despite the best efforts of the Russophone Harmony party). The initial source of the ethnic cleavage was the reluctance of Latvian politicians to adopt a citizenship law until 1994, leaving around one-quarter of the population (approximately 600,000 people) without automatic citizenship. A 'windows' system for citizenship applications was created according to age and length of residence in Latvia, in addition to language and history examinations. These rules were only loosened in 1998, following a national referendum. The citizenship issue was then replaced by language rights. A 1992 language law had made Latvian the official state language, and amendments over the following years saw all street names, railway timetables and other public sources of information converted to Latvian. Latvian was made the official teaching language of state-funded universities, and Russian was demoted to the status of just another foreign language in Latvian language schools.

A controversial switch to Latvian as the primary language of instruction in minority schools was introduced in the 2004–2005 school year and mobilised Russophone NGOs and movements to organise several public demonstrations and marches. The years 2010 and 2011 saw ultimately unsuccessful attempts by Latvian nationalists to collect enough signatures in order to hold a referendum on switching to 100 per cent teaching in Latvian in all state-financed minority schools, while a rival attempt by Russian-speakers to collect enough signatures to have a referendum on introducing Russian as an official second language in Latvia was successful and led to a polarising vote in February 2012. As a result, the only major cleavage in Latvia is ethnic. Russophones vote for Russophone parties distinguished by the passion of their pro-Russia rhetoric. Ethnic Latvians vote for parties similarly differentiated largely by the extent of their nationalism. However, in addition to this overarching ethnic cleavage, Latvia also has a political divide in its ethnic Latvian electorate that is perhaps best described as a corruption-fighter versus oligarch divide (see Pettai, Auers and Ramonaitė, 2011; Auers, 2013). This is a values cleavage, with one set of parties placing law and order issues as above all else (seeing the rule of law as a pre-requisite for economic development), while the oligarch parties argue that corruption is exaggerated and that the main focus should be on good technocratic management. This culminated in the early 2011 parliament election, which the then-president of Latvia, Valdis Zatlers, had initiated by calling for a recall of parliament (eagerly approved in a referendum by Latvia's voters) as a stand against Latvia's triumvirate of oligarchs. In the subsequent September 2011 election the Latvian electorate overwhelmingly voted against the oligarch parties with only one – the Green/ Farmer's Union party – making it over the 5 per cent threshold.

In contrast to Estonia and Latvia, ethnicity is not a major cleavage or political divide in the Lithuanian party system (although minor conflicts between Lithuanians and the small Polish minority can occasionally flare up, and there are parties representing Polish interests in the Lithuanian parliament). Kjetil Duvold and Mindaugas Jurkynas (2013) have convincingly argued that the major contemporary political conflict is between left and right and based on traditional socio-economic issues (taxes, healthcare, pensions). These issues also dominated party politics in the 1990s, although at that time they were perhaps better understood as a communist versus anti-communist cleavage that also contained elements of a clerical versus anti-clerical divide. The two big political parties of that era – the left-wing LDDP and the right-wing Homeland Union – structured these relatively straightforward cleavages.

In this sense it is quite similar to the ethnic cleavages in Estonia and Latvia, which were also essentially regime divides. The arrival of new political parties in the landmark 2000 and 2004 parliamentary elections shattered this stability and heralded the growing salience of additional divides that can be best described as 'territorial politics' (ibid., p. 142). These include growing rural/urban conflicts that are also reflected in nationalism versus cosmopolitanism as well as traditional versus modern values. The 2012 parliamentary election also threw up a curious, anti-elite populist party, The Way of Courage (*Drąsos Kelias*), which was formed around a single issue – popular outrage over a judge who allegedly delayed legal procedures in a high-profile pedophilia case that saw a number of prominent businessmen and public figures accused of running a pedophilia ring – but also reflected exasperation with the growing divide between those who had benefitted from the regime change and those who continued to struggle. This hardly makes up a political divide at the moment, but does reveal the continuing potential for populist parties to make electoral gains.

The Baltic states do have cleavages in the traditional sense – they reflect a major social division with which individuals identify and are expressed through an organised political party – although the ethnic cleavages in Estonia and Latvia, the corruption/oligarch divide in Latvia and the regime cleavage in Lithuania are very specific to the Baltic historical experience. One of the political outcomes is that some of these political parties are difficult to identify in a comparative party family classification: The Way of Courage, for example, or the Russophone Harmony party in Latvia, which has claimed that it is a member of the social democratic party family (largely in order to expand its electorate beyond Russophones), but has key economic and values policies that are right of centre. There is a gap between what parties *say* they will do and what they *actually* do. Many of the new generation of parties are driven by populist, anti-establishment sentiments that feed on the popular dissatisfaction and distrust towards the political class that has spread across Europe, not just the Baltic states.

At the same time, it is clear that all three Baltic party systems are well stocked with centre-right political parties. Indeed, the centre-right has monopolised political office in Estonia and Latvia, although there has been more of a political pendulum in Lithuania. Lithuania also has a large centre-left party, and a few smaller ones, and Estonia has a small social democratic party. Estonia and Lithuania have liberal parties, and all three have had agrarian parties, although the strongest agrarian party is in Latvia. The Green Party has only intermittently (2007–2011) been represented in the Estonian parliament and never in Lithuania. Although the Latvian Greens have been in the parliament since the 1990s thanks to an electoral alliance with the agrarians, they are very much the junior partners in this coalition. Finally, Latvia has unique Russophone and Latvian nationalist parties. The following section will consider how far these parties have been influenced by the laws and institutions that shape their activities.

3.3.3 The rules of the game

Electoral laws, parliamentary traditions and other 'institutions' govern and shape party activity in a party system. Although there is little variation in what the three Baltic constitutions have to say about political parties, there is much greater variety in the laws that specifically govern political parties. Three sets of legislation are particularly relevant: (a) Laws on political parties; (b) political party financing; and (c) election campaigning regulations. In addition, the electoral laws discussed at the start of this chapter also influence the behaviour of party's and politicians.

The three laws on political parties and public organisations lay out the basic conditions for their creation and operation. The major barrier to the creation of new parties is a minimum membership criterion. Here we see great variety in the requirements. On the one hand, Latvia requires only 200 signatories to form a political party, although sometimes new parties have problems gathering just a few hundred members. In 2005 a new party, the New Democrats (*Jaunie Demokrāti*), only recruited 200 signatories at its second attempt at a founding congress. Moreover, newspapers reported that a large proportion of the 200 founding signatories were students from the maritime academy who spent most of the time loudly and excitedly discussing the evening entertainment being laid on for them by the party (Delfi, 2005a). At the other end of the scale, Estonia has since 1996 had a large minimum membership criterion of 1,000, reduced to 500 in 2014 (a public register is checked annually). Lithuania is somewhere in the middle, requiring 400 people to register a party. These rules have resulted in political parties that are significantly larger in Estonia than in Lithuania, while Latvia has extremely small parties. Comparative data on party membership is rather sketchy, and in the case of Latvia and Lithuania relies on information from the party's themselves, although a number of different articles provide data for 2003 and 2004. The two biggest parties in Estonia in 2004 were Pro Patria, with a membership of 8,500, and the Centre Party with 7,600 (Mikkel, 2006, p. 33). In 2000, four Lithuanian political parties had a membership of more than 7,000: the Homeland Union, the Democratic labour party, the Christian Democrat Party and the Union of Political Prisoners and Deportees (Smith-Sivertsen, 2004, p. 232). At the same time, the biggest parties in Latvia in 2003/2004 were the LSDSP, which claimed a membership of 2,700, and the People's Party, which claimed 1,800. However, it is interesting to note that the party that won the 2002 election and formed a new government after that poll – New Era – had just 400 members at that time (Auers, 2006, p. 137).

Table 3.8 compares the levels of national party membership as a percentage of the electorate. Latvia not only has the smallest share of party membership in the Baltic states, but the smallest membership level in Europe as a whole (van Biezen and Mair, 2012). In the 1990s Estonia also had a relatively small party membership, but the imposition of the 1,000 minimum membership quorum as well as state financing for parties led to parties gradually building their organisational structures. As Table 3.8 indicates, total party membership in Estonia rose by over 50 per cent in the half decade between 2002 and 2008, perhaps because the earlier introduction of state financing for parties gave them the financial freedom to strengthen their organisational base between elections rather than simply binge on electoral advertising at election time. In contrast, Latvian parties have had little need for large memberships, rather relying on corporate donations and expensive media advertising in elections. However, the limits to party campaigning expenditure and the introduction of state financing for parties are likely to lead to Latvian parties also focusing on membership structures. Finally, Lithuania already had larger membership-based parties in the 1990s, largely due to the explicitly ideological orientation of the party system, with clear left, right and liberal parties and regularised competition between them. It is interesting to note that the fragmentation of that system did not lead to a fall in party membership. Rather, Table 3.8 shows that party

Table 3.8   National levels of party membership in the Baltic states

	Year	Total membership	As % of electorate	Change in membership
Estonia	2008	43,732	4.87%	+1.53% (since 2002)
Latvia	2004	10,985	0.74%	n/d
Lithuania	2008	73,133	2.71%	+0.61% (since 2004)
European mean (n=27)	–	–	4.65%	–

Source: van Biezen and Mair (2012); Saarts (2011).

membership continued to grow in Lithuania in this period, indicating that the new parties followed the, by then, well-established tradition of Lithuanian parties having large memberships and mobilising new activists into their parties.

As is the case elsewhere in Europe, the burden of financing political parties has moved from private hands to the public purse, something that has been welcomed by anti-corruption campaigners but much lamented by the Baltic public, who dislike parties and do not like to see them receiving public funds. Estonia's 1994 law introduced public financing to the party system from 1996 onwards. Initially, only parliamentary parties received these funds, but the law was later amended to support all parties polling over 1 per cent in parliamentary elections, although parliamentary parties receive much larger funds per voter. The year 2004 saw a sizeable jump in the size of public funds available to parties, accompanied by a ban on corporate donations and severe restrictions on other forms of private financing (Sikk, 2006). Latvia has followed a similar path, albeit much more gradually. The first Latvian political party financing law was passed in 1995 and allowed for annual individual and corporate donations of up to 36,000 euros a year, but banned donations from foreign or anonymous sources. The limit was later slimmed down to 15,000 euros. Some changes to the law on political party financing were made following the expensive 2002 election, limiting spending to 20 santimes per voter and banning corporate donations. In 2010 the parliament adopted legislation that introduced state financing for eligible parties from 2012, although private donations are still accepted (with this, Latvia became the last post-communist state in the European Union to adopt state financing of parties). Indeed, individuals can still annually donate up to 30,000 euros to a party. Parties polling over 2 per cent in national parliamentary elections receive an annual 0.71 euro for every vote polled in the election. Lithuania introduced state financing in 1999, after Estonia but before Latvia. All parties polling over 3 per cent of the vote in parliamentary, municipal or European Parliament elections receive a subvention based on the number of votes they have attracted. In 2012 Lithuania banned corporate donations to parties. Private donations from individuals are limited to 10 per cent of their annual income. In all three countries, state financing now makes up the bulk of party income. Bertoa and Spirova (2013) argue that the turn to state financing is critical in terms of ensuring long-term party survival and, thus, consolidation and institutionalisation of the party system.

Party funds are primarily directed towards election campaigning. In the 1990s there were few limits to television, radio or newspaper advertising, and parties used media advertising heavily in their campaigns. Parties often also utilised concerts and plays as well as festivals to attract voters – for example, in Latvia in 2002 the Green-Farmers Union organised a series of beer festivals, while the LSDSP hired television situation-comedy stars to tour the country, enabling politicians to attract substantially larger audiences than usual. Latvian parties also worked hard to recruit popular and charismatic personalities who could attract voters. Raimonds Pauls, a popular Soviet-era composer of artless tunes, was elected to five different parliaments in three different parties (Latvia's Way, the New Party, and the People's Party), and featured heavily in the election advertising of all three parties. One particularly memorable advert from the 1998 parliamentary election campaign saw two old women sipping tea in a café and declaring their intention to vote for Pauls simply because they enjoyed his music so much.

All three states tightened up and restricted political campaigning in the twenty-first century. The 2007 parliamentary election in Estonia saw the imposition of a ban on outdoor political advertising in the final 40 days before the vote (Solvak and Pettai, 2008). This ban does not cover T-shirts or balloons, and parties have increasingly utilised their members in getting their names and logos onto the streets in the run-up to the poll. In 2013 Latvia imposed even harsher limits on political advertising, banning party adverts on television for 30 days before an election. The 2013 municipal and 2014 European Parliament elections were the first under these new rules. However, parties competing in the poll do receive equal and free time for party political broadcasts in the run-up to the poll. Lithuania had introduced similar limits in its 2008 election, limiting outdoor advertising as well as banning party advertising on television and radio. This prompted the Order and Justice party to make a movie that could be shown in cinemas across the country (Jurkynas, 2009). Nevertheless, these laws were rescinded in advance of the 2012 election, giving Lithuanian parties the least campaigning restrictions in the Baltic states.

To conclude this section: There has been a clear and relatively steady tightening up of the rules structuring party competition over the last two decades. All three countries have moved from private to state financing of parties (although private donations are still legal in all three states) and limited party campaigning (although Lithuania moved to loosen its regulations in 2012). Together with a high minimum membership threshold, these rules have led to an institutionalisation of the major parties in Estonia and increasing consolidation of the Latvian system. Although Lithuania's party system was highly volatile at the turn of the twenty-first century, it has since gradually moved towards increasing consolidation.

3.3.4 Party organisations

The least-researched dimension of Baltic political parties is the internal one: parties as organisations. This is largely due to the inherent difficulty of studying party organisations: 'We know much less about the internal management and the organisational functioning of political parties than we do about their socio-cultural base, and their external history of participation in public decision-making' (Lipset and Rokkan, 1967, p. 4). Political parties have several separate, occasionally competing, levels. Howard Scarrow (1967, p. 779) differentiated 'between party as a non-parliamentary "outside" organisation, and party as a group of "inside" elected officials'. Anthony King (1969, p. 114) later refined this to three different and competing elements existing within successful political parties: the party in the electorate; the party organisation; and the party in office.

Party organisations were particularly weak in those parties that had been founded by a charismatic personality. As Angelo Pannebianco (1998) pointed out, the presence of a charismatic leader during the construction of a political party is potentially destructive because a strong leader resists any institutionalisation that might weaken that leader's own position in the party. Indeed, when the party leader exits the political stage the party typically disappears. The parties in the Baltic states that have survived the longest have been those that have succeeded in moving beyond a single party leader. This has typically been achieved by a name change or the fusion of a number of political parties into one consolidated party. Thus, Einar Repše's New Era fused with a number of other parties to emerge as Unity.

Parties in the Baltic states are particularly opaque, having traditionally been seen as top-heavy and more reliant on centralised leadership than on the rank-and-file membership. Moreover, they were often difficult to join because leaders feared the loss of control and the possibility of 'alien takeovers' that might result from an enlarged membership (Smith-Silvertsen, 2004, p. 239). Latvia's parties had a number of administrative obstacles that applicants need to overcome in order to join up. For example, New Era required that all potential new members have references from two existing members (no easy achievement when membership in 2003 was just 400), and be interviewed by a panel that sought to ensure ideological compatibility.[17] Moreover, expensive and virtually unlimited campaign advertising placed a great deal of authority in the hands of the party central office that was typically both geographically and in staffing terms tied up with the party in office.

However, the long-term trends of: growing party membership; increased reliance on state financing; as well as limits on media advertising, all point to a future increase in the relevance of rank-and-file members. Indeed, Estonia's and Latvia's recent elections have seen an increase in the number of young party members agitating in the streets with party paraphernalia (circumventing the ban on street advertising), while research on the electoral success of political parties in Lithuania has found that party members are just as crucial to the persistence and consolidation of political parties as is money (Ibenskas, 2012). Parties have increasingly used the regular flow of funds from the state to set up permanent offices outside their legislative power bases and to strengthen the party's structure. However, policy-formulation remains a weak link, with parties typically relying on bureaucrats (when in office) and party cadres to structure policy, rather than create and utilise think tanks. The Johannes Mihkelson Centre, allied to the Social Democrats in Estonia, was an exception, although its ability to influence policy debates has weakened since its 1990s heyday. Indeed, Baltic parties have forged greater links with foreign foundations – such as the Friedrich Ebert foundation that financially supported the development of Harmony Centre's economic programme prior to the 2010 parliamentary election – than they have supported the development of domestic institutions.

Conclusions

Over the last two decades, elections have been free and fair and are a normal part of the political cycle in Estonia, Latvia and Lithuania. At the same time, the Baltic party systems have taken great strides towards institutionalisation, establishing increasingly 'routine, predictable and stable' patterns of behaviour between the parties operating within the confines of a party system (Bertoa, 2014, p. 17). Electoral volatility has been in decline and, in the case of Estonia, has reached a low level that matches, and in some cases even exceeds, the mature democracies of Western Europe.

Parties in the Baltic states increasingly resemble cartel parties rather than the Americanised electoral machines that Klaus Von Beyme (1996) predicted in the post-communist region in the mid-1990s. However, there are differences. The nature of political competition in Estonia and Lithuania is more ideological, with socio-economic debates being particularly strong in Lithuania, despite the re-framing of the party system that began with the 2000 election. Latvia, in contrast, has a mix of 'thick and thin' political parties. Dominant parties are 'thick' in terms of income, but 'thin' in terms of membership and ideology.

Although parties have been strengthening, there remains a strong anti-party feeling in the Baltic states, as the Eurobarometers indicate. This has also resulted in strong support for independent politicians. Presidents in Latvia have traditionally been independent (and only one, Guntis Ulmanis, was actually a member of a political party when elected to the post). More recently, Dalia Grybauskaitė, elected to the Lithuanian presidency in 2009 and 2014, won without the aid of a political party. In 2009 and 2014, Estonians elected an independent candidate to the European Parliament.

Nevertheless, data on volatility, the effective number of electoral and parliamentary parties and other measures of party institutionalisation all point towards maturing party systems. New, strange parties, such as Lithuania's Way of Courage, are remarkable for their exceptionalism rather than for being the norm. As the trends in increasing state financing for parties and cuts in campaign spending opportunities raises the barrier for entry to the party system, further institutionalisation should be expected. The established parties are already clearly using the regular flow of funds from the public purse to invest in their organisations, opening party offices outside legislatures and finding increased utility in larger memberships.

4
Civil Society, Corruption and Ethnic Relations

In 2007 the Estonian government began to relocate a highly contentious Soviet era war memorial from the centre of Tallinn to a nearby military cemetery. The 'Bronze Soldier' was erected in 1947 to honour the memory of the fallen Soviet soldiers who had fought in the battles that liberated Tallinn from German forces during the Second World War. At that time it was known as the 'Monument to the Liberators of Tallinn'. An eternal flame was added in 1964. Following independence, Estonian authorities rededicated it to all soldiers who had died during the war and dismantled the eternal flame in an attempt to depoliticise the memorial. For ethnic Estonians, however, it remained an acrimonious symbol of annexation and repression, although Russophones viewed it as one of the few remaining public symbols of Soviet victory over fascism. The April 2007 exhumation of Soviet soldiers buried below the monument triggered an unprecedented two days of Russophone rioting and looting in Tallinn.

The Bronze Soldier incident revealed the enduring salience of the titular–Russophone divide in Baltic society. More than 20 years of nation-building, language laws and integration policies have had only partial success in Estonia and Latvia. On the other hand, the rioting also pointed towards the increasingly assertive and confident civil society that has emerged in the twenty-first century in Estonia in particular, but progressively also in Latvia and Lithuania. In the 1990s political observers noted that, similarly to other post-communist countries, the Baltic states had weak civil societies with: few significant nongovernmental organisations (NGOs); low political participation; and little trust in state institutions or in each other. While trust remains a problematic issue, especially in Latvia and Lithuania, the number of NGOs has grown and citizens increasingly participate in various communal, social-capital-building events. A growing number of social entrepreneurs have adopted both traditional approaches and seized new information technology (IT) opportunities to engage Estonian, Latvian and Lithuanian society.

This chapter evaluates the development of civil society in the Baltic states. It begins by briefly recalling the vibrant civil societies that emerged in the three Baltic states in the latter years of the Soviet Union and drove the Baltic independence movements. It then moves on to discuss the significant economic, political and social challenges that the sector faced in the decade after 1991, before turning to the resurgence of civil society in the twenty-first century. The second part looks at the continuing salience of corruption in Latvia and Lithuania and considers its negative impact on civil society's development. The third and final part focuses on the ongoing division between the Russophone and titular communities, especially in Estonia and Latvia, and considers the paradox that much of civil (and 'uncivil') society is spurred on by enduring differences between these two communities.

4.1 Civil society

Civil society is the expansive 'realm of freedom' between state and individual that upholds and promotes freedom of expression through multiple competing and cooperating organisations, groups and communal activities (Keane, 1998, p. 114). These activities develop social capital by promoting vertical links between public and government as well as horizontal links between organisations and individuals, encouraging exchange of the tools and skills that foster civic activism (UNDP, 1996, p. 83). In countries with sharp ethnic divisions (such as Estonia or Latvia) these horizontal links also boost inter-ethnic contact and nation building.

Civil society in the Baltic states has gone through several phases of development since the communist era. The Soviet regime had largely eradicated independent civil society by taking full control of the space between society and the individual: 'The Communist Party assumed responsibility for everything that is happening in society; therefore it [felt] obliged to direct and control the whole of social life' (Vajda, 1988, p. 339). However, in the 1980s the growing public freedom, encouraged by *perestroika* and *glasnost*, led to the creation of a great number of cultural, economic and political organisations, many eventually operating under the broader umbrellas of the three popular-front parties or, in Estonia and Latvia, the more nationalist Citizens' Congresses. However, this was typically civil society fostering disorder and revolutionary change and working *against* the state (Keane, 1998, p. 6).[1] The adjustment to a more cooperative spirit after the fall of communism proved to be difficult in all three countries.

Renewed independence in the Baltic states was accompanied by an unexpected slump in civic activism. Post-1991, Baltic civil society could initially draw upon the 1980s as well as the collective memory of the inter-war era for inspiration. Many inter-war organisations were renewed after 1991 with differing levels of success.[2] However, participation remained stubbornly low. While the final years of Soviet rule had seen regular pro- and anti-independence rallies gathering hundreds of thousands of people, the first years of independence saw few similar displays of civic activism. Trade unions shed members, NGOs were few as well as poor, and people withdrew from the public space. This independence hangover lasted for much of the 1990s.

Marc Marje Howard's influential 2002 *Journal of Democracy* article offered three possible explanations for the weakness of civil society in post-communist Europe. First, he argued that a deep distrust of NGOs and communal activities was carried over from the communist to the democratic era. In this sense, the civil society of the late 1980s was seen as an era of extraordinary politics and had little impact on the ex-communist public's deep-rooted negative opinion of civil society. Second, Howard claimed that widespread popular disappointment in the social, political and economic transformations that followed the collapse of communism further alienated people from the public sphere. Finally, Howard maintained that the persistence of communist era informal friendship networks often negated the need for structured organisations.

Howard's first point was that the post-communist publics' distrust of NGOs is rooted in the previous communist regime's policy of expecting citizens to volunteer their time for official state organisations or meetings. After 1991 this distrust was carried over into cynical attitudes to the type of shared voluntary civic organisations and activities that lie at the heart of civil society. This, then, is reflected in low levels of trust in civil society. There were few pan-Baltic polls on trust in civil society in the 1990s (not least because the phrase had yet to enter public discourse). Trust in trade unions at least partly reflects public opinion on wider civil society. The New Baltic Barometer (NBB) surveyed respondents, split between titulars and Russophones, to express their trust in trade unions, in 1993, and then again in further surveys in the 2000s. As Figure 4.1 indicates, between 1993 and 2004 trust in trade unions grew among Estonians, Latvians and Lithuanians, but fell among Russophones in Estonia and Lithuania, perhaps because of growing titular influence over the unions after independence. To put this into context, Figures 4.2, 4.3 and 4.4 show public trust in parliament, government and political parties between 1993 and 2012. The data indicate that trust in these political institutions has

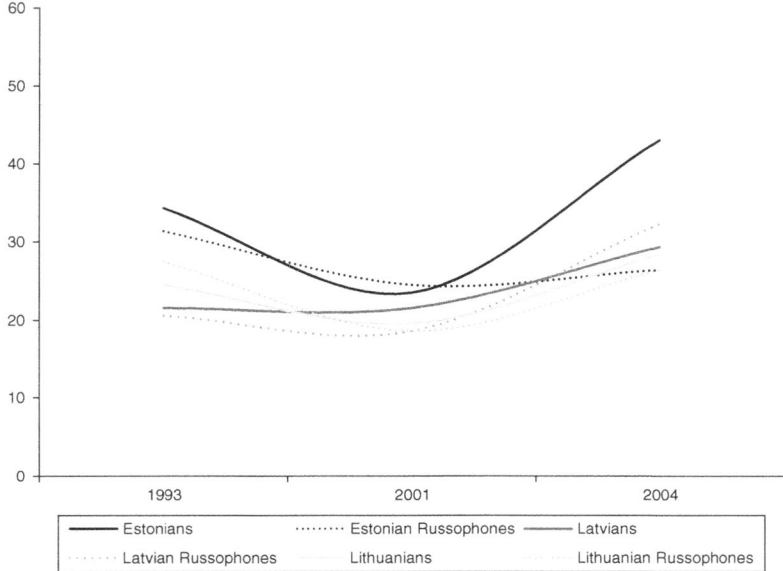

Figure 4.1   Trust in trade unions. 'Tend to trust' (%), 1993–2004

Source: New Baltic Barometer (1993, 2001, 2004).

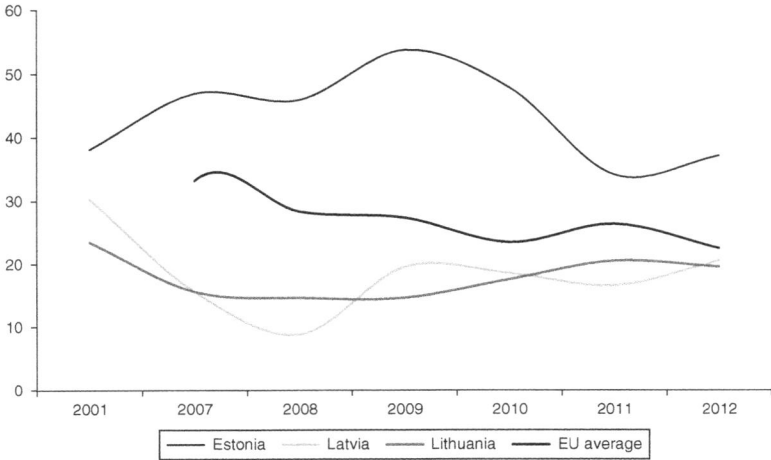

Figure 4.2   Trust in national government. 'Tend to trust' (%), 2001–2012

Source: Candidate Countries Eurobarometer (2001); Eurobarometer (2008–2013).[3]

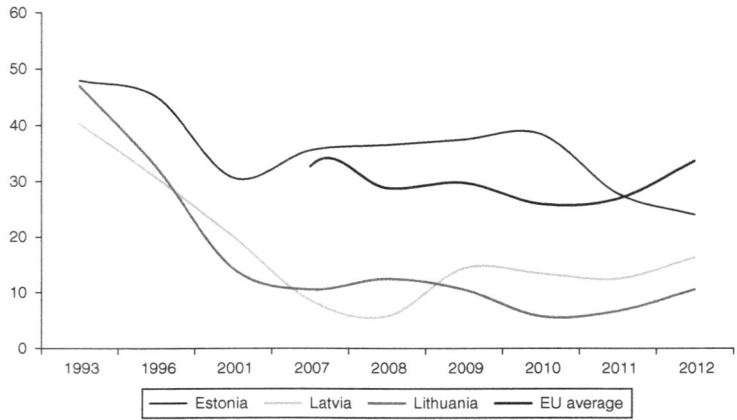

Figure 4.3   Trust in national parliament. 'Tend to trust' (%), 1993–2012

Source: New Baltic Barometer (1993, 1995, 2001); Eurobarometer (2008–2013).

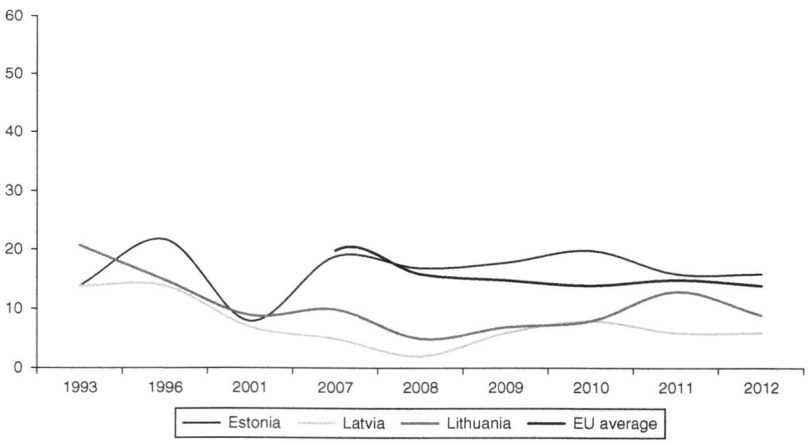

Figure 4.4   Trust in political parties. 'Tend to trust' (%), 2007–2012

Source: New Baltic Barometer (1993, 1995, 2001); Eurobarometer (2008–2013).

typically been far lower than that for trade unions. The partial exception is Estonia, which has had consistently higher trust in its political institutions than have the other two Baltic states.

It is not just attitudes towards civil society and the political system that influence participation in civil society. Trust in other individuals – social capital – is another crucial factor. Figure 4.5 shows that trust in others rose from the mid-1990s to the mid-2000s (except among Lithuanian Russophones). Growing trust is a necessary background condition for greater participation in civil society.

However, this growth in trust is challenged by the generally negative attitude towards civil society displayed by political elites in the Baltic states. In the twenty-first century, prominent national politicians still debated the purpose and role of civil society in the political system. In August 2004, towards the end of her second term in office, Latvian president, Vaira Vīķe-Freiberga, expressed concern about protests organised by the Latvian branch of Transparency International (*Delna*), which opposed the nomination of the speaker of parliament, Ingrīda Ūdre, as the Latvian European Commissioner.[4] Vīķe-Freiberga argued that

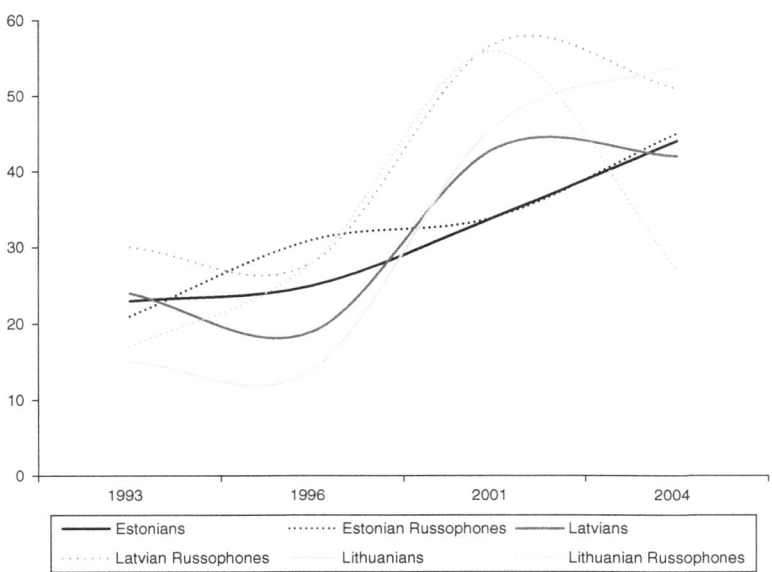

Figure 4.5 Trust in other people. 'Tend to trust' (%), 1993–2004

Source: New Baltic Barometer (1993, 1996, 2001, 2004).

Latvian NGOs involving themselves in the political process in Latvia should re-register as political parties, with all the financial declarations and other controls that this process imposes. In other words, she appeared to imply that only political parties could express political opinions. This shocked the Latvian NGO community because hitherto Vīķe-Freiberga, with her long career in Canadian academia and North American Latvian émigré society, had been seen as someone generally supporting and nurturing Latvian civil society. One observer on Latvian politics was even prompted to compare Vīķe-Freiberga to the authoritarian Belarussian president, Aleksandr Lukashenko (Kalniņš 2004).

The confrontation between the Latvian political elite and civil society accelerated after this incident. A triumvirate of newspapers – *Neatkarīgā Rīta Avīze, Latvijas Avīze* and the tabloid *Vakara Ziņas* – published a stream of articles attacking the activities of the Soros Foundation in Latvia as well as various individuals connected to the foundation. In a series of cynical front-page articles in January 2006, *Neatkarīgā Rīta Avīze* accused George Soros of attempting to 'capture' the Latvian state through his foundation's support for NGOs, academics, and policy-makers since 1991. The Soros Foundation has indeed been the best-funded NGO in Latvia and provided financial support for *Delna* and other major anti-corruption initiatives. Ainārs Šlesers (Latvia's First Party, LPP), at that time serving as transport minister, further accused George Soros of attempting to organise a coup against the Latvian government. In an interview with a Russian-language newspaper, Šlesers argued that Soros 'wants to control power in Latvia' and 'overthrow the cabinet' (Eglitis, 2004). The interior minister, from the same LPP party as Šlesers, then threatened to launch an investigation into the local chapter of Transparency International (which had received funding from the Soros Foundation) as well as other Soros-financed NGOs in Latvia. In a later interview, Šlesers also challenged the independence of the media, arguing that 'it is not normal that every night [Latvian public television's news broadcast] *Panorama* washes citizens' brains, saying how bad the government is, at the same time keeping almost completely quiet on the achievements of the cabinet' (Jansons, 2004). In January 2006 Šlesers proposed new legislation limiting the scope of operation for NGOs funded by foreign donors, seemingly inspired by similar laws that had recently been passed in Russia. This would have effectively neutered civil society, particularly the primary anti-corruption vehicles, Providus (a think-tank off-shoot from the Soros Foundation-Latvia) and *Delna*, which survive largely from foreign donations and grants. In Latvia, the anti-Soros rhetoric has particularly emphasised the role of 'liberal' American-Latvians and presented their values as something unnatural and threatening to the future existence of a traditional Latvia (Zake, 2010). In his anti-Soros rants, Šlesers had identified the then head of Latvian television, American-Latvian Uldis Grava, as one of the chief pro-Soros figures, interfering in the neutrality of Latvian television news reporting (Eglitis, 2004).

This anti-Soros rhetoric has not been limited to Latvia. In 2005 the Lithuanian *Respublika* daily newspaper published a series of articles that attacked civil society in general and the Soros Foundation in particular. Similarly to Latvia, activists and politicians who have received some kind of administrative or financial support from the Soros Foundation were identified as 'Sorosists' or 'Sorosologists' and either directly or indirectly charged as being agents of a foreign power (Soros's Jewish background was frequently held against him) who are attempting to eradicate the traditional values of the state (Donskis, 2006, p. 25).[5] The anti-Soros campaign was given further credence when members of the Lithuanian Liberal Democrat (*Liberalų Demokratų Partija*, LDP) and Labour party (*Darbo Partija*, DP) joined the attack and even suggested that NGOs linked to Soros should be investigated by prosecutors and the security services (McLaughlin and Trilupaityte, 2013).

The anti-Soros media and political elite have presented civil society as something that is essentially alien, and even threatening, to the existence of the Baltic states.[6] This curious anti-Soros rhetoric has been damaging in both Latvia and Lithuania because much of the NGO landscape in the Baltic states has been influenced by the Soros Foundation, which had targeted the fostering of civil society as a central aim as it set up local foundations in the Baltic states in the early 1990s.[7] The anti-Soros discourse also undermines anti-corruption initiatives, which were another priority undertaken by the foundations, particularly supporting the setting up of local branches of Transparency International. It is ironic that the Soros Foundation, which did so much to develop civil society, has in itself become an inadvertent barrier to the consolidation of civil society in the Baltic states.

While the anti-civil society discourse has been less prevalent in Estonia, it has not been entirely absent. Following his successful re-election to the European Parliament in May 2014, independent Estonian MEP Indrek Tarand launched an attack on Estonian NGOs, arguing that the largest organisations had become little more than extensions of the political system (and political parties) that were free-riding off state subventions (Estonian Public Broadcasting, 2014). However, the Soros

Foundation and the organisations that it has supported in Estonia have rarely been criticised.

It is difficult to measure what impact this anti-civil society rhetoric has had on the public in Latvia and Lithuania. At the very least, it has created a seed of doubt about the aims and work of the Soros Foundation. This elite-fuelled cynicism towards civic endeavours was boosted and exacerbated by what Marc Marje Howard described as widespread disappointment and disenchantment with the systemic transformation. Chapter 5 describes the extent of the economic crisis in the months and years that followed independence. In January 1992, the European Union sent emergency food aid to the Baltic states through its PHARE technical assistance programme. In the same month, the Estonian parliament declared a state of economic emergency. After sovereign independence had been achieved, dealing with the deep economic crisis (or taking advantage of it) saw individuals withdraw from the public space and focus on the transformation at the private level. The economic crisis also meant that few individuals had the financial resources to donate to civil society activities. International nongovernmental organisations (INGOs), such as the Soros and Ford foundations. moved in to fill the void.

In the same way, the Baltic states' return to economic growth in the second half of the 1990s and then the long economic expansion of the 2000s, were accompanied by a general strengthening of civil society. Indeed, it strengthened so much as to avoid a crisis during the economic recession of 2008–2010. Growing professionalism and experience in project applications and management have allowed NGOs to successfully compete for national and international funds. Corporate and private donations grew, and Estonia saw an increase in private donations to NGOs throughout the 2000s (Kasemets and Lepp, 2010, p. 17). Between 2007 and 2010 the percentage of individuals in Lithuania making donations to charity rose from 45 per cent of the population to 56 per cent, although corporations are still the biggest source of donations (90 per cent in Lithuania in 2012) and most donations are targeted towards sports teams or cultural organisations such as choirs or dance troupes (Leontjeva, 2013). Indeed, most civil society organisations operate in the cultural sphere (choirs, dance groups, sports clubs), while politically oriented organisations are relatively few and passive. The number of NGOs has also increased throughout the 2000s, although the number of participants has remained largely static, meaning that the same active individuals are spreading themselves thinly across more organisations (Civitas, 2006).

Accession to the EU and NATO initially had a harmful effect on the sector as many state donors and INGOs withdrew from the Baltic states, seeing accession as the moment that civil society could stand on its own. This took away the regular core funding that many NGOs relied upon and forced them to construct their budgets on a project-based foundation. This has had the disadvantage of often redirecting them from their core activities. On the other hand, accession to the EU has resulted in NGOs assuming a greater role in the formal decision-making processes, as an increased number of working groups and interest-group participation was urged and supported by the EU.

At the urging of the EU, the Baltic states adopted broadly similar models of interest representation. Tripartite councils (representing employers, trade unions and governments) were established in all three Baltic states in the 1990s, mimicking the corporatist models in the Nordic states. However, all three councils have met irregularly and generally lacked substantive influence over policymaking. While the economic crisis of 2008–2010 prompted Baltic governments to revive the councils, they once again proved to have little substantive influence in the policymaking process. Although only Lithuania has statutory legislation governing lobbying, all three Baltic states have powerful organised interests that influence policy through interaction with political parties, the executive and the legislature. This weakens the role and function of the tripartite councils.

At a comparative European level, organised interests are relatively weak in the Baltic states, with the region having one of the EU's lowest levels of trade union concentration and collective-bargaining intensity. Trade unions initially suffered from weak legitimacy and low membership because of their years of subordination to the communist parties. Moreover they were caught in a 'Catch-22' situation:

> On the one hand, they are identified by the neoliberal ideology as one of the main culprits for economic "rigidity", a "special interest" threatening economic efficiency. On the other hand, trade unions face a dilemma when confronted with the intemporal trade-offs inherent in market-oriented reforms: accepting these trade-offs is a highly demobilizing strategy with regard to the rank and file; rejecting them appears to be, and often is, irresponsible. (Przeworski 1995, p. 56)

However, after tailing off in the 1990s, union activity began to rise in the new century. The largest trade union in Latvia, the Latvian Free Trade Union (*Latvijas Brīvo Arodbiedrību Savienība*, LBAS) claims a membership of 170,000 people, approximately 20 per cent of the working population. However, in September 2005 it was only able to mobilise 6,000 people (and many attendees were pensioners and students, not trade union members) for what it hoped would be Latvia's biggest post-1991 demonstration. In March 2012, 16,000 teachers demonstrated in Tallinn, demanding a 20 per cent rise (and getting 11 per cent). A three-week strike by medical workers in October of the same year also resulted in an improved deal for the strikers. In the same year Lithuanian unions banded together and successfully lobbied and protested against the adoption of a new labour law. Trade unions (which are particularly strong and activist in Lithuania) and particularly business associations are probably the two most influential contemporary organised interests in the region.

The 2000s also saw an increasing number of rallies, demonstration and street protests. Estonia's Bronze Soldier riots in 2007 were followed by a small riot in the Riga Old Town on 13 January 2009. In response to the sharp economic slowdown and resulting austerity policies of the Latvian government, a small opposition party (Society for a Different Politics, *Sabiedrība Citai Politikai*, SCP) had banded together with a number of trade unions and NGOs to organise a public meeting in Doma Square in the heart of the Riga Old Town. It brought together approximately 10,000 people calling on the president to recall parliament. After the rally, a few hundred people made their way to the Latvian parliament building where they started throwing bricks and bottles. It took the police a few hours to take charge of the situation. A week later the rioting was repeated in Vilnius, where an anti-government and anti-austerity rally ended in limited rioting (Barry, 2009). However, this type of violence remains unusual and rare in the Baltic states.

Public mobilisation has remained largely peaceful as it has increased. The 2007 Latvian 'umbrella revolution' – which saw several thousand protesters turn out in foul wintry blizzards to protest Prime Minister Aigars Kalvītis' decision to fire the popular head of the anti-corruption bureau, Aleksejs Loskutovs – is rather more typical of the new activism. Indeed, these public protests have proved to be an effective weapon, with the umbrella revolution directly leading to the fall of the Kalvītis government, which had been re-elected to office just one year previously.[8]

Lithuania's curious anti-pedophilia movement is another example of increased citizen activism, albeit of an extremely unorthodox nature. The saga began in 2009, when Drąsius Kedys accused three prominent individuals in Kaunas of molesting his five-year-old daughter. Kedys publicised a video recording of his daughter describing the horrific experience. Two of the accused pedophiles were later murdered, as was Kedys himself. These dramatic events mobilised several thousand people to rally behind the Kedys family and prevent the police relocating Kedys's daughter from her father's family to her mother's family, as a court had decreed. A permanent community vigil was organised outside the house of Kedys's sister, a judge who was looking after his daughter. This guard fought off the police's first attempt to take the daughter but failed at the second attempt, when 250 heavily armed police turned up to fulfil the court order. This movement was eventually turned into a political party (Way of Courage – *Drąsos Kelias*, DK) that won 8 per cent of the vote in the 2012 parliamentary election.

The first decade of the twenty-first century has also seen the issue of gay-rights explode into domestic Baltic politics and mobilise large numbers of people around both sides of the issue. Article 121 of the Soviet criminal code made homosexuality illegal, and sexual minorities were not a visible community in the Soviet era Baltic states. The majority of Baltic society remains very conservative, and gay-rights groups struggle to find broad domestic support for their initiatives. The Latvian constitution was amended in order to explicitly state that marriage is between a man and a woman, falling into line with the Lithuanian constitution. In 2010 Estonia adopted the new Family Law, which also did not recognise same-sex marriages. However, 2014 saw a gradual change in policy. First, in October 2014 the Estonian parliament passed a new law recognising same-sex partnerships (albeit by a narrow 40–38 margin). A few weeks later Latvia's popular Foreign Minister, Edgars Rinkēvičs, became the first major Baltic politician to come out as gay. This prompted renewed debate on legislation to recognize same-sex partnerships in Latvian law.

'Gay Pride' marches have been the major vehicle for promoting the rights of sexual minorities. The first gay pride events took place in Estonia in 2004 and in Latvia in 2005, although the first event in Lithuania was not held until 2010. The marches have been marred by virulent opposition rallies. The first Latvian event was attacked by radicals throwing excrement and eggs at gay pride participants. The following year the event was limited to a hotel and counter-demonstrators forced to chant on the street outside the hotel lobby. The 2006 Estonian event was attacked by counter-demonstrators and since then, similarly to Latvia, gay pride has been accompanied by 'No Pride' counter-demonstrators. In May 2010 Vilnius hosted the first pan-Baltic 'Pride' march, now an annual event, which involved over a thousand marchers and included two parliamentary deputies.

Indeed, there has been an increasing tendency for pan-Baltic activism. In protest of continued direct payments to Baltic farmers that remain well below the levels received by farmers in older member states, farmers from all three Baltic states came together to demonstrate in Brussels in 2012 (Baltic News Network, 2012).

The 2000s also saw a rise in the number of communal civic activities. The environmental sphere in particular has seen a great number of initiatives. The annual 'let's do it!' (*Teeme Ära!*) campaign began in Estonia in 2008 (as part of a global campaign) and was later adopted in Latvia (*Lielā Talka*) and Lithuania (*Mes Darom*). The 2014 action saw 40,000 Estonians participate in various clean-up campaigns. Environmental campaigns remain enduringly popular in the Baltic states and, between 2007 and 2010, the number of Lithuanians participating in environmental clean-ups rose from 31 to 50 per cent of the population (Leontjeva, 2013).[9]

The Baltic states are evolving other innovative NGO activities. A 2012 corruption case in Estonia led to a series of small public demonstrations and petitions demanding changes and more public oversight of party financing in Estonia. This eventually led a group of NGOs to set up a crowd-sourcing initiative, the People's Assembly (*Rahvakogu*), where the public could propose, debate and vote on various ideas to improve the political system.[10] In 2013 Estonia organised its first 'opinion festival' in Paide, bringing together politicians, journalists, scholars and the general public in order to debate politics and policy. My Voice in Latvia has been similarly innovative in creating an online forum for preparation and discussion of citizens' initiatives, as well as the collection of signatures and subsequent submission of these projects to parliament. Charitable donations websites have also been set up across the Internet. One Lithuanian charitable donations website had received almost 3.6 million litas in donations by the middle of 2014 and funded more than 100 different projects.[11]

Independent media are another critical component of civil society. Media informs, involves and even mobilises public opinion as well as acts as a watchdog. Much of the public understands politics through the prism presented by the media. After independence, the Baltic media market, which had already started expanding with new independent media in the late Soviet years, grew fast. First print increased, then radio and finally the television markets. Estonia's first privately owned radio station, for example, was launched in 1992, and a year later there were a dozen private radio stations and three new privately owned television stations (Ruutsoo, 1996, p. 103). Latvia's first private radio station, *Radio SWH*, was launched in 1993.

All three Baltic states enjoy a vibrant contemporary media landscape. In the case of Estonia and particularly Latvia, this also extends to Russian-language media. However, in retrospect the 1990s and the early 2000s were the golden era for Baltic media. There were many national and local daily newspapers, magazines, radio stations and television channels. For a brief period in the mid-2000s, there were even three Baltic MTV channels with native language presenters. However, a combination of long-term and short-term factors chipped away at the media market. In the long term, the rise of popular free Internet news portals that primarily rely on republishing agency reports and have few of their own reporters, saw newspapers and magazines shed subscribers.[12] Estonia's print media shed 5–11 per cent of its circulation in 2013. The print publication of Latvian newspapers has been limited to just five days a week since 2012. A short-term catalyst was the economic crash of 2008–2010 that saw many publishers lurch into economic crisis, shed staff and cut back on printed pages and days of publication. In addition to falling audiences, the Latvian and Lithuanian media had to fight government plans to increase the rate of VAT paid on newspapers. In Lithuania, VAT on newspapers was quadrupled to 21 per cent (the usual rate) during the economic crisis, although it was later cut to 9 per cent. Changes in personal tax laws made journalists liable to pay social insurance tax on their income.

Despite these challenges, and in stark contrast to trust in political institutions, Estonians, Latvians and Lithuanians have generally held high levels of trust in their media throughout the independence era. Indeed, this trust has typically been above the EU average (see Figures 4.6 and 4.7).[13]

This high public trust in the media has made media organisations tempting acquisitions for businessmen wishing to influence the political agenda. There are clear trends in terms of ownership of media structures in the Baltic states. Estonian media has typically been owned by Nordic media companies, although this has started to gradually change. At the end of 2013 Norway's *Schibsted* sold the *Postimees* newspaper to the domestically owned *Eesti Meedia* Group. Latvia's newspapers are owned by an often-murky mix of Latvian and Russian businesses, while Lithuania's media market is typically domestically owned (Jegelevicius, 2013). The ownership structure also influences editorial independence, with Western investors typically supporting editorial autonomy, while local investors often play a more direct hand in shaping editorial policy that can reduce media to little more than political instruments. Indeed, the print media in Latvia has become increasingly politicised as it has

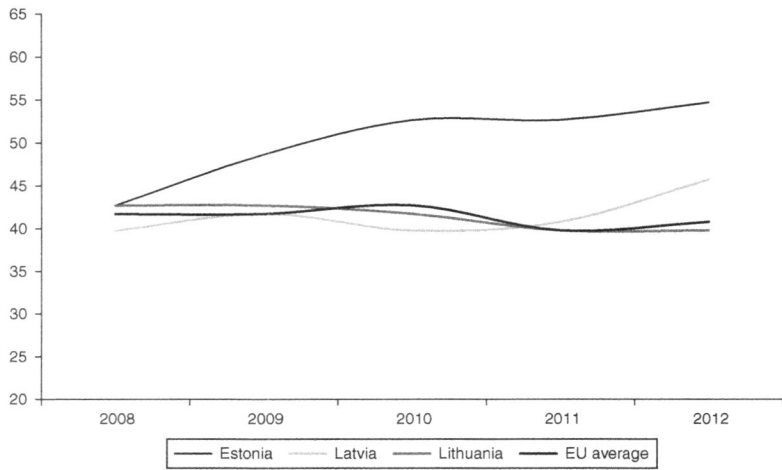

Figure 4.6   'Tend to trust' the press (%), 2008–2012
Source: Eurobarometer (2009–2013).

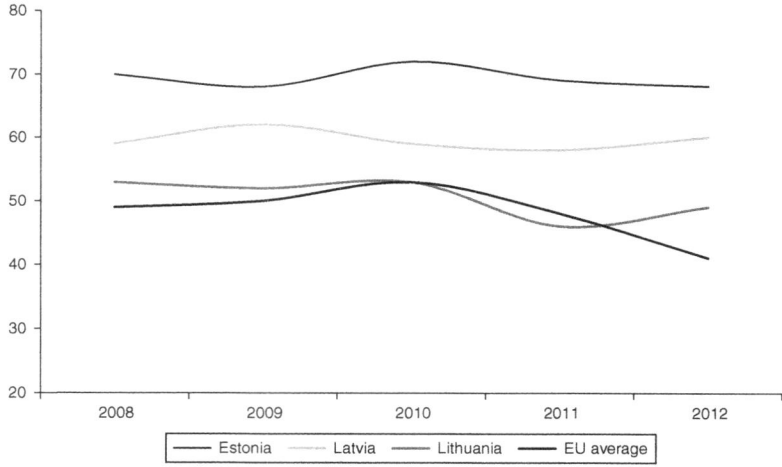

Figure 4.7   'Tend to trust' TV (%), 2008–2012
Source: Eurobarometer (2009–2013).

become unprofitable (Hõbemägi, 2013). Since the mid-2000s the press in Latvia has increasingly clearly sided with particular political interests (related to its specific ownership) and presents an unbalanced picture of the greater political issues.[14]

Examples of media dependence in Latvia and Lithuania abound. In April 2005 it was revealed that the press releases of Aivars Lembergs (mayor of Ventspils and a Latvian *eminence grise*, who is discussed in more depth later) were composed on computers used by journalists from *Neatkarīgā Rīta Avīze* (Galzons 2005). Formally, there is no link between the two, although it has long been alleged that *Neatkarīgā Rīta Avīze* and other newspapers are owned by Lembergs through off-shore companies. The Lithuanian media was similarly wracked by scandal following a Wikileaks revelation, from a leaked 2007 US embassy in Lithuania report, that two major Lithuanian newspapers – *Respublika* and *Lietuvos Rytas* – habitually intimidated and extorted politicians and business leaders into paying bribes for positive stories. Failure to pay would result in negative press (Jegelevicius, 2011). Estonia has mostly been immune to this sort of scandal, although Culture Minister Rein Lang (Reform Party) was forced to step down in late 2013 after claims he had used his influence in a political appointment to a culture magazine (*Postimees*, 2013). This difference between the states is also reflected in Freedom House's (2014) Freedom of the Press Index. In the 2014 report Estonia is ranked 15, with Lithuania following in 39 and Latvia 49 (an improvement on their 2013 rankings of 40 and 55 respectively).

Russian-language media composes 40 per cent of the Latvian media market, but has a much smaller presence in Estonia. The Estonian daily *Postimees* publishes a Russian-language translation of its Estonian daily, something that was tried and which failed by *Diena* in Latvia in the 1990s. Indeed, the Russian and Latvian-language media are very distinct, with each reporting political and social issues in very different ways. The readerships of these publications do not overlap. A 2001 survey revealed that while 29 per cent of citizens read the Latvian-language daily *Diena* and 20 per cent *Lauku Avīze*, only 5 per cent and 1 per cent of non-citizens do so. While, respectively, 21 per cent and 20 per cent of non-citizens read the leading Russian-language dailies *Subbota* and *Vesti*, the respective figures for citizens were 6 per cent and 3 per cent. This pattern was also reflected in local newspapers, with 42 per cent of citizens and 4 per cent of non-citizens reading Latvian-language local newspapers, while 5 per cent and 13 per cent read Russian-language local newspapers, as well as both radio and television (Latvian Naturalisation Board 2001, p. 39).

Although independent media has weakened in the 2000s, civil society in the Baltic states has gradually strengthened, overcoming the negative

Soviet cultural heritage, the fall in participation as the transition crisis took hold in the 1990s, and the criticism that civil society has received because of its relationship with international donors, particularly George Soros (Uhlin, 2010). The USAID comparative Civil Society Organisation (CSO) Sustainability Index allows for a comparison of the strength of the NGO sectors in the Baltic states. Broadly speaking, Estonia (2.0) has outperformed Latvia and Lithuania (both 2.7) in the evaluation. This is largely because Estonian NGOs are seen to have stronger organisational capacity and financial viability. Indeed, the Estonian National Foundation for Civil Society disburses over €7 million annually from the state budget to support NGOs. The Ministry of Culture performs a similar function in Latvia, albeit with a much smaller budget. Money still remains quite scarce for many NGOs, but then the Baltic states remain among the poorest in the European Union. As individual incomes rise, so will donations to civil society.

4.2   Corruption

After 1991, the Baltic states, particularly Latvia and Lithuania, experienced an inevitable increase in corruption – defined here as the use of public office for private gain. The transition to new laws governing the market economy created unplanned (or sometimes intended) gaps and grey areas that were exploited by underpaid (and occasionally unpaid) politicians, bureaucrats, judges, cash-rich criminals and the rising new class of entrepreneurs. These early years of transition often drew parallels with the violent American Wild West of the nineteenth century or Al Capone's Chicago.

Corruption seemed to be everywhere in these early years. The initial conditions were not especially promising for the Baltic states. Opaque personal networks, as well as backroom deals and bribery, were structural characteristics of administrative dealings in the Soviet system. *Blat* – 'the use of personal networks and informal contacts to obtain goods and services in short supply and to find a way around formal procedures' – was an established part of daily life in the Soviet Union (Ledeneva, 1998, p. 1). Moreover, living in three small states most residents of Estonia, Latvia and Lithuania had myriad informal contacts. For example, during the Soviet era the overwhelming majority of judges, prosecutors, lawyers and other actors in the legal profession gained their education in the law faculties at the three national universities (University of Tartu, University of Latvia and Vilnius University). It was not unusual for former classmates to sit together, albeit on opposing sides and as the arbiter, in a court case. The opportunity to make informal arrangements that circumvent the law must have been extremely tempting if not even inevitable. Moreover, corruption was also entrenched by the presence of well-organised criminal networks, many originating from neighbouring Russia. Sten Berglund et al. (2001, p. 37) argued that 'the East European model might compensate for the lack of [NGOs] by mobilizing pre-democratic clientelistic networks to a much greater extent than is – and was – customary in the [W]est'. This was certainly the case in the 1990s.

Corruption is hidden and difficult to measure. Nevertheless, there are a few sources of information available. The Transparency International Corruption Perceptions Index (CPI, a composite study that draws on surveys of business people, the general public and country analysts over a rolling three-year period) allows us to track the performance of the Baltic states over multiple years. The index is based on *perceptions* and thus is an indicator of the extent to which people consider institutions and political actors to be operating outside the rule of law rather than being an accurate reflection of the *actual* extent of corruption in the Baltic states. However, it is a useful indicator because, if people perceive corruption to be widespread, they themselves are more likely to participate in it. As Figure 4.8 clearly indicates, Estonia has regularly outperformed both Latvia and Lithuania in the CPI, Estonians are also less likely to offer a bribe (Figure 4.9).

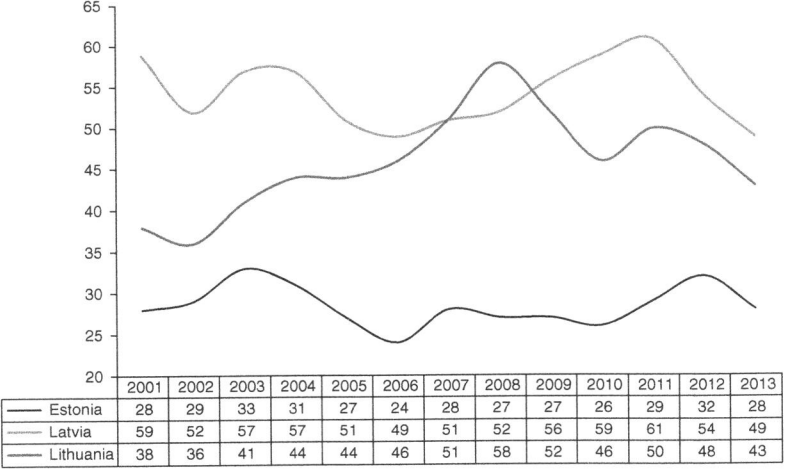

	2001	2002	2003	2004	2005	2006	2007	2008	2009	2010	2011	2012	2013
Estonia	28	29	33	31	27	24	28	27	27	26	29	32	28
Latvia	59	52	57	57	51	49	51	52	56	59	61	54	49
Lithuania	38	36	41	44	44	46	51	58	52	46	50	48	43

Figure 4.8 Corruption Perceptions Index. Ranking of the Baltic states, 2001–2013

Source: Corruption Perceptions Index (2014).

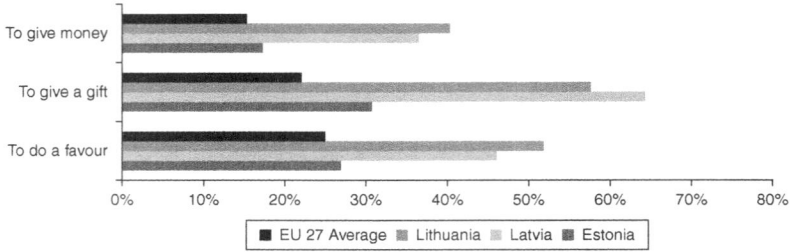

Figure 4.9   If you wanted to get something from the public administration or a public service, to what extent do you think it is acceptable to do any of the following?

Source: Eurobarometer 79.1 (2014).

Corruption takes place at many levels, although a distinction is typically made between political (when private actors attempt to illicitly influence lawmakers and executives) and administrative corruption (bribe-taking by civil servants, typically at the point of service-delivery). As the American-Latvian political science professor Rasma Kārkliņš (2005) pointed out, not all corruption is the same. While undoubtedly harmful in the long term, petty administrative corruption probably contributed to a stabilisation of the Baltic systems in the first post-Soviet years. The opportunity to supplement low salaries with bribes allowed state institutions to retain staff and limited social strife. However, systemic corruption, which undermines and distorts the rule of law and good governance, is undoubtedly harmful, not least because it has the potential to set a damaging example of corrupt behaviour among the general population.

However, while corruption was perceived to be deep-seated throughout the 1990s and early 2000s there were few cases, and even fewer convictions. One rare example came in 1995 when Lithuanian prime minister, Adolfas Šleževičius (LDLP), and other cabinet ministers were found to have enjoyed higher-than-average interest rates at a bank that collapsed in 1995 (although all the politicians had managed to withdraw their deposits before the bank collapse). The economic transition and especially the mass privatisations of the 1990s had created huge opportunities for graft, but weak oversight meant that few cases were prosecuted. A 1998 World Bank report wrote that:

Economic power in Latvia has become concentrated in a small number of conglomerates. Business and political interests have become intertwined in a complex and non-transparent way, and businesses are increasingly active in political parties. Excessive concentration of economic power, due in part to weak enforcement of competition legislation, drains efficiency from the economy and presents the risk that Latvia could become prone to high-level corruption. (Anderson, 1998, p. 22)

These conditions fuelled the rise of the Baltic oligarchs.

Unsurprisingly, the oligarch phenomenon is the weakest in Estonia, which has both the lowest levels of corruption and the most developed civil society in the region. Mel Huang (2002) explains the absence of oligarchs from Estonia as being the logical result of Estonian support for privatisation to outsiders that rapidly brought in Western managers and owners who both rejected corrupt practices and, in any case, were not members of any close-knit Estonian networks. The Estonian economy also created new IT, services and banking businesses that were the basis for domestic tycoons who, as a result, had little use for illicit political influence.

Latvia has three major figures known in the domestic discourse as 'oligarchs', although this is a term rejected by all three (Kuris, 2012). Aivars Lembergs has been the mayor of Ventspils since the late 1980s. His local political vehicle – For Latvia and Ventspils (*Latvijai un Ventspilij*, LuV) – has been partnered with the Green/Farmers Union party since 2002, giving Lembergs political influence at the national level. His primary form of economic influence has been through control of the city of Ventspils, a major oil transit port. Through much of the 1990s and 2000s Lembergs's main rival was Andris Šķēle, who rose to prominence in the mid-1990s as he used his insider knowledge (he was formerly a high-ranking official in the Ministry of Agriculture) to acquire much of Latvia's major food processing enterprises through a murky privatisation process (Huang, 2002). In 1998 Šķēle, who had already served as prime minister, created his own political vehicle, the Peoples Party (*Tautas Partija*, TP), which went on to win the parliamentary election later that year. That same election saw the emergence of Latvia's third oligarch, Ainārs Šlesers. In contrast to his two peers, Šlesers derived his wealth from his partnership in Norwegian retail and real estate investments in Latvia. Similarly to Lembergs and Šķēle, though, Šlesers also created a string of political parties: in 1998, the New Party (*Jaunā Partija*, JP); in 2002, Latvia's First Party (*Latvijas Pirmā Partija*, LPP); in 2010, For a Good Latvia (*Par Labu Latviju*, PLL); and, in 2014, United for Latvia (*Vienoti Latvijai*, VL). All three individuals are alleged to have control over different parts of the Latvian media as well as a shared interest in the *Diena* newspaper group (Petrova, 2011).

The Lithuanian case is not as clear-cut as the Latvian. In 2009, then presidential candidate, Dalia Grybauskaitė, claimed that Lithuania was also dominated by a small clique:

> I tried to calculate how many people actually ruled Lithuania. According to my calculations the number is around a hundred. Fifteen individuals are at the very top – they govern almost all the main political parties, and there are a few people in the government and parliament. (Urbonas, 2009, p. 83)

However, this is an *elite* rather than an *oligarchy* in the sense of wealthy businessmen controlling both a political vehicle and a media. In Lithuania, former prime minister Bronislovas Lubys (who died in 2011) used his wealth from the early privatisation of a chemical plant and his influence in the Confederation of Lithuanian Industrialists to exert control over the privatisation process in the mid to late 1990s, and was probably the closest individual to being an oligarch (Huang 2002).

The influence of the Latvian oligarchs has been gradually under-mined as the state toughened up its anti-corruption instruments. All three Latvian oligarchs have been charged or implicated in major corruption scandals, although as of 2014 none had yet been found guilty. Aivars Lembergs was the first to experience legal problems when he was arrested in 2006 and charged with money-laundering, bribery and abuse of office as well as with the more technical crime of failing to declare property for tax purposes. He was suspended from the post of mayor but has gone on to be re-elected to the Ventspils local authority in two local elections (2009 and 2013) and has continued to fulfil the public functions of mayor, regularly hosting municipal events and representing the city on Latvian television news and chat shows. Both Šlesers and Šķēle were caught up in the 'Jurmalagate' scandal that saw a former mayor of the wealthy beach resort impris-oned for bribery. Šķēle was additionally implicated in the 'Digitalgate' or 'Kempmayer Case', which alleges an illegal plot surrounding the purchase of equipment to digitalise Latvian television. Finally, Šlesers played a central role in the recall of the Latvian parliament in the summer of 2011, a turning point in Latvia's fight against corruption. It was parliament's refusal to suspend his parliamentary immunity (following a request to raid Šlesers's private residence) that led to President Zatlers triggering a referendum on the recall of parliament.

This prompted a number of NGOs to put together an 'Oligarchs Funeral' celebration in Riga. Indeed, the subsequent early election saw Šlesers's political vehicle fail to pass the 5 per cent threshold, while Šķēle seemed to sense which way the wind was blowing and did not compete in the election (the People's Party then went into liquidation). Only Aivars Lembergs's Green/Farmers Union was re-elected and, while it was initially kept in opposition, it helped form a new government coalition in 2014.

The fight against political corruption in Latvia began long before President Zatlers recalled parliament in 2011. Attention was drawn to the issue in 2000 when the World Bank published an extensive report on 'Anticorruption in transition: A contribution to the policy debate'.[15] The report analysed two types of corruption in the post-communist world: administrative – where distortions appear in the implementation of laws by both state and non-state actors – and systemic state capture – whereby actors 'influence the formation of laws, regulations, decrees, and other government policies to their advantage as a result of the illicit and non-transparent provision of private benefits to public officials' (World Bank 2000, p. xv). Latvia was categorised as a country with a high degree of state capture (fifth highest among the twenty East-Central European and Commonwealth of Independent States surveyed), but with significantly lower levels of administrative corruption than Estonia and Lithuania. The World Bank argued that the high level of state capture was caused by national wealth in Latvia being concentrated in one key area (transit of natural resources from third countries), and detailed that those who control this area sought to maintain their influence through the capture of state institutions.

Coupled with negative reports from the European Commission (which argued that corruption had to be reined in to allow candidate states to succeed in the European single market, for cross-border actors to receive a fair hearing in foreign courts and as a key element of the battle to build administrative and legal capacity in order to absorb high levels of EU funding) and NATO concern that corruption would impact the Baltic states' ability to manage NATO secrets, this international criticism prompted vigorous anti-corruption campaigns and the creation of new institutions in Latvia and Lithuania in particular. At that time the EU did not have any clear anti-corruption programme or framework that could be transferred to the candidate states. Rather, there was a high level of flexibility for states to adopt different types of anti-corruption initiatives. Indeed, it could be said that the most important thing was to be seen to be doing something.

There was also domestic momentum to tackle corruption in Lithuania as well as Latvia. As discussed elsewhere in this volume, all three Baltic states saw anti-corruption White Knight political parties emerge in the early twenty-first century, all promising a new kind of politics, contrasting themselves with the tarnished elite (see Chapter 3). While this type of anti-corruption party died out in subsequent Estonian parliamentary elections, they have continued to thrive in Latvia and Lithuania.

The three Baltic states have addressed corruption through different institutional choices and directions although the policies, despite different origins, have converged (Johannsen and Pedersen, 2011). Estonia and Lithuania, for example, created specialised parliamentary committees with greater powers than their Latvian equivalent to investigate cases of political and administrative wrong-doing. Latvia and Lithuania created dedicated independent anti-corruption agencies based on similar institutions in Hong-Kong and Singapore. In contrast, Estonia has an anti-corruption programme coordinated by the Ministry of Justice. Lithuania's Special Investigation Service (STT) was created in 1997, initially as a unit of the Ministry of the Interior, but from 2000 as an independent institution accountable to the president and parliament. The Latvian anti-corruption agency (KNAB) was set-up two years later in 2002 after feisty political debate. Both independent agencies have investigative and law-enforcement powers, but the Latvian agency also has the right of legislative initiative and legislative review as well as control and oversight over the funding of political parties (which has led to several sizeable fines being imposed on political parties). In short, the Latvian KNAB tackles both administrative and political corruption while the Lithuanian STT is limited to administrative corruption tasks. Nevertheless, both agencies have established themselves as major players in the political system. In the decade between 1999 and 2009 the STT saw the number of cases it had 'solved' annually rise from 160 to 424, and the number of whistleblowing reports from the public increase from 215 to 878 (Velykis, 2010, p. 5). The Latvian KNAB has also seen an increase in its workload, from investigating 18 cases in 2003 to 33 in 2013 (KNAB, 2013, p. 13). As Figure 4.10 indicates, the Latvian and Lithuanian publics trust the two specialised anti-corruption agencies to deal with corruption more than they trust the national police.

Johannsen and Pedersen (2011) argue that Latvia and Lithuania have created independent agencies to tackle the corruption issue at least partly because the perception among lawmakers is that corruption has greater salience in these two states. They found that a higher number of Latvian and Lithuanian ministers have personal experience of attempted bribery

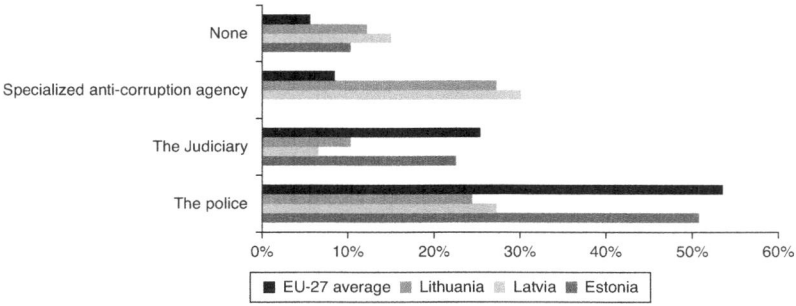

Figure 4.10   If you want to complain about a case of corruption, whom would you trust most to deal with it?

Source: Eurobarometer 79.1 (2014).

and these same ministers agree that the misuse of high office is more prevalent there than in Estonia. As a result, Estonia had less of a need for a powerful independent anti-corruption institution. Moreover, Estonia received a much more favourable initial evaluation of its readiness to join the EU in the Agenda 2000 reviews, and this gave it greater leeway to choose an anti-corruption mechanism while Latvia and Lithuania, which were initially placed in the secondary category of potential member states, had to be much more open to international leverage in order to get into the EU.

While there is no doubt that corruption continues to exist in Latvia and Lithuania, it is no longer a fundamental, existential threat to democracy in the region. The corruption rate in Latvia and Lithuania was particularly striking because of their Baltic Sea location. The Baltic states' Nordic neighbours are regularly ranked as the most open and least corrupt states in the world. Certainly the example of the northern neighbours helped in the fight against corruption in the 2000s. The frequency with which businesses in the Baltic states paid bribes fell significantly between 2002 and 2005, when they were making their final push for EU membership (Anderson and Gray, 2006, p. 11). Powerful anti-corruption institutions emerged to fight state capture and uncover graft. Citizens have protested against corruption, and NGOs have entered the debate. While much remains to be done – particularly when we compare the Baltic states to their close Nordic neighbours – great strides have undoubtedly been taken. Of course, corruption also began to decline as the opportunities for graft became limited by the end of the mass privatisation campaign, an era when it had been all but impossible for the media, civil society and law enforcement to keep a check on what was going on. While there are still large enterprises left to privatise, the rarity of the process and the accompanying public scrutiny make it much more difficult for the process to be hijacked by corrupt actors.

While Latvia has typically been seen as the Baltic laggard in fighting corruption, recent reports have pushed Lithuania ahead of Latvia in terms of both the public's perceptions of corruption and actual experience of giving or receiving bribes (European Commission, 2014). Estonia's continuing exceptionalism is typically explained by its enthusiastic adoption of various e-government tools that have contributed to the transparency of the public sector as well as by Estonia's cultural proximity to Finland. In a study of corruption in Estonia, Margit Tavits (2010) found that people engage in corruption as a result of social learning – in other words, when corruption is seen as an acceptable practice and when people perceive that it is widely practiced in their community. If this is generalised to Latvia and Lithuania, the decline of state capture corruption should be accompanied by a general decrease in bureaucratic corruption.

4.3   Russophones and other minorities

Ethnic polarisation, and its impact on the Baltic states' political systems, has been a reoccurring theme throughout this volume. It has also had a significant impact on civil society. On the one hand, strict new citizenship laws in Estonia and especially Latvia limited the number of Russophones who could participate in early elections and ethnicity remains a strong predictor for participation in civil society, with Russophones being less likely to be active (Aasland, 2002; Schulze, 2014). On the other hand, ethnicity is a major mobilising issue for Baltic civil society, with the annual 16 March and 9 May events in Latvia rallying thousands of participants.

In 1991 the titular Baltic and Russophone communities were divided by language as well as by support for the independent states. A 1991 survey by the Estonian Language Board had found that only 4 per cent of Russophone school-leavers had mastered the Estonian language (Baltic Independent, 1991). A snap telephone poll, just days after independence was renewed in August 1991, found that while 99 per cent of ethnic Estonians supported independence, just 54 per cent of Russophones did, and 19 per cent were opposed to it (Baltic Independent, 1991A).[16] A 1992 survey of Riga residents found that Russophones were both more positive about the past and more fearful of the future than were ethnic Latvians (Schafer and Schafer, 1993).

Estonian and Latvian society became increasingly heterogeneous as a result of the mass migration of Russophones to Estonia and Latvia after the Second World War. This resulted in a major remaking of the ethnic composition of the Baltic populations. The Russophone-titular cleavage had been marginalised during the inter-war era because 'when the Russian Empire retreated from the Baltic in 1915–1917 it took much of the imperial industries (those dependant on the Russian hinterland) and their workforces with it' (Lieven, 1994, p. 61). In the mid-1930s, ethnic Estonians made up 88 per cent and ethnic Latvians 77 per cent of their respective states (Norgaard, 1995, p. 170). By 1989 ethnic Latvians were barely a majority in the Latvian SSR (see Table 4.1). In contrast, ethnic Lithuanians constituted over 80 per cent of the Lithuanian SSR, and Poles, rather than Russophones, were the largest minority in the republic (although the two minorities are now a similar size). Minorities felt particularly threatened in the early years of independence, when the nationalist rhetoric was intemperate and few decisions had been made on citizenship and language laws. This sense of unease even infected Lithuania when, just a few days after the collapse of the Soviet Union, the Lithuanian government disbanded and later imposed direct rule on the municipal governments of Vilnius and Šalčininkai, the two regions in Lithuania with the largest Polish populations, and accused their leaders of supporting the Moscow coup (Snyder, 1995).

Russophone migrants were primarily industrial workers employed in the new urban manufacturing enterprises set up by the Soviet Union. Russophones still outnumber Estonians and Latvians in a number of major cities. In Estonia they are clustered in the capital Tallinn and the north-east region around the cities of Narva and Kohtla-Järve. The main

Table 4.1 Ethnic composition of the Baltic states, 1989–2009 (%)

	Estonia			Latvia			Lithuania		
	1989	2000	2009	1989	2000	2009	1989	2000	2009
Titular	61.0	67.6	68.7	52.0	57.7	59.3	79.6	83.5	84.0
Russophones	34.6	28.9	28.9	42.0	36.4	33.9	12.3	8.2	6.6
Poles	0.2	0.2	0.2	2.3	2.5	2.4	7.0	6.7	6.1

Source: Estonian Human Development Report 2011, p. 45.

Russophone areas in Latvia are the capital Riga and the eastern region of Latgale, especially the city of Daugavpils. The titular and Russian-speaking populations lived separate and parallel lives from the very beginning of the Soviet period. A Radio Free Europe/Radio Liberty (1954) interview with a 70-year-old [Latvian] female, who had arrived in the UK from Latvia in November 1953 to be reunited with her daughters, indicates prevailing Latvian attitudes at that time:

> She says that the morale of the Latvian population is very low. Apathy and weariness prevail[;] ... the Russians, of whom there are many in Latvia, are the privileged class. They have the best jobs, possess or have at their disposal many cars (Pobieda or Moskvich) and are well dressed and fed. There is scarcely any social intercourse between them and the local population; they avoid each other and even in public parks sit on separate benches. On the Latvian side this is motivated by deep resentment. As to the Russians, they are, it seems, encouraged by the authorities to keep up an aloof attitude.

This reveals the resentment felt by many individuals at that time as their social status was undermined and the Baltic languages were gradually, if not entirely, replaced by the use of Russian in the public sphere. There was a clear cultural dimension to the division between Balts and Russian-speakers. This is captured by a 1987 survey of cultural habits in Estonia that reveals particularly contrasting attitudes towards the environment and the arts. Russophone migrants tended to live in insular communities, go to Russophone schools, read Russian newspapers, watch Russian-language television broadcasts and attend Russian theatres (Ilves, 1991, p. 75). There was little interaction between the two communities. Integration had not been of any concern to the Soviet Union at least partly because much of the migration to the Baltic states had been transitory. In the case of Estonia, during the Soviet period there were 80 departures for every 100 arrivals (Taagepera, 1993, p. 103). In contrast, the Polish community in Lithuania was much more integrated, especially in terms of language knowledge.

Ethnic relations dominated much of the post-1991 domestic discourse in the Baltic states. Although it quickly lost salience in Lithuania and had appeared to become less relevant in Estonia, ethnic relations has consistently shaped the Latvian political system since 1991. The 1990s were initially dominated by attempts to regulate the status of Russophones in the Baltic states. The initial challenge was to pass citizenship legislation, followed by updated language laws. Although both were achieved by the mid-1990s, they continue to be challenged in Latvia, where a referendum on the status of Russian was held in February 2012, and a citizens' initiative on liberalising the citizenship law was submitted to the electoral authority that same year. Nevertheless, after the legal status of the minorities had been ratified in the 1990s, political attention was increasingly focused on the issue of social integration. New programmes and ministries were created, albeit with a mixed impact. Society remains particularly divided in Latvia, with ethnic Latvians and Russian-speakers occupying different information spaces (e.g., linguistically based newspapers, radio stations, and television channels). The situation in Estonia has been moderated by more inclusive political parties.

The political rhetoric against Russophones was initially very sharp after August 1991. In September 1991 the Latvian minister of finance proposed economic assistance for Russophones ready to quit Latvia (Mole, 2012, p. 83). However, although the language was eventually tempered, the writing of new citizenship laws attracted further controversy in Estonia and Latvia, causing both internal and external dissent. The pro-Russophone political opposition was particularly harsh in Estonia, where the former prime minister and leader of the popular front, Edgar Savisaar, claimed that the law would institutionalise 'ethnic cleansing' and 'apartheid' (*Baltic Independent*, 1993, p. 3). Neighbouring Russia's response was similarly virulent, with President Boris Yeltsin threatening that Estonia has 'forgotten about some geopolitical and demographic realities, but that Russia has the ability to remind them of it' (Ott, Kirch and Kirch, 1996, p. 22). In July 1993 the Russophone north-eastern cities of Narva and Sillamäe held referendums on regional autonomy supported by 97 per cent of voters.

In contrast, Lithuania had quickly adopted a 'zero-option' model that granted citizenship to all individuals fulfilling certain conditions. Estonia readopted its 1938 citizenship law in 1992 but then quickly introduced new residency and civic-knowledge conditions in order to apply for Estonian citizenship. The process was far more drawn out in Latvia where the citizenship law that was finally adopted in 1994 was very different to that adopted during the first independence era. While the essential principle behind the initial 1919 law was one of *jus solis*, where citizenship is based on the place of birth, the 1994 law was based on the principle of *jus sanguine* where nationality is acquired through descent from the parents. Following the renewal of independence in 1991, there had been two possible routes that Latvian policymakers could follow: a zero option that would give all Latvian residents citizenship, or a more restrictive law based on ethnicity. Latvian policymakers chose the latter path, and citizenship was granted to those individuals that were citizens before the Soviet occupation of 17 July 1940, and their direct descendants. This position was based on a legal restorationist view of independence.[17] Those people who had moved to Latvia in the Soviet era (approximately 700,000 people, overwhelmingly Russophones) were denied automatic citizenship. In 2014 approximately 282,000 individuals, or around 17 per cent of the Latvian population, remained non-citizens. Among EU member states in 2011, only Luxembourg (43.1 per cent) and Cyprus (20 per cent) had a higher non-citizen population than Latvia (third with 17 per cent) or Estonia (fourth with 15.7 per cent) (Eurostat, 2012).

The citizenship issue dominated Latvian politics in the early 1990s and drew in many different actors.[18] Aside from parliamentary parties, international actors such as the Organisation for Security and Cooperation in Europe (OSCE), the European Union, the Council of Europe and the Russian government were all vocal in the initial debate, encouraging an inclusive citizenship law. The OSCE took the leading role as the 'eyes and ears' of the international community (Galbreath, 2003, p. 40), deploying both long-term missions to Estonia and Latvia as well as a high commissioner on national minorities (Max van der Stoel, who rapidly became somewhat of a *bête noire* for Estonian and Latvian nationalists). There was particularly strong international criticism of an idea floated by the Latvian National Independence Movement (*Latvijas Nacionālās Neatkarības Kustība*, LNNK) promoting a quota system that would significantly delay the naturalisation process for the majority of non-citizens. The 1994 law maintained naturalisation as a gradual process through the creation of age-group 'windows' (the youngest coming first).

The rate of naturalisation under this system proved to be very slow. A survey by the Latvian Naturalisation Board (2000) attempted to explain the initially low take-up rate. A poor level of Latvian-language knowledge (59 per cent) and lack of preparedness to tackle the history exam (54 per cent) were the two major reasons given by respondents, indicating insufficient information and funding for the naturalisation programme. The expense of taking the exam was mentioned by 47 per cent of respondents, while another 8 per cent did not wish to serve in the Latvian armed forces (Latvia had compulsory conscription until 2006). Latvian citizenship was also viewed as an impediment for travel to Russia (20 per cent); 73 per cent believed that there is 'no difference between citizens and non-citizens', and 26 per cent stated that they did not consider it important to participate in elections. Increased international pressure was placed on Latvia's policymakers. Subsequent amendments saw the abolition of age limits and the automatic granting of citizenship to children of non-citizens born in Latvia (if requested by the parents). These were put forward in a referendum on 3 October 1998 (the same day as the parliamentary election) and approved by 53 per cent of voters. As Figure 4.11 indicates, over subsequent years there was a marked increase in the rate of naturalisation, particularly in the mid-2000s when non-citizens were motivated to take-up Latvian citizenship because of the perceived benefits of European Union citizenship after accession. Estonia experienced a peak of naturalisation in the early and mid-1990s. However, the number of individuals naturalising in Latvia (and Estonia) has drastically fallen since then (Regelmann, 2014). Three factors have contributed to this fall. First, Russophones have the option of gaining Russian, rather than Estonian or Latvian, citizenship. Second, aliens in Estonia and non-citizens in Latvia have almost the same social and economic rights as citizens (and in Estonia aliens can vote in local elections), reducing the need for citizenship. Finally, more than a decade in the EU has shown aliens and non-citizens from the region that, in terms of EU mobility, there are few additional advantages to be had in holding Estonian or Latvian citizenship. As a result, incentives for naturalisation have been reduced.

Those who did take up citizenship tended to be active participants in the Latvian democracy. A 'survey of newly naturalized citizens' carried

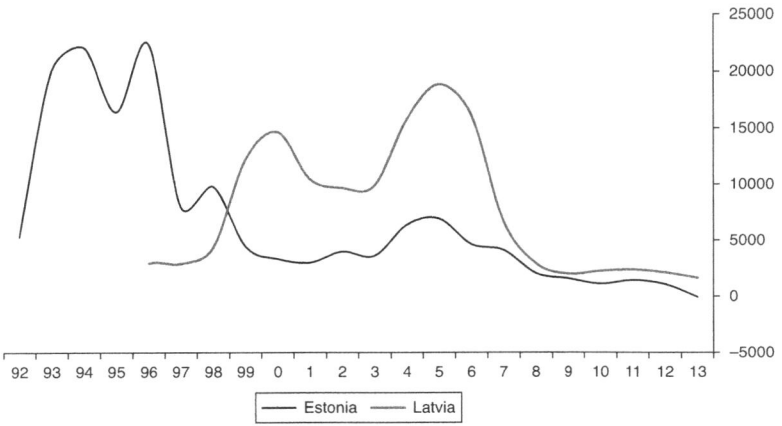

Figure 4.11   Rate of naturalisation in Estonia and Latvia, 1992–2013

Source: Estonia.eu (2014); Latvian Naturalisation Board (2014).

out by the Baltic Institute of Social Sciences (2001) compared political attitudes between three social groups: recently naturalised citizens, citizens and non-citizens. New citizens tended to be more interested in politics than were the other two groups and were generally more satisfied with the development of democracy in Latvia. Moreover, they had greater trust in the parliament, cabinet of ministers, trade unions, political parties and NGOs than did the other two groups.

While citizenship issues stirred most controversy in Latvia, language policy was a battleground in both Estonia and Latvia. The Russian-language was initially dominant in both Estonia and Lithuania. During the Soviet era it was taught in all schools (whereas Estonian and Latvian were usually not taught in Russophone schools) and dominated radio and television. Career progression demanded knowledge of Russian. As a result, the titular populations learnt to speak Russian, while Russophones had no economic or political push or motivation to learn the Baltic languages. This caused severe resentment among the titular populations, who felt that their core culture was being undermined.

The Baltic states had initially adopted new language laws in the late 1980s declaring the titular languages as the only official republic languages. New 'thick' language policies encompassing a great number of laws, regulations and institutions were adopted after independence, introducing professional Estonian, Latvian and Lithuanian language requirements for certain categories of public- and private-sector employees and tight control of language use in the public sphere. This caused some outcry at the time, as it affected professions, such as the police, which had traditionally been dominated by Russophones. These policies certainly contributed, possibly intentionally, to a changing of the guard in the police and other professions, but they also caused much resentment – especially in Latvia where the state paid for neither Latvian-language courses nor the Latvian-language exams that individuals had to pass. Language continues to be politically salient. Latvia's 2012 referendum on introducing Russian as a second state language polarised ethnic communities. In 2014 Lithuanian politicians debated whether bilingual street signs should be allowed in regions heavily populated by minorities, with Prime Minister Algirdas Butkevičius being forced to state that 'there will be no two languages in regions, there will be no bilingual signs' (BNS, 2014).

Estonia drafted a social integration policy between 1997 and 2000, with Latvia following a few years later. However, integration – defined here as 'a process of unifying society by promoting participation, non-discrimination and intercultural control' – has generally been quite weak

in both states (Muižnieks, 2010, p. 279). Continuing low rates of naturalisation and high numbers of remaining aliens and non-citizens indicate the lack of a common political community. Estonian Russophones
are less spatially and socially integrated than their Latvian peers, and
both states still have some 20 per cent of the population lacking titular
language skills – primarily located in the minority-dominated cities and
regions close to the Russian border. Moreover, the Russian-language press
in Latvia, as well as media produced in Russia, generally paint a different
picture of politics, society and the wider world than do Latvian media,
leading to two separate, often conflicting, information societies in Latvia
(Šulmane, 2010). The school systems in both Estonia and Latvia are still
structured by language, although Russian-language schools now teach
the majority of the curricula in the titular languages. The Latvian political system is also structured by an ethnic cleavage, encouraging further
polarisation. A 2007 survey of ethnic non-Estonians found that almost
one-third (32%) had experienced discrimination in job hunting, getting
a raise (26%) and even in access to health services (16%) (Lagerspetz
et al., 2007). An earlier study had also found that Estonian Russophones
were far more likely to be threatened by social exclusion, although this
was not the case for Russophones in Latvia (Aasland, 2002). Another
outcome is that Estonian Russophones are less likely to vote and be
active in civil society than ethnic Estonians (Schulze, 2014). Moreover,
Russophone NGOs also have less influence on government, being identified with the political opposition in Latvia and with non-citizen interests
in Estonia (Agarin, 2011). Lithuania has not been entirely unaffected.
Charles Woolfson (2010) pointed out a contradiction between empirical
survey evidence that, on the one hand suggested lower perceptions of
discrimination in Lithuania (respondents did not see 'belonging to a
different ethnic group' as a disadvantage) versus high levels of hostility
to certain ethnic groups and evidence of systematic discrimination in
the labour market. Woolfson argued that Lithuanians actually have relatively deep levels of antagonism towards others, although this is not
seen as an important issue by most of the population because there are
so few visible minorities in Lithuania.

In contrast to much of Europe, the Baltic states have indeed seen little
non-European immigration (rather, the Baltic states have experienced
emigration). The annual combined number of asylum seekers and refugees in all three Baltic States is only in the double digits. Between 2000
and 2007 just 10,326 persons migrated to Estonia (Kovalenko et al, 2010,
p. 10). More than half of these migrants were non-visible immigrants
from neighbouring Finland (31%) and Russia (24%), as well as migrants

from neighbouring Ukraine, Belarus, Moldova and Georgia. There are no more than 500 practising Muslims in Lithuania, a country of over three million people, and many of the Muslims are ethnic Lithuanians (Racius, 2009).

There are very few visible minorities in the Baltic States and, resultantly, few registered racist attacks. Indeed, their very scarcity means that attacks are given a relatively high profile in the press. Nevertheless, as Kovalenko et al. (2010) and Woolfson (2010) note, there is a prevailing attitude towards intolerance of minorities in the Baltic states. Hans Glaubitz, the Dutch ambassador to Estonia, left the country after complaining that his black partner had suffered constant casual racist and homophobic abuse at the hands of skinheads and the Estonian public (BBC News, 2006). In another case an Estonian journalist, Rein Sikk (2007), posed as a black woman calling in at the virtual Estonian embassy that the Estonian Foreign Ministry had opened on the online Second Life platform. He recounted that he was both racially abused and ridiculed by the staff at the virtual embassy. An African member of *Los Amigos*, a popular Latvia-based reggae band founded the *Afrolat* organisation after experiencing discrimination in Latvia, including being attacked by skinheads in the heart of the Riga Old Town and unwittingly being used in an anti-immigration TV commercial by a political party (Zariņa, 2009).[19] Black US embassy employees have been targeted in all three Baltic States, as have diplomats from other non-European states. The Chinese ambassador to Lithuania's car was torched in Vilnius in December 2009. Students from visible minorities have also been targeted (Nimmo, 2007).

Anti-semitism is rare but still present in the region. There are occasional attacks on holocaust memorials and other Jewish monuments in all three states. In 2010 leading Latvian nationalist political activist, Jānis Iesalnieks, publically argued that 'intelligent anti-Semitism' should have a place in the public discourse – he was subsequently forced to take a (very) brief step back from public life. In 2004 the Lithuanian daily newspaper *Respublika* had a notorious front page depicting a globe and two individuals – one gay and the other a stereotypical crooked-nosed Jewish male – and posed the question: 'Who controls the world?' This was a part of a series of explicitly anti-semitic (and homophobic) editorials published by the paper. This is representative of what Leonidas Donskis has called a specific old-fashioned Lithuanian anti-semitism: 'Unequipped with more "sophisticated" forms of anti-Semitism, such as Holocaust denial or revisionist versions of Second World War history, Lithuanian anti-Semitism remains deeply grounded in a sort of ideological and political demonology that was characteristic of the second half of the nineteenth century and the beginning of the twentieth century' (Donskis, 2006, pp. 13–14). This is not a systemic pattern, and both racist and anti-semitic incidents are rare and unusual, although they may well become more frequent if large numbers of non-European immigrants begin to settle in the region.

Conclusions

Civil society in the Baltic states is no longer weak and ineffective, although it does remain flawed. Restrictive citizenship and language policies curbed the participation of Russophones and gradually polarised civil society. Competing ethnic historical narratives drive the biggest regular rallies in Latvia and, as the Bronze Soldier riots revealed, can also mobilise in Estonia. It is clear that integration policies in Estonia and Latvia have had little success in constructing unified political communities in these states. Russophones rarely identify with Latvia and Estonia, and a majority (including Russophone Estonian and Latvian citizens) refer to themselves as 'Russians' (Duvold and Berglund, 2013). Moreover, the status of the Baltic languages continues to be challenged. Despite two decades of marginalisation and restriction of the use of the Russian-language in the Baltic states, a rising number of businesses, particularly those in the services sector, look to recruit employees with Russian-language skills. This now puts young Russophones in an increasingly privileged position in the labour market. They have learnt fluent Latvian at school (in addition to the Russian also taught at school and typically used at home) while a growing number of young Estonians, Latvians and Lithuanians have chosen to learn English or German rather than Russian.

At the same time the capabilities and political role of NGOs have grown. Steadily rising funding, both in terms of donations and success in attracting project funding, has led to increased professionalism. NGOs are increasingly integrated into working groups at the ministerial level and in parliamentary committees. The falling corruption rate, and the continuing demise of Latvia's oligarchs, means that civil society has fewer challengers. A rapid increase in the number of voluntary activities, particularly in the environmental sphere, has seen the expansion of civil society events and rising levels of trust (albeit not, in Latvia and Lithuania, towards political institutions).

5
Economic, Social and Welfare Issues

In late 2008 the three Baltic states were thrust into the heart of an intensely polarising international public debate on strategies to tackle the growing global economic crisis. The previous four years, following accession to the European Union (EU) in 2004, had witnessed rapid economic growth across the region, indeed the three recorded the highest GDP growth in the EU. Banks eased lending restrictions, foreign direct investment (FDI) inflows surged and Baltic businesses and consumers binged on cheap, readily available credit. Hubristic politicians increasingly talked of the inevitability of economic convergence with Western Europe. However, a gradual slowdown from late 2007 declined into a deep recession in 2008 following the bankruptcy of Lehmann Brothers investment bank in the United States that September. The collapse and subsequent public bailout of *Parex Bank*, Latvia's second largest commercial bank, brought on a recession that humbled the 'Baltic Tigers'.[1]

The Baltic states' governments responded with policy approaches collectively dubbed austerity (severe cuts in government spending) and internal devaluation (strategies designed to improve competitiveness). These policies proved so controversial that at one point Estonia's president, Toomas Hendrik Ilves, who has never shied away from a fight, clashed with Nobel Prize–winning American economist Paul Krugman, an event so celebrated in Estonia that it was quickly turned into an opera (Kangsepp, 2013). As taxes were raised and public-sector salaries, benefits and other spending were cut, international journalists expressed amazement at the Baltic states' readiness to make enormous short-term sacrifices in return for potential long-term gain. However, this simply revealed an ignorance of recent Baltic history and contemporary politics. The Baltic states had experienced a far deeper and more traumatic economic collapse in the years immediately after independence was regained. In the drive to forge links with the West and build market economies, Baltic governments have long proved to be strong, while trade unions, interest groups and civil society have proved weak. Moreover, internal devaluation was a logical continuation of the neo-liberal economic policies that the Baltic states have consistently adopted, albeit with varying degrees of enthusiasm, since 1991 (Kattel and Raudla, 2013).[2] These factors combined to make austerity policies possible.

This chapter initially discusses the Baltic states' economic transition from communism to capitalism and considers their economic performance over the last quarter century. Initial high expectations of a successful rapid transformation to a West European style market economy (based on education and urbanisation indicators pointing to high levels of modernisation) were dashed as the Baltic states, especially Latvia and Lithuania, experienced huge GDP dips in 1992 and 1993, before returning to growth in the mid-1990s. Inflation surged. Banking failures and the Russian currency devaluation of 1998 caused further economic trauma. Then came a long boom as the years immediately before and after accession to the European Union saw unprecedented economic growth, with both foreign investment and cheap credit flowing into the Baltic States. Estonia (especially) and Lithuania adopted anti-cyclical fiscal policies, while the Latvian government failed to impose fiscal discipline and was hit particularly hard by the 2008 post-Lehman brothers economic dip. The Baltic states saw cumulative output declines of 14–24 per cent between 2008–2010. However, Lithuania was initially less affected than Estonia and Latvia, reflecting the larger size of its economy as well as the greater structural changes carried out after the Russian rouble crisis at the end of the twentieth century (Purfield and Rosenberg, 2010). Moreover, Lithuania had also experienced less of a pre-crisis credit boom than its two northern Baltic neighbours. Estonia drew on its rainy-day fund (at that point worth approximately 9 per cent of GDP) to cushion its recession. Latvia was most affected and needed to be bailed out by a group of international lenders led by the International Monetary Fund, the European Commission and a number of EU states (including, humiliatingly for Latvia's political leaders, Estonia), and experienced the largest dip in GDP of any state in the recent crisis. Nevertheless, all three emerged from the crisis with brisk rates of economic growth and attracting fresh waves of foreign investment.

The economic crisis exacerbated the already high levels of inequality that have dogged Baltic society and are the focus of the second part of this chapter. The early years of the transition had seen society polarise into groups of winners (entrepreneurs, the young, those with in-demand skills such as English-language knowledge or information-technology skills) and losers (pensioners and those on benefits, farmers, low-skilled manufacturing workers). Poverty rates rose as the quality of social services nosedived, particularly health care and education, following cuts in funding. Although the second decade of independence saw increased public-sector investment (not least because of access to European Union funding sources such as the European Social Fund), the Gini coefficient measure of inequality in all three states has remained high (indeed, by this measure Latvia and Lithuania have had the highest inequality in the European Union since 2008; see Figure 5.5). Reforms to pension systems, health care, unemployment and other benefits, education systems, as well as worker rights and other elements of the European welfare model have been adopted, albeit with diverse models and to differing extents in all three Baltic States. However, a broadly comparable Baltic social model has emerged.

5.1   Economic development

The move towards a market economy was targeted by all three Baltic states even before sovereign independence was regained in August 1991. Estonia, and to a lesser extent Latvia and Lithuania, had already experimented with market reforms in the latter years of the Soviet era, creating independent central banks and moving forward with modest privatisation initiatives. Market reforms were a key part of the strategy to gradually divorce the Baltic states from the Soviet Union and modernise the Baltic economies. It was expected that this would rapidly lead to higher standards of living in the region. At this point there were lively, albeit abstract, debates within the popular fronts on the type of market economy that should be adopted (with fuzzy notions of a redistributive Nordic social model central to the discussion). All mainstream political actors agreed that as well as fuelling economic development, the introduction of the market would consolidate both democracy and integration with Western Europe. In this sense the economic reforms can clearly be deemed a success, with accession to the EU accomplished in 2004 and democracy firmly consolidated as the only valid political system.

However, these early debates did not envisage how long and how traumatic the economic and social transformation would prove. There was a (in retrospect) naive belief, shared by both Balts and Western observers, that the pre-conditions for market reforms – an educated workforce, developed infrastructure and established law-and-order system – would lead to a swift economic transition. However, this did not prove to be the case. The workforce was not as relevantly educated or as productive as had been assumed. The transportation, communication and urban infrastructure was decayed and in need of huge investments. The Soviet model of politically and personally, rather than constitutionally oriented, justice has proved far more entrenched and difficult to reform than outsiders had expected. A quarter century after the break with the Soviet Union all three Baltic states are still much poorer than their Nordic neighbours and incomes remain well below the European Union average.

This is not to say that on these terms the economic transformation has been an absolute failure. The Baltic states *have* experienced periods of extremely rapid economic growth. Indeed, their annual GDP growth has typically been higher than that found in the established West European market economies, as standard economic theories of convergence would predict. They *have* closed the income gap on Western Europe. Any contemporary visitor to the dynamic Baltic capital cities can see the positive visual changes that have taken place since 1991. However, the economic transition was far less linear and much more painful than had been expected.

5.1.1 The Transformation

The initial preconditions for a successful transition to the market were mixed. On the one hand, the three states have almost no significant natural resources (barring Estonia's oil shale, which is still the state's major source of energy, and the forests that cover some 40 per cent of Estonia and Latvia and a quarter of Lithuania), and in 1991 they had very few foreign reserves. Trade was oriented towards the Soviet Union, with resultingly low quality standards and, in any case, a chaotic and rapidly shrinking market. On the other hand, the Baltic economies were quite diverse – agriculture and food processing, textiles, industrial manufacturing, forestry and pharmaceuticals were among the major economic sectors – and the region was considered to be the most developed part of the Soviet Union. At the same time, during the latter years of the Soviet Union it was clear that the Baltic states' economies were performing poorly. Estonia had had a similar level of economic development to neighbouring Finland in the 1930s, but the two had diverged significantly by the 1980s. While comparative measures are difficult to formulate due to complications with the accuracy of Soviet-era data, one comparison found that in 1988 Estonians had to work 547 hours to afford a colour television, while Finns worked just 92 (Erixon, 2010, p. 7). The poor performance of the economy was ultimately to the benefit of the market reformers, who could lobby for public support for radical reforms by pointing out the obvious economic failure of communism in the Baltic states.

Since 1991 all three Baltic states have experienced broadly similar patterns of GDP decline and growth, inflation, unemployment and other macroeconomic indicators (although, as a broad rule of thumb, Estonia has until very recently performed significantly better than Latvia and Lithuania). Economic development has not been linear. The Baltic states' economies have experienced periods of deep recession followed by brisk economic growth. The depth of both downturns and upturns has generally been far greater than that seen in West European economies. As Figure 5.1 indicates, the first years of the economic transition were marked by a deep depression that in terms of both length and depth far exceeded that of 2008–2010. Economic output in the Baltic states fell by 50 per cent as the old markets of the Soviet Union closed, demand fell and new tariffs and taxes appeared at borders that were now manned by guards and officials. At the same time, strong Western competition, with typically superior consumer products, entered the market – while Baltic goods also struggled to find new Western markets. During the Soviet era, exports outside the Soviet Union were worth just a few percentage points of total GDP for the three states, and the race to identify new markets for Baltic products proved rather more difficult than initially thought. One of the major industrial concerns in Soviet Latvia had been the Riga Autobus Factory (*Rigas Autobusu Fabrika*, RAF), based in Jelgava. It manufactured vans and minibuses under the 'Latvija' label. The collapse of the Soviet Union led to the destruction of RAF's existing supply chains and the erosion of its markets. At the same time, the vehicles produced were far too shoddy and outdated for European markets, and the RAF market niche was too small to attract an international investor. RAF shed staff, regularly changed owners and in 1998 was at last declared bankrupt. Other, smaller companies shared similar fates.

The economies of the Baltic states picked up in the mid-1990s as economic reforms began to kick in and privatisation began. Estonia saw particularly sharp economic growth as foreign investors rushed to take advantage of the many economic opportunities that privatisation offered. However, the collapse of the Russian rouble in 1998 had a knock-on effect on Baltic markets, which were still reliant on trade with Russia at that time.[3] In the long term, however, the 1998 crisis had a positive effect on the Baltic states as it motivated them to seek Western markets for their products. The 2000s saw a near decade of economic growth that led to the three being dubbed the 'Baltic Tigers'. However, all this came tumbling down between 2008 and 2010, when the three states once again experienced economic catastrophe – indeed, the sharpest economic downturn of any region in the world, with Latvia in particular experiencing the biggest fall in GDP of any industrialised state since the US Great Depression in the 1930s.

Despite these extreme ups and downs, the end goal of Baltic economic reforms has always been clear: to create open, Western-oriented market economies to facilitate economic growth, increase the standard of living and, in the long term, enable accession to the European Union. Estonia had perhaps the clearest vision of the model that its economy should adopt. Its political elite was largely unified in supporting the creation of a market environment favourable for Western investors to bring capital, innovation and ideas and offer multiple links with the West. In contrast, Latvia and (especially) Lithuania, were more divided on the extent to which they should open up to foreign investors and reject Eastern markets for the West. The major Latvian ice-free ports and rail-links with Russia mean that the transit between East and West has remained a major economic sector with influential links to political parties. Russia has also remained a major market for Lithuania's agricultural exports. Nevertheless, even in Lithuania, the only Baltic state with an electorally strong left-wing party, the debate was on how *quickly* the market reforms should be introduced, rather than on the *direction* of those reforms. In the same way, the Estonian Moderates/Social Democrats have been coalition partners in governments executing explicitly pro-market reforms, weakening centre-left public economic discourse. In Latvia anti-market voices are inextricably tied together with the Russophone parties that have been in political opposition since the 1993 'founding' election. As a result, all Baltic governments since 1991 have essentially been pro-market and pro-West.

Thus the initial economic strategy was quite straightforward. The Baltic markets were small and initially with few links to Western markets. A simple tactic to make the domestic environment more attractive to investors was to open up the economy. In combination with a cheap and relatively educated labour force as well as a reasonably developed infrastructure, politicians hoped that these first steps would attract outside investment.

The reforms were shaped by a combination of domestic elites and international advisors from the international financial

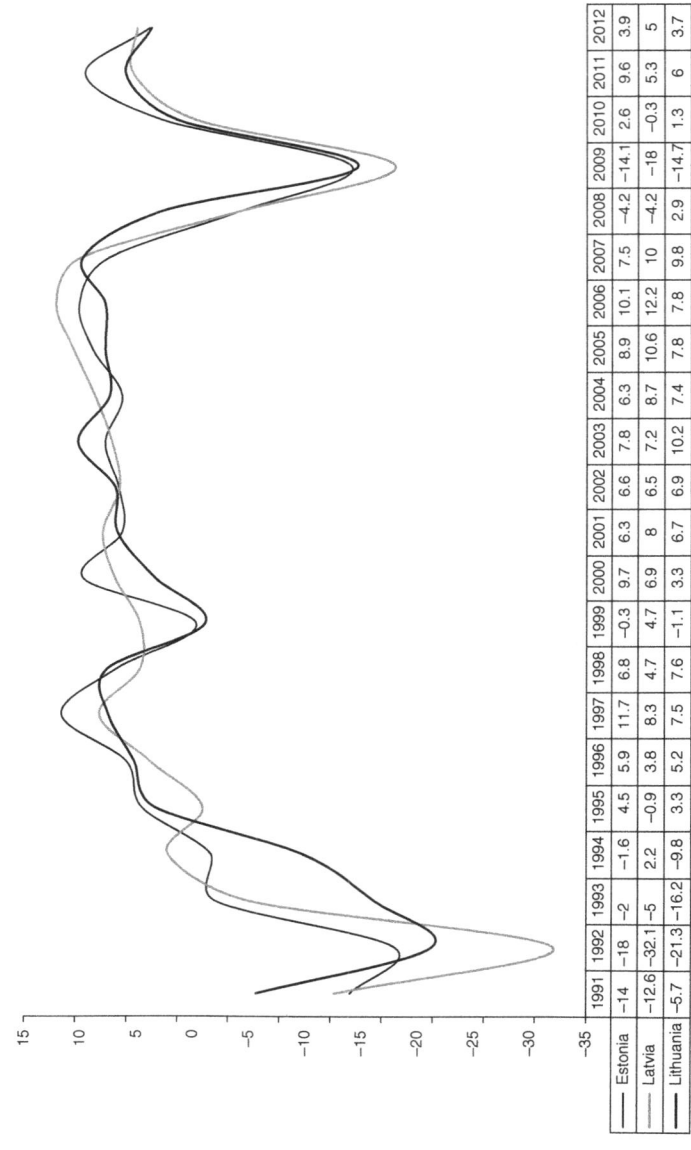

	1991	1992	1993	1994	1995	1996	1997	1998	1999	2000	2001	2002	2003	2004	2005	2006	2007	2008	2009	2010	2011	2012
Estonia	−14	−18	−2	−1.6	4.5	5.9	11.7	6.8	−0.3	9.7	6.3	6.6	7.8	6.3	8.9	10.1	7.5	−4.2	−14.1	2.6	9.6	3.9
Latvia	−12.6	−32.1	−5	2.2	−0.9	3.8	8.3	4.7	4.7	6.9	8	6.5	7.2	8.7	10.6	12.2	10	−4.2	−18	−0.3	5.3	5
Lithuania	−5.7	−21.3	−16.2	−9.8	3.3	5.2	7.5	7.6	−1.1	3.3	6.7	6.9	10.2	7.4	7.8	7.8	9.8	2.9	−14.7	1.3	6	3.7

Figure 5.1   GDP growth in the Baltic states, 1991–2012

Source: World Bank, World Development Indicators (2014), and Norgaard et al. for Estonia 1991–1994.

institutions – particularly the International Monetary Fund and the World Bank – as well as 'technical assistance' from the European Union and neighbouring Nordic states. The larger and wealthier European states as well as the United States also provided ad hoc aid and advice. This 'Washington Consensus' urged an initial focus on macroeconomic stability, aiming for currency reform, trade and price liberalisation, privatisation and budget discipline. The reforms were initiated with great gusto, largely following the 'shock therapy' approach in terms of economic liberalisation, rapidly destroying old Soviet-era economic structures and quickly setting about building new ones (Åslund 1994, Barr 2005). However, the three states quickly started to differ in their enthusiasm for reform, as Estonia moved forward especially quickly while Lithuania adopted a more gradualist approach (Feldman 2001). As so often, Latvia found itself somewhere between the two.

Estonia had actually initiated economic reforms before breaking away from the Soviet Union, liberalising some prices in late 1989 and cutting the share of goods with a fixed price from 90 per cent to 60 per cent. This was continued by the popular front's Savisaar government that took office in 1990. By August 1991, only 10 per cent of prices remained to be liberalised, and that was quickly accomplished. This inevitably led to inflation, not least because prices were liberalised on goods that, in many cases, were in short supply. A further shock came in 1992, when energy prices were liberalised in Russia, leading to much higher payments for energy in all three Baltic states. Indeed, price liberalisation led to huge falls in Russian-Baltic trade, which in 1992 had still made up 90 per cent of the Baltic states' external trade.

Inflation was disastrously high in the early 1990s, reaching a peak in 1992 and 1993 before swiftly declining to double and then single digits by the mid- to late-1990s (see Figure 5.2). However, inflation began to crawl upwards as accession to the European Union approached in 2004, reaching double digits again as the economies began to overheat in 2006–2007. Since then Baltic inflation has been among the lowest in the European Union, allowing all three to fulfil the Maastricht Criteria and join the Eurozone between 2011 and 2015.

The Baltic states were quick to adopt the core institutions of the market, beginning with new independent central banks and a move away from the Soviet rouble and towards new currencies. The Bank of Estonia was created in January 1990, following the 1989 Law on Soviet Economic Independence that had granted increased economic autonomy to the Baltic states. The other two central banks were created later that year. They had few functions at that time, but played absolutely crucial roles

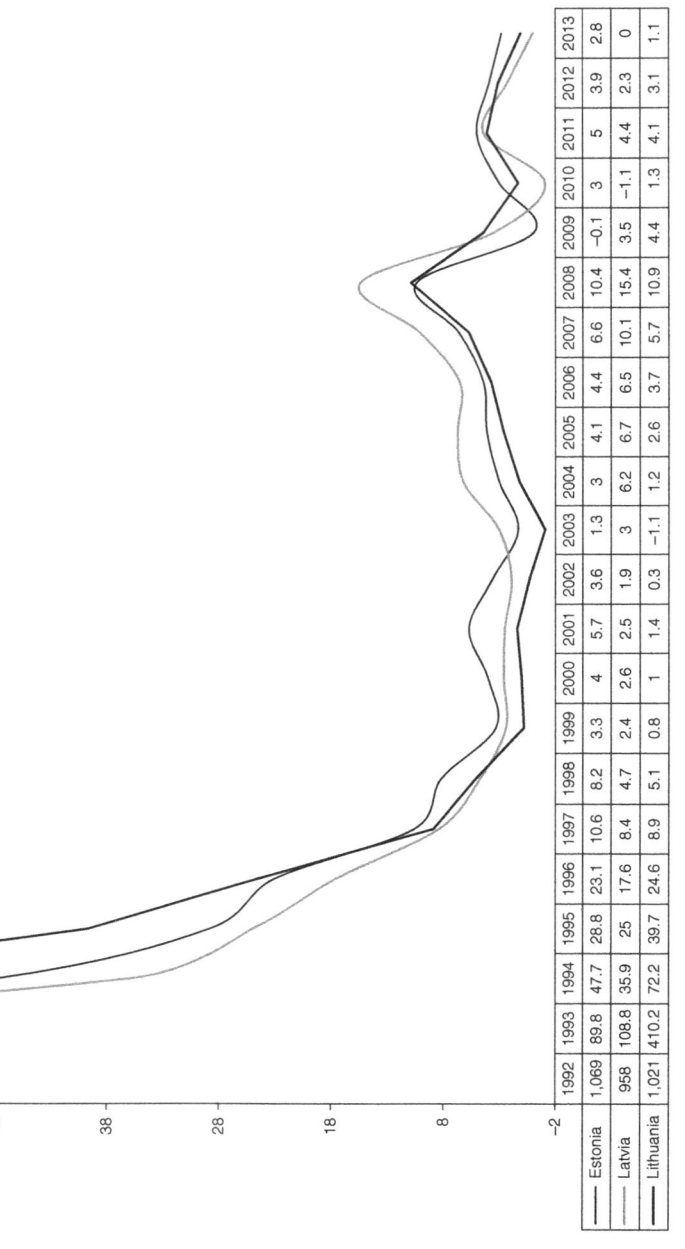

	1992	1993	1994	1995	1996	1997	1998	1999	2000	2001	2002	2003	2004	2005	2006	2007	2008	2009	2010	2011	2012	2013
Estonia	1,069	89.8	47.7	28.8	23.1	10.6	8.2	3.3	4	5.7	3.6	1.3	3	4.1	4.4	6.6	10.4	-0.1	3	5	3.9	2.8
Latvia	958	108.8	35.9	25	17.6	8.4	4.7	2.4	2.6	2.5	1.9	3	6.2	6.7	6.5	10.1	15.4	3.5	-1.1	4.4	2.3	0
Lithuania	1,021	410.2	72.2	39.7	24.6	8.9	5.1	0.8	1	1.4	0.3	-1.1	1.2	2.6	3.7	5.7	10.9	4.4	1.3	4.1	3.1	1.1

Figure 5.2 Inflation (consumer prices, annual percentage). Baltic states, 1992–2013

Source: World Bank, World Development Indicators (2014), and Norgaard et al for 1992–1993.

in debating and planning the road to currency independence. The foreign exchange reserves of all three states were strengthened when the Bank of England and the French central bank returned gold reserves held since the Second World War (Estonia saw the return of 11 tonnes of gold in 1992).

The central banks quickly moved to create new currencies. Inflation had begun to rise, and Russia, which anchored the rouble zone, was experiencing a rocky economic and political transformation. Baltic businesses and individuals were switching to US dollar transactions and starting to place funds abroad (OECD, 2000). As a result, all three banks were under public and political pressure to introduce new, domestically controlled currencies. This took place over a number of stages in Latvia and Lithuania but, as in so many other economic issues, Estonia moved first and most decisively. It broke from the rouble zone to establish its own currency, the Estonian kroon (EEK) in June 1992, just ten months after the collapse of the Soviet Union. Roubles were exchanged for kroons at the rate of ten roubles for one kroon, with banks closed for five days to allow for the redenomination of rouble accounts. Latvia introduced an interim currency (the Latvian rouble, known affectionately as the repsitis after the central bank Governor Einars Repše) in May 1992, exchanging Soviet roubles for Latvian roubles at a one-to-one rate. The new Latvian currency, the lat, was introduced a year later in March 1993 at an exchange rate of 1:200 for the Latvian rouble. Lithuania's approach was similar to Latvia's two-step currency exchange. First, an interim currency – the Lithuanian talonas – was introduced in May 1992 at a 1:1 rate with the rouble. Then the litas was introduced in June 1993.

All three Baltic states eventually elected to peg their currencies. Estonia adopted a currency board model designed to bring a sharp halt to inflation, build investor confidence and attract badly needed FDI.[4] International advisors from the World Bank and Sweden, and most particularly the influential economist Jeffrey Sachs, had recommended this model (Erixon, 2010, pp. 21–22). The kroon was anchored with the German DM at a rate of 8:1. Latvia initially chose a floating regime but the lat appreciated strongly and was subsequently informally pegged to the IMF's Special Drawing Rights (SDR) from February 1994 onwards. Lithuania followed Estonia in adopting a currency board model that pegged the litas to the US dollar at a 4:1 rate from April 1994 onwards. All three currencies were later pegged to the euro until the euro's adoption as the national currency between 2011 and 2015.[5]

Commercial banks quickly sprang up after 1991. A number were reconstituted and privatised Soviet-era specialised banks that had served specific parts of the economy. However, a greater number were newly created and licensed banks that banking regulators hoped would bring greater competition to the banking sector. Initially the banks were loosely regulated, not least because the Baltic states simply lacked the skilled and educated human capital to staff the regulatory institutions that were then located in the central banks, and the financial costs of entry to the system were low (at that time Estonia demanded just five million roubles, about $40,000, as the minimum start-up capital for a commercial bank). By 1992 there were 43 licensed commercial banks in Estonia, and in 1993 there were 60 in Latvia and 27 in Lithuania.

Some of them [Latvian banks] were 'pocket' banks owned by state enterprises, some were purely private but were dedicated mainly to raising deposits to on-lend to the owners, and some were set up with specific functions in mind (Olympia bank was set up to help finance the Latvian Olympic team). All of these private or quasi-private banks were allowed to develop with little supervision from the Bank of Latvia initially. (Fleming, Chu and Bakker, 1996, p. 5)

Under these conditions of loose, inexperienced regulation, banking collapses were almost inevitable. Estonia's banking crisis came first, in 1992, as the Moscow-based central branches of the previously Soviet state-owned banks froze the assets of all non-Russian banks, including the Estonian Savings bank, which held 85 per cent of all Estonian household assets. At the same time, the currency switch to the kroon led to a tighter monetary policy that eventually revealed liquidity problems at a number of Estonia's largest commercial banks. While the Bank of Estonia chose to save the banks whose assets had been seized in Moscow, the others were liquidated. Licenses were reviewed and by 1993 the number of banks in Estonia was cut to 23. Banking crises in Latvia and Lithuania followed in 1995, largely as a result of regulators beginning to demand greater auditing standards from the banks, which led to fundamental flaws being revealed in the banking system. In the case of Latvia, 40 per cent of the banking system's assets were revealed to be at risk, leading to a run on the banks. A number of banks were eventually declared insolvent, and individuals who had seen their savings whittled down by high inflation now saw their savings largely disappear. Creditors were limited to a ceiling of $1,000 in compensation. The biggest scandal surrounded *Banka Baltija* in Latvia, the biggest commercial bank in the Baltic states, which had depositor assets of $500 million in 1995 but saw $260 million disappear, never to be recovered. This led to lengthy, drawn-out criminal trials resulting in (short) prison sentences for the bank's owners.

The weak regulatory system was eventually addressed through the creation of specialised financial regulators in Estonia and Latvia – Latvia's Financial and Capital Market Commission was created in 2001, and Estonia's Financial Supervision Authority in 2002 – although Lithuania elected to tighten up the central bank's regulatory authority, perhaps because it had experienced only lesser banking crises in the 1990s. However, this was not the end of banking crises in the region. Latvia's *Rigas Komercbanka* failed in 1998, *Parex bank* went bust in 2008, although it was subsequently bailed out by the state, while Lithuania's *Snoras bank* (and its Latvian subsidiary, *Latvijas Krājbanka*) were declared insolvent in 2011. Two years later *Ukio bank*, Lithuania's sixth-largest bank by assets, was also declared insolvent.

The Baltic banking systems were greatly stabilised by the entry of Nordic banks into the three states beginning from the late 1990s. The small size of the Baltic states relative to their Nordic home markets coupled with Nordic banks' readiness to win market share in the Baltic states by offering low interest rates led to an ever-increasing flow of capital into the Baltic states, and commercial banking in the region took off. The small size and flexibility of the Baltic markets allowed the Nordic banks to experiment with Internet and mobile-banking applications. They also offered a seeming solidity to a Baltic public scarred by banking collapses. By 2009 they dominated commercial banking, controlling approximately 90 per cent of assets in Estonia, 80 per cent in Lithuania and 60 per cent in Latvia (Hansson and Randveer, 2013, p. 6).

The Baltic states also moved quickly to establish financial markets. The Vilnius Stock Exchange (VILSE) and the Riga Stock Exchange (RIGSE) were established in 1993, with the Tallinn Stock Exchange (TALSE) following in 1996. The small Baltic capital markets, as well as the international trend for consolidation and unification of stock exchanges, has seen the three exchanges move ever closer. In 2001 the Helsinki Stock Exchange (HEX) purchased TALSE and then RIGSE the following year. In 2003 HEX merged with OM, the Swedish stock market operator, to create OMX which bought a majority stake in VILSE in 2004. All three Baltic stock exchanges are now owned and operated by Nasdaq-OMX and share a common trading platform. Both trading volume and market capitalisation (which in mid-June 2014 was approximately six billion euros) remain small, and the stock market is a minor financial player in the Baltic region.[6]

Reforms of financial markets opened up increased investment and trade opportunities, particularly with the West. As small states with few natural resources there was little opportunity to create wealth without interaction with international markets. Indeed, as Aldis Purs (2012) pointed out, economic development in the tsarist and inter-war independence eras had been stalled by a lack of access to capital for investment. Although the Soviet era saw heavy investment in ports, energy and other capital-intensive infrastructure projects, the communist system was not well placed to take advantage of these assets. It was hoped that opening up trade opportunities would allow FDI to flow in and domestically produced goods and services to flow out to Western markets. This actually called for a radical restructuring of the status quo because, broadly speaking, the Soviet Union had not prioritised the export side of trade, valuing imports of products not domestically available far higher than wealth-creating exports.

The three states quickly moved ahead with different trade models. Estonia adopted an extremely open Hong-Kong–like model with almost no tariffs on imports. Indeed, when Estonia began negotiating accession to the World Trade Organisation and the European Union in the late 1990s, almost uniquely it had to reintroduce tariffs on a number of products. Estonia began to eradicate import quotas, licenses and tariffs, although in 1991 the Soviet system had few tariffs to remove, and most tariffs were eradicated by 1997 (just taxes on the import of tobacco, alcohol and fuel remained). Latvia and especially Lithuania took longer to act and maintained a far larger range of tariffs. In 1999 Latvia still had a range of fourteen tiers of tariffs (Feldman 2001).

Agriculture is a case in point. All three Baltic states have relatively large agricultural sectors, with agriculture taking up over 25 per cent of Lithuania's GDP in 1990. Moreover, agriculture, as a representation of rural sentiment (it is often said that *real* Balts are to be found only outside the cosmopolitan cities), is often given high political priority in the region. This explains why Estonia was the only Baltic state to rapidly move to a free-trade regime in agricultural products, adopting only occasional anti-dumping measures, while Latvia and especially Lithuania remained far more protectionist. The latter two states were the most reluctant to negotiate the 1997 second Baltic Free Trade Agreement that opened up tariff-free movement of agricultural products between the Baltic states (the first part of the agreement, for free trade in industrial goods, had been signed in 1994). In 1999 the Baltic states briefly experienced a 'pork war' when the Latvian parliament passed legislation introducing a 70 per cent tariff on pork imports (regardless of origin) after the Latvian market had been swamped by what parliamentarians declared as cheap Estonian pork. Estonia introduced a broad range of agricultural tariffs only as a part of the EU accession process, bringing its trade policy in line with the EU's Common External Tariff.

Opening up to trade was only the first part of the puzzle. The second, trickier, phase was the reorientation of trade away from the former Soviet and communist states of the COMECON trading bloc and towards the West. Once again Estonia did this much faster than the other two. By 1993 only 20 per cent of Estonia's trade was with Russia, while the corresponding data was 30 per cent for Latvia and 60 per cent for Lithuania (Feldman 2001). Finland became Estonia's key trading partner, although trade with the other Nordic states, as well as intra-Baltic trade, increased. Latvia traded mostly with the Nordic states and Germany, while Lithuania's biggest trading partner became Germany. Over the last 20 years the main trading partners for the Baltic states have been their neighbours around the Baltic Sea. However, Russia's economic rise in the twenty-first century saw it resume an increasingly significant role in Baltic trade. As the European Union began debating sanctions on Russia in early 2014 the initially hubristic comments of Latvian politicians began to pale as Prime Minister Laimdota Straujuma argued that heavy economic sanctions on Russia could lead to a fall in Latvia's GDP of up to 10 per cent (*Latvijas Avīze*, 2014). At the same time Lithuania was in the middle of an economically harmful 'Milk War' with Russia after the latter had partially banned Lithuanian dairy imports after questioning the quality and sanitation of these goods on the eve of a major EU summit in Lithuania that was to offer an EU association agreement to Ukraine (Gutterman, 2013). Approximately 85 per cent of Lithuania's dairy exports go to Russia. While the initial momentum to increasingly trade with the West rather than Russia had been successful, the Baltic states had not escaped Russian influence altogether.

Privatisation was another cornerstone policy of the reform agenda. However, it could only begin once a set of appropriate laws – on property rights, bankruptcy, commercial laws and so on – as well as effective law-and-order institutions had been put in place to regulate the private sector. Political elites also needed to settle on the method of privatisation. As a result, the bulk of privatisation took place several years after independence. The necessity for reform was clear. Soviet-era enterprises were extremely large – in 1990 the average enterprise in Estonia had 790 employees, Latvia 760 and Lithuania 840, compared to a Western

European average of 160 (OECD, 2000, p. 27) and tied into disintegrating post-Soviet supply and distribution networks. Enterprises needed investment and expertise in order to take advantage of the new trade opportunities that were opening up.

The Baltic states had the advantage of beginning their comprehensive economic transformations a few years after the new Central European democracies, allowing them to learn from the mistakes and successes of the first wave of post-communist privatisation. Czechoslovakia (later the Czech Republic and Slovakia) and East Germany in particular had initiated an early and swift privatisation (while Hungary and Poland adopted a more gradual approach) that the Baltic states largely elected to follow. Estonian and Lithuanian enterprises were privatised en masse, leading to claims that both the old and new elites were benefiting from insider knowledge of privatisation for economic gain. Latvia's enterprise privatisation took place far more gradually.

Restitution proved to be the least contentious method of privatisation, although this was primarily used for land and housing. After all, prior to 1940 most property had been in private hands and in an act laden with symbolism, those who had had their property 'stolen' by the Soviet Union had it handed back to them. Although a labour-intensive approach it was not considered to be overly contentious, and the majority of property had been returned to pre-1940 owners by the mid-1990s in all three states.

All three states established specialised agencies to oversee the privatisation process, with a particular focus on attracting international strategic investors who had both the money and the expertise required to reform the Soviet-era enterprises. The Estonian Privatisation Office (later Agency) was established in 1992 and primarily used direct sales and buyouts to privatise Estonia's enterprises. International tenders were particularly favoured, largely because it was clear that Estonia lacked both the capital and the expertise to restructure and invigorate the private sector. The first such international tender was organised in December 1992 – having been delayed from earlier in the year after the German appointed to head the process had been found to be favouring German investors above others – and 38 large enterprises were subsequently privatised. Small and medium-sized enterprises were sold through domestic auction procedures.

The Latvian Privatisation Agency was created two years later, in 1994. Privatisation took longer in Latvia because of the greater density and size of manufacturing enterprises, making them trickier to privatise, although it had been mostly completed by the end of the twentieth century (Zile and Steinbuka, 2011). The privatisation of small enterprises in Latvia was largely completed by 1995, although the privatisation of larger enterprises only began in 1994. Part of the gas monopoly, *Latvijas Gāze*, was sold in 2002, and in the following year stakes in the large Latvian shipping company *Latvijas Kugniecība* and the Latvian savings bank *Latvijas Krājbanka*, were also sold. The sale of the state's remaining 39 per cent stake in the oil-transit firm *Ventspils Nafta* was completed in late 2006. However, the electricity company Latvenergo is still to be privatised, as is the national airline airBaltic and the government's remaining 51 per cent stake in the profitable former telecommunications monopoly, *Lattelecom*.

In 1995 Lithuania was the last Baltic state to set up a privatisation agency (later restructured and in 1997 renamed the State Property Fund). Indeed, Lithuania's privatisation was markedly different to that in Estonia and Latvia in that it was far more egalitarian and also favoured domestic actors over international investors (Norgaard, Hindsgaul, Johannsen and Willumsen, 1995, p. 132). Between 1991 and 1995 Lithuania had privatised property and small and medium-sized enterprises using vouchers that were distributed to citizens according to their age, while land was returned to pre-1940 owners. A second phase began after the adoption of a new privatisation law in 1995. This saw the privatisation of enterprises for cash, but in the first two years less than half of the enterprises up for privatisation had been sold. Lithuania's reluctance to sell to international investors clearly affected the willingness of foreign actors to invest in the state. This attitude only began to change towards the end of the decade.

Thus the Baltic states essentially used three basic approaches in privatising medium-sized and large enterprises. Estonia's model was largely based on sales to outsiders (the secondary approach in Latvia and very much rarer in Lithuania), while Latvia and Lithuania initially used vouchers followed by management–employee buyouts (European Bank for Reconstruction and Development, 1997), although Latvia eventually also adopted a sales to outsiders approach. The privatisation programmes brought in significant revenues to the Baltic states' governments. Moreover, these revenues came at a time when the Baltic governments had few other forms of income, as the economies were contracting and then only just beginning to recover. At the same time privatisation aroused a certain amount of controversy. In Latvia and Lithuania in particular the process was seen as opaque and open to corruption. Three-time Latvian prime minister Andris Šķēle was often alleged to have used his insider knowledge as a leading civil servant at the Ministry of Agriculture in the early 1990s to spontaneously privatise huge swathes of the food processing industry (at that time, before the creation of the Privatisation Agency, line ministries organised privatisation leading to a great many opportunities for insider privatisation). In Lithuania, former prime minister Bronislovas Lubys was also accused of insider privatisation when taking control of the Azotas chemical plant in 1992–1993 and then KLASCO, the largest stevedore enterprise in Klaipeda port, in 1999 (Huang, 2002). Lubys persuaded the privatisation agency to both lower the price and allow the deal to be structured as a leveraged buyout, allowing him to pay for the company through future profits.

Differences in the pace, depth and direction of Baltic privatisation has had long-term consequences on society and the political system as well as on economic development. Aleksander Lust (2009) argued that Estonia's openness to outside investment and Lithuania's more insular and protectionist approach led to different levels of public support in the referendums on EU accession in 2003. He claimed that the 91 per cent 'yes' vote with which Lithuanians embraced the EU, and the more modest 67 per cent that supported accession in Estonia, were shaped by the extent to which their respective economies had interacted with outsiders:

> Lithuanians saw EU membership as a *solution* to Lithuania's – and their own – economic problems. They hoped that EU membership would help their country to *develop* by encouraging foreign investment and trade and making Lithuania eligible for EU subsidies. ... By contrast, many Estonians thought that Western integration (e.g., the sale of state-owned enterprises to foreigners and free trade with the West) was the *cause* of their (country's) difficulties. They worried that joining the EU would make Estonia *dependent* on the West by driving domestic producers out of business and allowing foreigners to buy up Estonian economic resources. (Lust, 2009, p. 342)

Although the Estonian economy had performed better than the Lithuanian, the primary domestic perception was that it still lagged behind that of its Nordic neighbours. While Lust's analysis is contentious, it does serve as a reminder that strategic economic decisions have effects far beyond the economy.

Nevertheless, privatisation was just one part of the creation of a private sector in the Baltic economies. Equally important was the formation of new private enterprises needed to provide the goods, and especially services, that were unavailable in the communist economic model. These small and medium-sized enterprises were crucial in changing the visible face of the Baltic states. New bars and restaurants contributed to the creation of new forms of social life and organisation and developed the infrastructure needed to invigorate the tourist industry. Entrepreneurship was supported through new laws that legalised these previously banned activities. New hugely popular business and economics education programmes were created in Baltic universities in order to prepare the next generation of entrepreneurs and managers (although the same Soviet-era economists taught the now-renamed courses). Entrepreneurs opened new business colleges, sometimes of dubious quality, to cater for this large, new market. At the same time, the Baltic states opened up to trade and investment, hoping to attract international investors to enter their economies.

A legal framework for FDI was established by the end of 1991, guaranteeing full repatriation of profits, although Latvia was initially more restrictive as regards the right for foreign entities to buy land as well as licensing procedures (Feldman 2001). Foreign investors were relatively quick to move to the Baltic markets, and there was some competition between the states in attracting foreign capital, which was much needed due to the lack of domestic funds as well as only developing capital markets and a financial system. The appearance of multinationals (such as McDonalds), while criticised by some for 'globalising' the Baltic states, also helped to internationalise and *normalise* them. Moreover, multinationals introduced international standards of management, staff training, health and safety and other norms that helped to raise standards across the board.

Estonia rapidly positioned itself as the most reform-minded and investor-friendly Baltic state and initially attracted the bulk of FDI flowing into the three countries. However, Latvia and Lithuania had caught up with Estonia by the end of the 1990s. The type of FDI coming into the Baltic states differed as to the capital and skill-intensive FDI that flooded into the Visegrad states. Rather, together with Bulgaria and Romania, the Baltic states 'became favored low-wage relocation sites ("sweatshops" may not be too strong a word) for West European light industries making clothes, shoes, and furniture, or assembling small electrical goods' (Bohle and Greskovits, 2009, p. 51), attracting foreign investors through low tax regimes and flexible labour-market policies. Although foreign investors had mixed experiences – Kellogg's acquired Ādaži Food Products, Inc., invested $22 million and opened a new food-processing facility making corn flakes and other breakfast foods for the

Baltic market in 1993 but then closed the plant in 1997, largely due to low demand for breakfast cereals in the region – the openness of the Baltic states, particularly Estonia and Latvia, led to a rapid internationalisation of the business environment.

While initial FDI inflows were for the purchase of privatised companies, they continued even after the privatisation programmes were completed, only slowing down during the global credit crunch. The biggest investors in the Baltic states have been from the Nordic region (especially Finland in the case of Estonia) as well as the United Kingdom, Germany and the United States. In recent years Russian investors became more active in taking over Baltic enterprises, with the financial sector proving particularly attractive in Estonia and Latvia. As was the case with increased trade flows, Russian investment aroused mixed emotions with the Baltic publics. On the one hand Russian money meant investment and jobs. On the other hand, the political and economic transformation had been intended to divorce the Baltic states from Russian influence.

FDI played an extremely important role in stabilising the region's public finances. Although the Baltic states inherited none of the Soviet Union's debt and ceased contributions to the centralised Soviet budget (to which Latvia in particular was a major contributor), the large output falls in the early 1990s contracted budgetary income at a time when

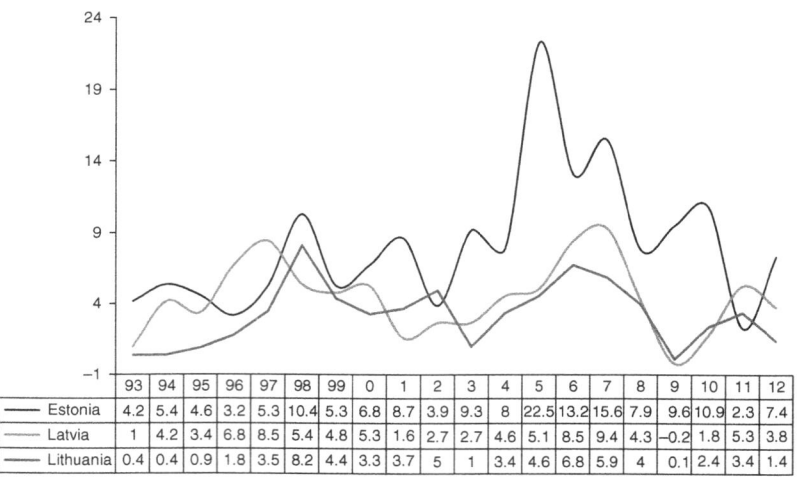

	93	94	95	96	97	98	99	0	1	2	3	4	5	6	7	8	9	10	11	12
Estonia	4.2	5.4	4.6	3.2	5.3	10.4	5.3	6.8	8.7	3.9	9.3	8	22.5	13.2	15.6	7.9	9.6	10.9	2.3	7.4
Latvia	1	4.2	3.4	6.8	8.5	5.4	4.8	5.3	1.6	2.7	2.7	4.6	5.1	8.5	9.4	4.3	-0.2	1.8	5.3	3.8
Lithuania	0.4	0.4	0.9	1.8	3.5	8.2	4.4	3.3	3.7	5	1	3.4	4.6	6.8	5.9	4	0.1	2.4	3.4	1.4

Figure 5.3   FDI, net inflows (GDP percentage). Baltic states, 1993–2012

Source: World Bank, World Development Indicators (2014).

there was increasing public demand for higher pensions and more benefits to compensate individuals for the fall in living standards. This led to the election of a left-wing government in Lithuania in 1992 (which continued the path of economic reform, albeit at a slower pace) and a populist electoral victory in Latvia in 1995.

Estonia's public finances have been far more prudently managed than those of the other Baltic states', even before the economic downturns of 2008–2010. Estonia's revenues have generally been higher, and the government budget deficit much smaller (OECD, 2012, p. 83). The nature of Estonia's currency board placed constraints on the extent to which the Estonian government could run budget deficits, and Estonia has had consistently lower public debt than its regional neighbours. Moreover, Estonia's 'stabilisation reserve fund' is the only one of its kind in the Baltic states, with excess budget resources, as well as revenues from privatisation, being invested abroad.

All three governments also introduced new taxation systems. VAT (initially defined as a turnover tax in Latvia), excise, property and corporate taxes were introduced early, as well as social insurance contributions. The general tendency has been for tax rates to decrease. For example, after initially adopting a progressive tax with a top rate of 33 per cent, Estonia attracted a great deal of international attention when it became the first European state to adopt a flat tax, for both individuals and corporations, of 26 per cent, which was then later lowered to 24 per cent. Estonia later adopted a corporation tax model that only places a duty on money taken out of companies – reinvested profits are not taxed, thus encouraging companies to innovate. Successive Latvian governments have also supported a flat income tax rate that hovers around the 25 per cent mark, while also gradually shifting to a system of indirect taxation, with almost 40 per cent of government tax revenue originating from VAT imposed on a wide number of goods and services. Similarly to Estonia, Latvia also moved to lower corporate tax to 15 per cent. The trend for lowering taxes has also been pronounced in Lithuania, where a flat income tax of 33 per cent that was introduced in 1994 had been lowered to a 2014 rate of 15 per cent (with corporate tax at the same rate).

The early 1990s were a period of economic flux and change. The change from Soviet-era norms and laws to those of the market economy created many gaps and opportunities for those prepared to bend the law. Law-and-order institutions and traditions were frail, impoverished and lacking direction. The opportunity to tackle the shadow economy (and crime more broadly) was weakened by the understandable closure of the KGB and other Soviet agencies equipped to fight crime. Perhaps the most long-lasting impact in the three states has been on the shadow economy, which still takes up a significant part of the Baltic economies. The Stockholm School of Economics in Riga has been publishing a Baltic Shadow Economy Index since 2009. The index 'combines estimates of misreported business income, unregistered or hidden employees, as well as unreported "envelope" wages to estimate the shadow economies as a proportion of GDP' (Putniņš and Sauka, 2014, p. 4). The long-term trend has been for the shadow economy in all three states to fall, although the size of the shadow economy in Latvia (23.8 per cent in 2013) remains far higher than in Estonia (15.7 per cent) and Lithuania (15.3 per cent).[7]

By the end of the twentieth century the Baltic states had privatised the overwhelming majority of formerly government-owned enterprises and real estate and also opened up for international trade, attracting significant and increasing flows of FDI. The key laws and institutions of the market had been either reformed or created anew, and the Baltic states were increasingly integrated with Western markets as the double accession to the European Union and NATO edged ever closer. Moreover, the macroeconomic position was broadly favourable as inflation reached low levels and the governments had little debt. All the preconditions were in place for a heady spurt of growth in the first decade of the twenty-first century.

5.1.2   Boom and bust

Indeed, the twentieth century saw the Baltic states experience the longest period of economic expansion in their history. Between 2000 and 2007 Latvia experienced average annual GDP growth of 8.8 per cent and a fall in unemployment from 14 per cent to 6 per cent (Blanchard, Griffiths and Gruss, 2013). Unemployment in Estonia and Lithuania fell to 4 per cent in the same period (Maslauskaite and Zorgenfreija, 2013). This economic boom was primarily driven by increased domestic demand, with the housing market particularly benefiting from increased liquidity, as Nordic parent banks eased borrowing requirements for their Baltic subsidiaries. Liberalisation of the financial sector had led to foreign banks buying up their smaller Baltic counterparts. By 2007 more than 60 per cent of banks in Latvia and 90 per cent in Estonia and Lithuania were foreign-owned, mostly Nordic. These large international banks – *Swedbank, SEB, Nordea* and so on – fought for market share in the region, transferring assets to the Baltic banks to be loaned out to enterprises and the public at the very low rates of interest being enjoyed all across Europe at that time. As the economy rapidly grew, and standards of living shot up, there was growing optimism, partly fuelled by politicians, that convergence with Western Europe was within reach, encouraging even more borrowing. Interest rates remained extremely low throughout this period, encouraging further borrowing. The real estate market was particularly overheated and construction accounted for as much as 40 per cent of the increase in employment in Latvia (Blanchard, Griffiths and Gruss, 2013). Between 2005 and 2007 real-estate prices in Riga rose by a vast 385 per cent (Blanchard, Mitali, Hamid, 2010). Between 2000 and 2008 household debt tripled in all three Baltic states, with much of the spending being on real estate. Moreover, much of the FDI that had flooded into the Baltic states had been in the non-tradable retail, construction and financial sectors, helping to feed the domestic consumption boom and further skewing the current-account deficit. As one economist wrote, 'The Baltic countries simply lost control over their macro economy', as political leaders became hubristic and complacent at the rapid economic growth and seeming economic convergence with Western Europe (Erixon, 2010, p. 3).

Signs of economic overheating appeared in 2006, as the price of domestic goods and wages in particular began to rise fast (as a result of expansionary government economic policies, wage increases and post-2004 migration to the United Kingdom and Ireland, exerting upward pressure on salaries) but were unaccompanied by gains in productivity, and the Baltic states began to lose international competitiveness (Blanchard, Griffiths and Gruss, 2013). All three states also experienced rising current-account deficits that by 2007 ranged over 20 per cent in Latvia and 15 per cent in Estonia and Lithuania (Kattel and Raudla, 2013). The Latvian government in particular was slow to react to the changing face of the economy. A 2007 anti-inflation plan detailed a number of measures aimed at slowing and harmonising the economy, including balancing future budgets and introducing a new property tax. However, these efforts were largely half-hearted, as indicated by the party campaigns in the October 2006 parliamentary election. One party in particular – Latvia's First Party – ran a bullish election campaign with the slogan 'put the [economic] pedal to the metal', claiming that convergence with Western European incomes was just a matter of time. These domestic voices proved far louder than international organisations such as the IMF, or foreign economists, who had started talking about overheating of the economy already in 2006, although international credit-rating agencies were far slower to react (Blanchard, Griffiths and Gruss, 2013).

The Baltic economic crash has been much discussed and reviewed. While there is broad agreement on the causes of the crisis – overzealous lending and borrowing, too-loose government fiscal policy leading to a real estate bubble and overheated economy – the Baltic governments' austerity policy response, and the extent that it could be deemed a success, arouses much more controversy. The remarkably deep recessions of 2008–2010 were marked by two phases. First, a contraction of the Estonian and Latvian economies in 2008 as the global financial crisis enveloped the region. Lithuania's economic contraction started later and was less pronounced. The low point of the recession came in the first quarter of 2009, when Latvia saw an annualised economic contraction of 18 per cent, Estonia 15.6 per cent and Lithuania 11.8 per cent (Erixon, 2010). Indeed, Latvia saw a nearly one-quarter fall in output over a period of less than two years. The Latvian crash was the largest, both because it experienced the largest credit boom and because of the need to bail out the domestically owned, and systemically important, *Parex Bank*. This was not a concern for Estonia and Lithuania where the Nordic states dominated the banking sector and would have to bail out the 'daughter' banks if the need arose. The Baltic states experienced deep but short recessions. Although Estonia and Lithuania had milder experiences than Latvia, their recessions were still extremely sharp when compared to other European Union countries. It is also striking that the output falls took place over two years, whereas it took Greece more than six years of recession to exceed Latvia's GDP loss.

The first phase began in 2007 as the Nordic banks reassessed their credit portfolios in the Baltic region and tightened access to credit. However, the boom had been so big that it took a while for this change in credit conditions to feed into the economy (Hansson and Ranveer, 2013). Nevertheless, 2008 saw a slowdown in domestic demand as well as a (less severe) fall in exports (Blanchard, Griffiths and Gruss, 2013). The trigger for the crash in Latvia was a run on *Parex Bank*, the largest domestically owned bank. Parex's deposits declined by a third in the second half of 2008, as rumours quickly circulated about the bank's weakness. The bank was eventually bailed out by the government, which split it into two parts and renamed both. The collapse of Parex brought a symbolic end to the post-Soviet era. The bank had been set up in the late 1980s and its owners, Valerijs Kargins and Viktors Krasovickis, have long been seen as two of the most influential political players in Latvia, being major donors to a number of political parties from the 1990s onwards. Moreover, both were symbols of ostentatious, murkily gleaned wealth, with a string of expensive properties, flamboyant cars and ever-younger girlfriends. The slowdown in Latvia was particularly dramatic and unemployment shot up from 5.7 per cent to over 20 per cent. Economists have categorised Latvia's recession as the second-deepest after the US Great Depression in the 1930s. However, the Latvian case was in a sense far more dramatic, as Latvia's GDP loss took place over less than two years, while the US Great Depression lasted for almost five (Weisbrot and Ray, 2011).

The extreme fall in output naturally had an effect on the 2008 and planned 2009 Latvian government budgets that had been put together on the basis of continued brisk economic growth rather than collapse. The Estonian fiscal situation was rather different to Latvia and Lithuania in that Estonia had maintained a balanced, and even surplus, budget in the years of growth. This rainy-day fund gave the Estonian government a reserve to draw on when the economy began to dramatically slow down. In contrast the other two Baltic states, particularly Latvia, had run deficit budgets even during the years of high growth. They had green-lighted expensive infrastructure projects as well as large salary increases for public-sector employees and, when real government income exceeded projections, budgets had been revised upwards. When the crash arrived Latvia, which had bailed out Parex Bank, was in a precarious financial position and forced to turn to international lenders for financial assistance. The low pre-crisis levels of public debt also allowed the Baltic states, particularly Latvia, to borrow in order to finance the shortfall between income and expenditure. Latvia was eventually granted 7.5 billion euros in committed bailout funds through a combination of the IMF, the European Commission and individual European states, although it only utilised 4.5 billion of this loan facility and even repaid the loan early, at the end of 2012.

In 2009 began a contentious debate, both domestic and increasingly international, on how the Baltic states should deal with the economic crisis. One school of thought, supported by some of the best-known global economists such as Paul Krugman and Nouriel Roubini, pushed for a currency devaluation.[8] They argued that this 'external devaluation' was the most straightforward approach, being far easier to coordinate and swiftly making Baltic exports more competitive. However, this advice was rejected by both central banks and the national governments (all three of which were nominally centre-right coalitions at that time) which preferred to focus on the ultimate goal of euro accession, which would be derailed by a currency devaluation. Moreover, the overwhelming majority of loans (80 per cent in Estonia and Latvia, 60 per cent in Lithuania) had been taken out in foreign currencies, especially the euro, and devaluation would have led to an even greater number of defaults. Central-bank economists also argued that Baltic exports had a high import content, meaning that the gains of devaluation would be short-lived, especially as exports declined globally as economic contraction kicked in. Finally, avoiding devaluation would de facto force the Baltic governments to tackle the *structural* problems inherent in their economies. Thus all three governments maintained a united front, fearing that contagion would set in if just one state were to wander off-track.

Of the Baltic states' international partners, only the IMF questioned this tactic (which went against its usual advice in situations of financial crisis), although it eventually went along with the approach. Some economists have speculated that the Swedish banks played a particularly important role in pushing for internal devaluation, thus trying to prevent potentially huge losses from the defaults that a devaluation would bring (Weisbrot and Ray 2011). However, this tends to underestimate the salience of the Baltic national elites' focus on European integration. As discussed elsewhere in this volume, the Baltic political elite has long been united in the strategy of entwining itself with Europe for security reasons. A devaluation would have put back the aim of euro accession, thus leaving Latvia outside one of the key integrating groups in the European Union, something that the national leaders could not countenance.

All three Baltic states followed the road of internal devaluation and fiscal consolidation. While the depth and extent of the economic crisis differed in all three, there were great similarities in the paths that they followed (Kattel and Raudla, 2013; Maslauskaite and Zorgenfreija, 2013). Austerity meant simultaneous expenditure and revenue measures (in other words, pro-cyclical cuts in government spending and tax increases). Estonia acted first and adopted measures in the first half of 2008 that focused on cuts to expenditure, such as lowering public sector wages, cutting pension contributions and limiting sickness benefits.[9] Between 2008 and 2011 Latvia's cumulative fiscal adjustment was estimated at 17 per cent of GDP, which involved 6.8 per cent on the revenue side but cuts of 10.2 per cent on the expenditure side (European Commission, 2012, p. 27). To achieve the cuts in expenditure Latvia took radical and hitherto unprecedented steps, reducing the average size of government ministries by one-third (23,000 people were laid off), cutting public salaries and pensions (which later had to be reversed after the Constitutional Court declared the cuts unconstitutional) as well as closing half of the state's agencies and consolidating their functions into other institutions. In the same way small rural schools and hospitals were closed down (115 mostly underused rural schools, some of the few remaining relics of the Soviet era, were closed), prompting almost the only public opposition to these measures (Kajaks, 2013). At the same time, both direct and indirect taxes were raised. Lithuania focused on cuts to expenditure, particularly public-sector wages and benefits, but also adopted stimulus measures, such as cuts in income tax (from 24 per cent to 15 per cent). Virtually all non-EU-financed capital expenditure projects were cut. Other measures were intended to make the Baltic states more competitive. Employers in the private sector cut costs by shedding labour, leading to sharp increases in labour productivity (thus the private sector shed labour rather than reduced salaries as the public sector did). Latvia began selling five-year residents' visas to foreign nationals ready to invest at least 70,000 euro in real estate. By 2013 this had brought some 600 million euros into the Latvian property market (Hecking, 2013).[10]

There was remarkably little internal discussion or public opposition to this approach. Baltic elites were entirely unified in their support for internal devaluation and, while other approaches were discussed by international experts and commentators, they were not treated seriously by Baltic decision-makers (Kuokstis and Vilpisauskas, 2010). The few organised protests were small and had little impact.[11] The only substantial negotiations between government and trade unions took place in Lithuania in 2009 and ended with no real concessions from the government side. Many Balts seemed to have realised that their wage increases in the previous years were a result of an overheating economy. Others used the exit option and migrated to European Union countries in search of work, especially the United Kingdom and Ireland.[12] The Baltic economic model, which sees low levels of interaction between political leaders and organised interests, meant that there were few formal instruments whereby society could express its discontent (Kallaste and Woolfson, 2013). Most importantly, the Baltic states actually have few mediating institutions – unions, NGOs, parties – capable of harnessing and mobilising the population into organised protests against the changes. Finally, Balts have time and again proven themselves to be remarkably resilient to economic change, having survived the far bigger economic crises of the early 1990s, the banking collapses of the mid-1990s and the Russian rouble collapse of 1998.

As they came out of recession in 2010 the Baltic states returned to economic growth. Moreover, this was an export-driven recovery much aided by the beneficial external environment. The Baltic states' major export partners (Poland, the Nordic states, Russia) had been much less affected by the global economic crisis than other European regions. Moreover, the Baltic states had seen large strides in competitiveness thanks to the internal devaluation. In an attempt to avoid a return to an unbalanced economy, the Latvian parliament adopted in March 2013 a fiscal discipline law, similar to Estonia's, to avoid excessive budget deficits in future years.

5.1.3   Future prospects

The last quarter century has seen these three Baltic economies transformed from closed and integrated parts of the Soviet system to open, economically liberal EU states. The World Bank's annual 'ease of doing business survey' ranks the three Baltic states in the top 25 among 183 countries surveyed. In 2013 Lithuania was ranked 17th, Estonia 22nd and Latvia 24th. The first key aim of the economic reforms – the creation of a market economy – has clearly been achieved in all three states. The second aim of pivoting from East to West has also been largely achieved, despite Russia's resurgence as a trading partner and a growing source of FDI and economic influence in the twenty-first century. Russian nostalgia for Riga black balsam (*Rigas Melnais Balzams*) and *Vana Tallinn*, traditional herbal liquors that were distributed and consumed all across the Soviet Union as a healthier alternative to vodka (the former is now owned by a Russian company), Latvian sprats, Lithuanian dairy products and other Baltic foods and drinks meant that the Baltic states maintained and perhaps even enlarged their markets in the East over the last quarter of a century. Russian tourists make up an ever-growing part of the Baltic tourist industry, and Russians have also been buying Latvia's five-year investment-for-residency visas.[13]

Estonia quickly became the Baltic frontrunner in terms of economic performance and enacting reforms. A number of factors explain Estonian exceptionalism. First, political leaders and *ideas* were initially more salient in Estonia, whose post-independence leaders were overwhelmingly young, economic liberals committed to following radical economic reforms. In a self-congratulatory article, Estonia's reformist prime minister, Mart Laar, emphasised the importance of elite political consensus and commitment to radical reform as well as the significance of acting quickly before the era of extraordinary politics comes to an end (Laar, 1996). Moreover, they were supported by the Thatcherite economic consensus of the early 1990s – shaped by the ideas of Friedrich Hayek and Milton Friedman – that supported a pro-market deregulatory and pro-privatisation agenda. In contrast, Latvia's first elected government was a potpourri of reformers, communist-era nomenklatura, émigrés and opportunists. Lithuanians elected a left-wing government that only half-heartedly continued the economic reforms already started. Estonia also had certain structural advantages over Latvia and Lithuania. The most important factor may have been its far lower density of heavy manufacturing and large-sized enterprises as compared to Latvia and Lithuania. This meant fewer complicated and awkward restructurings and privatisations (large enterprises proved far more challenging to privatise) and also a smaller blue-collar population to oppose the reforms. Moreover, Russophones were concentrated in the larger enterprises, and the political elite found them easier to ignore than the titular population (this was also true of Latvia). While Latvia and Lithuania ultimately followed Estonia's polices, this was done far more grudgingly and with less commitment.

The 2008–2010 crisis also thwarted initial hopes of convergence with the wealthier states of Western Europe. Figure 5.4 (below) reveals that the high rates of economic growth in the Baltic states have moved them closer to the EU–28 average rate of GDP per capita. However, economist Morten Hansen (2013) has pointed out that convergence is not inevitable and might, indeed, be unlikely unless the Baltic states invest more

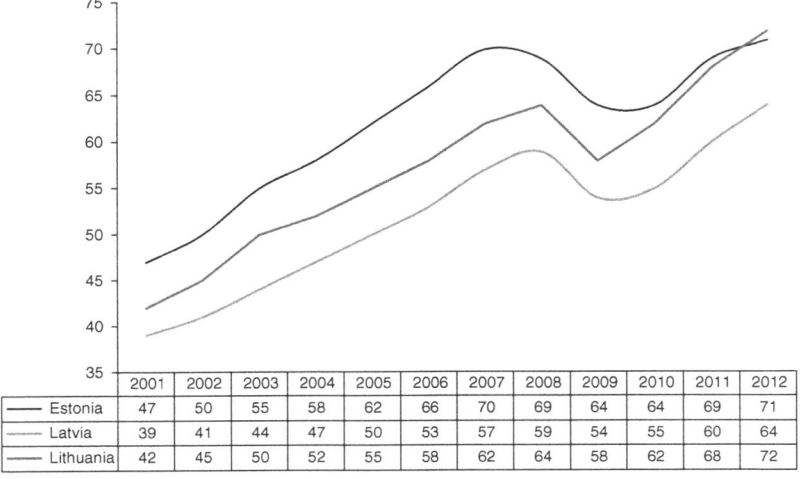

	2001	2002	2003	2004	2005	2006	2007	2008	2009	2010	2011	2012
—— Estonia	47	50	55	58	62	66	70	69	64	64	69	71
—— Latvia	39	41	44	47	50	53	57	59	54	55	60	64
—— Lithuania	42	45	50	52	55	58	62	64	58	62	68	72

Figure 5.4 Convergence with the European Union (GDP per capita. EU28=100). Baltic states, 2001–2012

Source: Eurostat (2014).

on research, development and innovation and put more resources into fighting corruption.

The neo-liberal nature of the economic reforms have not come without social cost. An inevitable result of austerity, with its cuts in government expenditure accompanied by higher taxes, is a rise in inequality. Already high before the crisis, both poverty and social exclusion rose in the Baltic states from 2008 onwards. The following section will consider these and other social issues in more detail.

5.2 Social issues

The radical economic transition had an equally transformative effect on society in the Baltic states. The boom-and-bust economic narrative was experienced at the individual level through changes in the labour market, migration, benefits, pensions, access to education and shifting health-care outcomes. For all its many fundamental faults, the Soviet economic model provided certain minimum standards of living for its populace: low levels of income inequality, roughly on a par with Sweden (Bergson, 1984; Smith 2007), supplemented by universal benefits, subsidised goods and many additional services and non-cash benefits provided by the state-owned enterprises. Unemployment rates were extremely low.

This was unsustainable in the medium term. The newly independent Baltic states did not have the public finances needed to maintain these generous benefits. Nor did they have the political will, having committed to move towards neo-liberal economic regimes with investor-friendly, low tax rates and flexible labour markets (Farkas 2011). Nascent civil societies, frail social democratic parties (particularly in Estonia and Latvia) and weakened trade unions meant that the Baltic governments faced little organised opposition to these reforms. Broadly stated, the new social models have gradually shifted responsibility for welfare from the state to the individual.

The pattern of social reform was similar in all three states. First, the inevitable rise in unemployment, an unavoidable side effect of the downturn in economic output. This was a severe challenge to societies that had seen full employment since the 1940s. While the economies picked up in the mid-1990s, employment levels would never reach the full employment of the Soviet era. Many of those who had received narrow vocational education and worked in manufacturing found it difficult to reorient themselves towards the rapidly growing services sector. Those still employed found their jobs far more tenuous than in previous years, with Estonia in particular quickly adopting business-friendly legislation with low firing costs for employers. These changes were difficult to explain to increasingly unhappy populations that were used to being the economic envy of the rest of the Soviet Union. At this point the Baltic states changed from being a region of heavy immigration to one shedding population.

All three Baltic states swiftly created a broad system of benefits, including unemployment and income-support benefits, child-support payments, maternity and paternity allowances. However, the payments are generally small, reflecting the low levels of overall spending on social protection in the Baltic states relative to the size of their economies. Total welfare payments are well below the EU average. In 2009 welfare expenditure in the EU–27 was, on average, 29.5 per cent of GDP, but in Estonia it was just 19.2 per cent, Latvia 18.8 per cent and Lithuania 21.3 per cent (Purju, 2013, p. 18). Indeed, together with Romania and Bulgaria, the three spend about half the per-capita amount that Slovenia and the Visegrad countries spend on welfare. Moreover, while the Central European states target the poor and especially pensioners, social spending in the Baltic states favours 'the young, the educated and the middle-class (whether in public or private jobs) rather than the elderly' (Bohle and Greskovits, 2009, p. 53).

Pensioners were particularly exposed to the risk of poverty, having few opportunities to gain alternative sources of income by re-entering the workforce. Pensioners in the Soviet era were characterised by receiving old-age pensions at a relatively young age (women retired at 55, men at 60, although numerous professions also had provisions for early retirement), as well as relatively easy access to disability pensions. The size of the pensions was not linked to previous salary or welfare contributions and financed on a pay-as-you-go basis. The Baltic states thus inherited a large number of working-age pensioners, but with no dedicated pot of money to pay for these pensions. As the number of pensioners in the population rose, but the number of tax-paying employed individuals declined, pension reform became an economic necessity.

The pension reforms undertaken in all three states are broadly similar. All three adopted a three-pillar system (Paas et al., 2004; Licmane and Voronova, 2013). Unusually, Latvia was the first to adopt this scheme. The first pillar is a pay-as-you-go scheme, and pays the basic state pension. The second level is a mandatory funded scheme and the third pillar is an optional supplementary scheme that is funded by individual contributions into a selected pension fund (in Estonia and Latvia the second level is managed by the state and the third privately, but in Lithuania both are managed by private actors). Final pensions are calculated by both the number of years worked and the level of income that social security contributions were paid on. The pensionable age in all three states was raised to over 60, although it remains well below the EU average.

Unemployment benefits are tied to the length of previous employment and, again, are rather less generous than those found in the older EU states or the Visegrad countries. Benefits are typically paid for no more than one year, and the size of the monthly payments gradually declines, although during the economic crisis the Baltic states temporarily extended the amount of time that these benefits could be received, and Latvia even adopted a temporary public works programme, largely funded by the European Social Fund, which employed some 120,000 people between 2009 and 2011 (participants were paid 150 euros a month).

Sickness and maternity benefits are also linked to previous earnings. In an effort to tackle the Baltic states' demographic decline, generous maternity and paternity provisions were introduced during the economic boom in the mid-2000s, although these were cut back during the following recession. Estonia and Latvia also have small, monthly child benefits (payments were between 11 and 19 euros per child in 2013). Lithuania opted for extensive means-tested benefits to assist with school meals, education and food costs, heating bills and other expenses. Means testing is much more limited in Latvia and almost non-existent in Estonia. Although broadly similar, there are differences in the generosity and targeted nature of the Baltic states' system of benefits:

> The family and child support system is more generous in Estonia than in Latvia and Lithuania. Lithuania gives support to families with children, based on their previous social insurance contributions or on the means-tested basis. Estonia and Latvia give support based on previous contributions and citizenship (residency). In addition, means-tested benefits are also available to poor families and individuals. (Aidukaite, 2013, p. 97)

Meagre benefits have inevitably resulted in rising inequality and poverty. The unemployed, rural dwellers, households with three or more children and pensioners, especially single older women, were the groups most exposed to the likelihood of poverty. Indeed, in sharp contrast to their Nordic neighbours, the three Baltic states together make up the region with the highest inequality in the European Union, with the Gini coefficient of all three states being well above the EU–27 average (see Figure 5.5). The number of severely materially deprived people has remained high, particularly in Latvia and Lithuania. It was on a downward trend during the boom years but was exacerbated by the recession (Figure 5.6).

There are also regional variations to the distribution of prosperity in the Baltic states, with wealth being very much concentrated in the

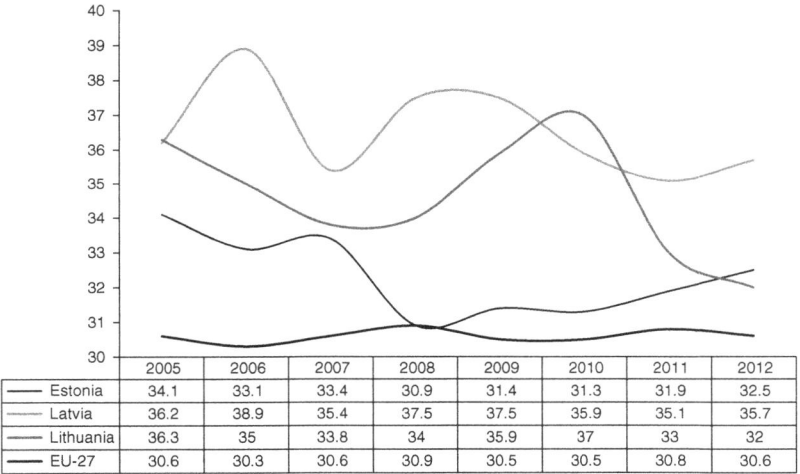

	2005	2006	2007	2008	2009	2010	2011	2012
Estonia	34.1	33.1	33.4	30.9	31.4	31.3	31.9	32.5
Latvia	36.2	38.9	35.4	37.5	37.5	35.9	35.1	35.7
Lithuania	36.3	35	33.8	34	35.9	37	33	32
EU-27	30.6	30.3	30.6	30.9	30.5	30.5	30.8	30.6

Figure 5.5 Gini coefficient of Baltic states and EU–27 average, 2005–2012
Source: Eurostat (2014).

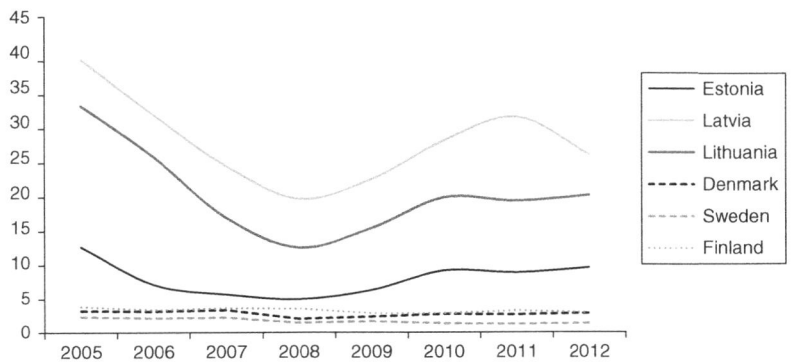

Figure 5.6 Severely materially deprived people (%). Baltic states and Nordic states, 2005–2012
Source: Eurostat (2014).

big capital cities of Tallinn, Riga and Vilnius. Estonia and Latvia have periphery regions blighted by unemployment and poverty. In both cases these are the eastern regions that are distant from the western capital cities that border the Baltic Sea and are also regions of Russophone concentration. North-east Estonia has high unemployment that even during the boom years ran at 10 per cent, double the national rate, reaching 25.8 per cent in 2010 (Purju, 2013, p. 7).

There is also a gender dimension to the transformation. Women have seen a sharp change in their social status with the transition from the communist regime. The Soviet Union had generally missed out on the 1970s sexual revolution and the rise in equality between the sexes. Women in the Soviet system were both horizontally and vertically segregated from men, working in different sectors and at different levels (Blackburn, Jarman and Brooks, 2000). Anatol Lieven (1994, p. 33) recounted that the English Faculty at the University of Tallinn at the end of the Soviet period had 27 female and just two male employees. However, the latter were the director and deputy director of the faculty. In the Soviet system women dominated the health care and education sectors. Analysis of the Baltic Labour Force Surveys from the early 2000s indicated that only Lithuania had moved towards less gender segregation, while such segregation had actually increased in Estonia and Latvia (Voorman, 2009). At the same time, however, the Baltic states have no unemployment gender gap, hinting at greater gender equality in the labour market – although this may also be explained by women's greater representation in the service sector which was less affected by the boom and bust of the Baltic experience in the 2000s (Bicakova, 2010).

Crime sharply increased in the 1990s, doubling in Lithuania between 1991 and 1997, and also changed in profile, with violent crimes (including murder) and organised crime becoming far more prevalent (Ceccato, 2008; Andresen, 2011). However, as the Baltic states began to increasingly Europeanise following integration with Western Europe, patterns of crime began to change, with the role of organised crime shrinking while economically and socially marginalised groups have become more active in criminality (Masso et al., 2012). Murder rates have remained high, although they are fast in decline. In the early 2000s the intentional homicide rate in all three states was about ten times higher than the rate in the neighbouring Nordic states, but these rates have approached Nordic levels since accession to the EU (see Figure 5.7 below). Both the economic development that came with accession, as well as the open borders that led to criminals seeking opportunities elsewhere in the union, help to explain these changes.

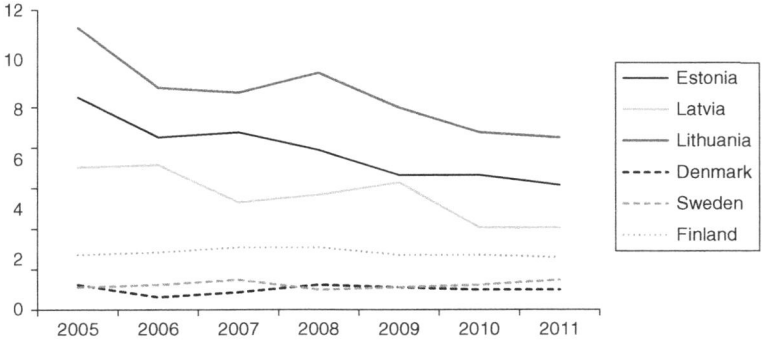

Figure 5.7 Intentional homicide rate per 100,000 population. Baltic states and Nordic states, 2005–2011

Source: United Nations Office on Drugs and Crime (2013).

The economic transformation inevitably affected health outcomes. Price liberalisation and the break with the Soviet Union led to growing prices for pharmaceutical products, and the fall in output and decline in real wages affected almost all health-care professionals (at that time employed by the state) as well as the general funding of hospitals and other health-care institutions. At the same time, the stress of the transformation – unemployment, increasing uncertainty about the future – affected people at the individual level. Moreover, the quality of health care in the Soviet Union had long been in decline, as evidenced by the falls in life expectancy for Soviet citizens between the early 1970s and the collapse of the Soviet Union. There was a further dip in life expectancy in the early and mid-1990s, before it once again started to grow in the late 1990s, although the Baltic states still lag behind life-expectancy rates in Central and Eastern Europe as well as Western Europe. This difference is largely explained by the higher levels of 'heavy and hazardous alcohol consumption' among men in particular leading, in combination with smoking, to high cardiovascular disease rates (Leon, 2011, p. 4; Prattala et al., 2011). Alcoholism has remained an ongoing problem in the Baltic states. All three are categorised as 'traditional vodka drinking cultures…characterised by non-daily drinking, irregular binge-drinking episodes (e.g., during weekends and at festivities), and the acceptance of drunkenness in public' (Popova et al., 2007, pp. 465–466). Consumption of alcohol, relative to the inter-war period, increased during the Soviet era, with Latvia and Lithuania having particularly high levels of alcohol consumption, which has continued into the post-communist period. These drinking patterns inevitably have a negative impact on health, with Lithuania having a particularly high incidence of recorded cardiovascular deaths at weekends and on Mondays, which is typically the result of binge drinking at the weekend (Chenet et al, 2001). Rural dwellers, especially men and those with less education, have had poorer health outcomes than those living in urban areas (Helasoja et al., 2006). Nevertheless, there is strong evidence that health outcomes began to improve hand-in-hand with economic development in the twenty-first century, and scholars have identified convergence between health patterns in the Baltic states and Finland (Finbalt Health Monitor, 2011).

Suicide rates rose sharply to be among the highest in the world. The trend has been the same in all three Baltic states, with a big spike in suicides in the early years of the transformation, peaking in the mid-1990s, followed by a gradual fall in the numbers before a small spike during the most recent economic downturn. Suicide has also remained far more frequent among men than women. Much of the rise in suicide rates came from the Russophone minority in Estonia and Latvia, which actually had much lower rates of suicide than the titular population before the post-1991 transition began. The loss of privileged jobs and housing, greater uncertainty and pressure from the titular populations has contributed to Russophone suicides (Pray et al., 2013).

Education, which provides one possible route out of poverty, has also seen many reforms. The initial expectation was that all was fine with education. After all, the Soviet Union had proven to be quite successful at opening up the higher-education system to sections of society that had not previously had access to tertiary-level education. However, as the transition to democracy and the market kicked in, it quickly became apparent that there was a mismatch of skills and that reforms must be undertaken (Barr, 2005).

Higher-education was a particularly tricky area to reorganise, not least because higher-education professionals (professors and senior administrators) were active in the new democratic politics, frequently holding senior positions in the Ministry of Education (including the minister's post) and acting as de facto defenders of reactionary interests. In the Soviet era the core elements of the new market-driven economies – entrepreneurship and economics, political science and public administration, law – had not been taught. Building modern educational programmes was hindered by lack of educated staff, money and experience in these new fields. However, the potential rewards (in terms of thousands of young people ready to pay to study these fields) led universities to create new programmes and to the mushrooming of a great number of new higher-education institutions, many catering to the Russian-speaking students that the public universities in Estonia and Latvia no longer catered for.

Education was also an area where international actors were prepared to invest money. Perhaps the most visible example in the Baltic states is the Stockholm School of Economics in Riga, initially funded largely by the Swedish government and the Soros Foundation, but now a self-sustaining institution that has proved to be extremely successful in educating and socialising a new business elite (Racko 2011). Other efforts attempted to reform the existing university institutions by providing visiting professors to teach and aid the construction of new higher-education curricula. Perhaps the most significant of these efforts was the EuroFaculty, a programme created by the Council of Baltic Sea States that targeted the construction of law, political science/public administration and economics programmes at the three classical national universities in the Baltic states – Tartu University, the University of Latvia and Vilnius University. EuroFaculty, despite its name, did not create a separate institution, but worked through the existing social sciences via close collaboration with the faculties in the different universities. It closed in 2005, following Baltic accession to the European Union and NATO.

However, the double accession did not mark the end of education reforms. While certain formal elements of the higher-education system have been internationalised (such as the move to the 3+2 year Bologna system for bachelors and master's studies) the Baltic states continue to face several important educational challenges, not least the great number of higher-educational institutions that continued to persist well into the twenty-first century. In 2012 Latvia had 60 higher-education institutions, Estonia 30 – down from 49 in 2002 – and Lithuania 45 (Ruin, 2012). All three Baltic states attempted higher-education reforms during and after the economic crisis. Estonia's 2012 education reform saw it move towards a model of fully state-financed higher education for those students studying full time and in programmes taught in the Estonian language. Lithuania passed a comprehensive higher-education law in 2009 that introduced more external evaluation of higher-education institutions, reorganised and reduced the number of research institutes and introduced a competitive funding model of students using vouchers to choose their programme rather than the state giving direct financing to the institution. In contrast, Latvia's politicians failed to adopt a comprehensive education reform plan. A modernising minister (Roberts Ķīlis, who gained his D.Phil in anthropology at the University of Cambridge) attempted to radically change the structure, financing, evaluation and other aspects of the higher- education system, but was brought down by the reactionary higher-education clique that opposed almost every element of Ķīlis's reform package. As a result, as of 2015 Latvia still has a system in which the state pays for a certain number of 'budget students' in certain higher-education programmes, and then these students study alongside other private, fee-paying students.

Since around 2010 universities have had to face the challenge of radical drops in student numbers as the demographic crisis, which began in the early 1990s when all three Baltic states experienced the start of negative natural population growth. At the same time, the opening up of European universities to Baltic secondary school graduates led to an increasing number of young Estonians, Latvians and Lithuanians seeking the adventure and challenge of taking a degree abroad. However, these young students make up just a small part of Baltic residents who have migrated westwards over the last quarter century.

In the Soviet era the Baltic states, particularly Estonia and Latvia, were areas of mass immigration. Between 1944 and 1949, 400,000 Russophones migrated to Latvia alone (Zepa and Klave, 2011, p. 68). Since 1991 the situation has reversed, and the Baltic states have become countries experiencing high emigration, particularly Latvia and Lithuania. In the early 1990s the first wave of emigrants was composed of Russophones moving eastwards, primarily to Russia. However, the longer wave of twenty-first century migration has been to the West. An exhaustive 2011 study found that:

> The recent history of emigration from the Baltic countries can be divided into three episodes: (i) the pre-accession period (which we loosely designate as 2000–2003, although it includes also the first four months of 2004); (ii) the post-accession period of economic growth, to which we refer as 2004–2008 (although the crisis hit Latvia in the last quarter of 2008, its effect on emigration appears only in the data of 2009–2010); (iii) The crisis period, 2009–2010. (Zepa and Klave, 2011, p. 77)

Surveys from the first period found that significant numbers of Baltic residents, particularly Russophones (who were in a weaker position in the labour market and also less identified with the new states), were ready to work abroad temporarily, or even emigrate to Western Europe, in search of better-paid work.[14] However, although there was a high potential for migration, the pre-EU accession institutional barriers were high, and there was relatively little movement. The situation changed radically after 2004, when an institutionally migration-friendly regime was introduced, and European Employment Services (EURES) advisors started operating in the Baltic states, and the European Mobility Portal also encouraged migration to other parts of Europe. The swift growth of budget airlines, such as Ryanair and EasyJet (which provided increased cheap travel links between the Baltic states and Europe), as well as developing migrant networks, eased the transition from the home to the host country and also enabled greater mobility flows. This process was accelerated after the economic recession began to kick in from late 2008, and rapidly rising unemployment, as well as severe cuts in wages in the public sector, led to an ever-increasing number of people seeking employment elsewhere.

Latvia and Lithuania were hard hit by these trends. Latvia lost 10 per cent of its active workforce, some 120,000 people, between 2009 and 2011, a total similar to those who had emigrated in the 2000–2008 period and which amounts to roughly a quarter of a million people, 9 per cent of Latvia's 2000 population (Zepa and Klave, 2011, p. 84; Hazans, 2013, p. 66).[15] Lithuania, which similarly to Latvia has long been an area of migration, saw 728,000 people emigrate abroad between 1990 and 2011, with the majority leaving in the twenty-first century and 83,500 registered departures in 2010 alone (Sipaviciene and Stankuniene, 2013, p. 49). Emigration did bring certain economic benefits at a time of economic crisis, limiting unemployment and other benefits. Indeed, remittances from those employed abroad made up over 4.5 per cent of Lithuania's GDP in 2010 and 2011 (Maslauskaite and Zorgenfreija, 2013, p. 61).

Estonia has seen the least migration. Estonia's data is more sketchy than the Latvian or Lithuanian figures (perhaps reflecting that this issue is less of political concern there), but total Estonian emigration since 2004 has been approximately 2.4 per cent of the population, or about 30,000 people, far less than in the other two Baltic states (Kaska, 2013, p. 31). Moreover, Estonians who have left the state to work abroad tend to head for Finland rather than the United Kingdom or Ireland, although there was an increase in Estonians migrating to countries other than Finland after accession to the EU (with Ireland and the United Kingdom as the most favoured destinations, as with their Latvian and Lithuanian neighbours). The geographic proximity of Finland, as well as language similarities, also opens up the opportunity to commute to work on a daily or weekly basis and around 3 per cent of Estonia's working population was employed in Finland in 2011 (Viilmann and Soosaar, 2012).

Estonian migrants also have a social profile different to their Latvian and Lithuanian peers in that they tend to have just a secondary education and blue-collar employment, whereas migrants from the other Baltic countries have a higher level of education (Kaska, 2013, pp. 32–33). In total the Estonian population declined by around seven per cent in the first two decades of independence (Kaska, 2013).

All three Baltic states have developed plans to aid the repatriation of their nationals. The Estonian government has developed the Our People Foundation, which operates under the Ministry of Culture, and pays out up to 2,000 euros to aid return migration (although this is only available to Estonian citizens and ethnic Estonians that have lived abroad for more than 10 years). However, this is a minor programme that in its peak year (2008) aided the return of just 242 people (Kaska, 2013, p. 36). A more typical annual return rate was in the double digits. The Latvian Foreign Ministry created a 'diaspora programme' that is aimed at both maintaining links with the émigré community as well as developing ideas and programmes that could ultimately tempt the departed to return to Latvia. However, only around 20 per cent of Latvia's migrants have any short- or medium-term plans to return to Latvia (Zepa and Klave, 2011, p. 89). Lithuania developed the Global Lithuania plan for 2011–2019 that aims not only to encourage the return of emigrants, albeit without cash benefits, but also to develop a diaspora policy that intends to use emigrant Lithuanians as a state asset, in terms of lobbying Lithuanian interests in their host country or aiding economic links between the two.

Conclusions: The Baltic Tigers – a common Baltic model?

Is there a single Baltic socio-economic system, analogous to the Scandinavian/Nordic or Anglo-Saxon models of capitalism, as some authors have claimed (Barr, 2005)? This chapter has outlined significant parallels as well as differences in the Baltic systems. Reforms were undertaken quickly, not least to rapidly break away from the Soviet Union and move towards the West. The small scale of the domestic markets also drove the Baltic states to open up relatively quickly (especially Estonia, the smallest market) in order to attract both the finance and international entrepreneurial expertise that was clearly lacking after a half century of a planned economy. Just as important was the final destination of the reform. The Baltic states very much saw themselves as a part of Europe, and a part of this identity construction was the need to create a market economy. While citizens often disputed the outcomes of this transition – rising inequality, falls in income, job insecurity – the blame for this was typically put on venal politicians and bureaucrats rather than on the vagaries of the market system itself. Moreover, in Estonia and Latvia the issue of national survival (of the national languages, what to do with the Soviet army as well as the large Russian-speaking communities) dominated the political discourse, providing the opportunity for radical reforms of the economy to be carried out in plain sight (Feldman, 2001). Working from a tabula rasa, the advisors of the institutional reforms had a great deal of influence. Latvia provides an instructive example in the case of Juris Vīksniņš and his 'Georgetown Gang' of cohorts. Vīksniņš, a professor of economics at Georgetown University, found stipends for a number of youngish Latvians to participate in the Pew Economic Forum Freedom Fellows Program at the university. These economists would later play a major role in the economic reforms, holding key ministerial posts (Finance and Economics) in the reformist governments of the early 1990s. Many still hold important posts at the Bank of Latvia. The Baltic states adopted neo-liberal economic and social policies because no real alternatives have been presented, neither in 1991 nor more recently during the 2008–2010 crisis. As a result, all three Baltic states can be described as small, open, liberal market economies that are heavily dependent on FDI and international trade in their continued development.

At a European level, the three states have broadly similar economies. Eurostat (2014) per capita GDP in PPS data shows the three clustered together, with only Hungary and Poland separating Latvia from its Baltic neighbours (Eurostat, 2013). Estonia is considered to have moved first and farthest because its elite was unified and had been preparing economic reforms from the mid-1980s, launching the IME (*Isemajandav Eesti*) programme in September 1987. IME envisaged economic autonomy for Estonia within the Soviet Union, including having its own currency. While the programme was not enacted, it did promote debate and discussion, and many of the people involved in writing it, including Siim Kallas (later governor of the central bank) came out of the process with a clear vision of how the Estonian economy should be constructed. Estonia also had certain structural advantages over Latvia and Lithuania, having more light industry, which is easier to restructure and privatise than the larger heavy industries that the other states inherited from the Soviet Union (Feldman, 2001). In terms of social policy, the Baltic states are the lowest spenders on social protection in the European Union.

They have adopted generally similar policy approaches, creating more individual and less state responsibility for welfare and accepting high income inequality as one of the inevitable outcomes of this approach (Aidukaite, 2011). The three Baltic states clearly make up a distinct economic and social policy region in Europe.

6
Foreign and Security Policy

In early 2014 the foreign and security policy discourse in the Baltic region was transformed as a resurgent and assertive Russia annexed Crimea and launched covert operations in eastern Ukraine.[1] Observers were quick to point out that events in Ukraine eerily paralleled the 1940 occupation of the Baltic states. The traditional security concerns about Russian intentions in the region that the Baltic states had increasingly suppressed over the previous 20 years once again rushed to the surface. The post-existential era of Baltic foreign and security policy that had marked the decade that followed accession to the EU and NATO seemed to have come to an end.

Prior to the events of early 2014, Baltic security seemed assured by membership in NATO and the EU as well as by rising Russian economic integration and political cooperation with the West. Latvia and Lithuania had radically cut defence and security spending during the economic recession of 2008–2010 (although it had never been particularly high; see Figure 6.1) and had been in no hurry to return to pre-crisis spending levels. The Baltic states' foreign and security policy focus had moved beyond simply defending Baltic borders to spreading the Baltic 'success story' of economic and political transformation to other post-Soviet states. They were in the process of recasting themselves as donors rather than recipients of international aid.

Baltic leaders acted quickly and assertively to the potential threats posed by Russian actions in Ukraine. They were clearly determined to avoid the failed inter-war policies of neutrality, inaction and simply 'hoping against hope' (Plakans, 1995, p. 142). All three states adopted activist and, initially, even hawkish approaches. Latvia and Lithuania promised to beef up defence spending. Baltic political leaders used their membership in the European Union and NATO to push for tough sanctions on Russia, although this was eventually moderated to targeted sanctions in order to minimise the impact on their economies, which were still tied up with Russia. The Baltic states also sought defence guarantees from NATO allies, particularly the United States. In April 2014 they welcomed US troops to the Baltic states and the long-standing NATO Baltic air policing mission was beefed up with Polish, Danish, French and British aircraft.

After the initial alarm, it became clear that the Baltic states enjoy a greater degree of external hard security than at any other previous point in their history. The long-standing twin challenges to Baltic security have been size and geography. Estonia, Latvia and Lithuania are small states located on the periphery of Europe with a large neighbour, Russia, that has long considered them to be an integral part of its territory (the 'near abroad') and never fully abandoned the idea of bringing them back into its sphere of 'privileged interest'. Both these challenges were met in the first decade of the twentieth century. The size issue was tackled by traditional diplomacy that in due course led to integration with the EU and NATO, the two key organisations pooling the resources of member states. The seemingly intractable geographic challenge was handled by a gradual, constructivist-driven change in the narrative of the region that has seen the Baltic states increasingly recast as part of the 'West' not the 'East' and more 'Nordic' or 'North European' than 'Post-Soviet' or Russia's sphere of 'privileged interest'.

This transformation was achieved by a mutually complimentary two-pronged foreign policy approach. First, a conscious decoupling of all possible political and, initially at least, economic and cultural ties with Russia and other Soviet successor states. This distancing was a precondition for the complimentary second action of enthusiastic open-armed integration with the West. No Western organisation was too small or marginal to join – the three Baltic states have been enthusiastic members of the European Broadcasting Union (EBU), with Estonia and Latvia even winning the Eurovision song contest organised by the EBU. Although Estonia initially sprinted ahead in the race for accession to the European Union, and Lithuania seemed best placed to join NATO first, all three states joined these two organisations together in 2004. This was achieved largely due to Baltic willingness to defer to international conditionality on a whole host of economic and political reforms as well as to their eagerness to join George W. Bush's 'coalition of the willing' in the 2003 Iraq war, provide troops for NATO's activities in Afghanistan and take part in other NATO military actions.

There have been three core elements of this shift to the West. First, NATO was seen as the only realistic guarantor of hard security. Second, accession to the EU would provide access to wealthy West European markets as well as the opportunity to reform and strengthen key institutions and consolidate democracy. Finally, increasing economic, political and cultural cooperation and integration with the Nordic states would lead to a gradual remaking and reorientation of Baltic identity from the (negative) post-Soviet to the (positive) North European/Nordic/Baltic Sea Region.

The strategic reorientation of the three states' foreign policies can be regarded as a major success story. Throughout the Soviet era the three Baltic republics had technically had their own foreign ministries. However, these were understaffed and clearly subordinated to the Moscow-based Soviet Ministry of Foreign Affairs. The Estonian Soviet-era foreign ministry provides an illustrative example. Until the late 1980s it employed just ten people and performed strictly limited, primarily regional, functions. Arnold Green, who ran the Estonian Foreign Ministry from the 1960s until 1990, explained that it occasionally had 'special representatives' in Soviet missions in Eastern Europe and in the Baltic Sea Region (BSR) states where the Estonian SSR had its own interests in the fields of 'culture, science and technology, education, health, sports and tourism' (Nichol, 1995, p. 129). The ministry was also responsible for overseeing contacts with Estonian émigré organisations and hosting oversees visitors to the Estonian SSR.

This began to change in 1990 after the Popular Fronts had won legislative elections and gained increasing political and administrative control of the Baltic Republics. With external recognition a political priority, Estonia, Latvia and Lithuania restructured their foreign ministries. They began by appointing new foreign ministers (Lennart Meri in Estonia, Jānis Jurkāns in Latvia and Algirdas Saudargas in Lithuania) who were not a part of the previous Soviet foreign-policy-making community. Staffing levels in the Baltic foreign ministries began to expand as old cadres were pushed out and a new, young generation of diplomats was recruited. By the end of 1990 each foreign ministry employed around 30 to 50 personnel. An Estonian diplomacy school was set up in order to meet the expected growing demand for diplomats. All three foreign ministries had also begun to create and steer foreign policies independent of Moscow. In October 1990 Lithuania opened an 'Information Bureau' (effectively a limited diplomatic mission) in Oslo, and in January 1991 Latvia opened a similar Information Office in Stockholm. A few weeks later a number of high-ranking Swedish government officials and parliamentarians visited Latvia (Lasas, 2008, p. 356). However, Moscow still held a great deal of leeway over the Baltic states and prevented other states from setting up any kind of recognised diplomatic missions in the region, not even information centres or cultural offices. Consular activities (most importantly issuing passports) still had to be coordinated with Moscow (Nichol, 1995, p. 112).

The role and importance of the foreign ministries increased substantially after independence in August 1991. They were charged with establishing bilateral relations with other states across the globe as well as coordinating Baltic membership in international organisations and setting-up and staffing diplomatic missions in key partner states. This took place under severe financial constraints, with all three ministries struggling to recruit and retain qualified staff. The foreign services could promise interesting and dynamic careers in the long-term (and many of those recruited in the early 1990s now hold key diplomatic posts and senior positions in international organisations), but only poor salaries and aged working conditions in the short term. Funding problems also limited the pace and extent to which foreign missions could be opened. Nevertheless, despite these significant start-up problems, the foreign services of all three countries were quick to establish them as sovereign state actors in the international system.

A crucial strategic moment came in late 1991, when the three Baltic states became the only former Soviet Republics to reject membership of the Commonwealth of Independent States (CIS). While the continued presence of tens of thousands of heavily armed Russian troops on their soil meant that Baltic political leaders continued to publicly hedge on the extent of their Westernising ambitions, the general framework for Western integration was set with this decision. This initially timid approach did cause some concern, as the post-communist states of Central Europe targeted accession to NATO and the EU with far greater gusto, and Baltic leaders feared that they would swiftly join both organisations and leave the Baltic states behind in a de facto grey zone of uncertainty between East and West that Russia might interpret as continuing to be in its traditional sphere of interest (Jamestown Foundation, 1996).

The shift to the West could only start with aplomb once the initially precarious security environment caused by Soviet/Russian troops on the territory of all three Baltic states had been resolved. Following fraught and extended negotiations, the last troops left in August 1994. This was the end of the period during which the three states maintained a façade of international neutrality in order to avoid antagonising Russia. As soon as Russian troops left, all three states' foreign policy elites pivoted to the

West. Other defence options were only briefly discussed. There had been some debate over creating a regional version of NATO by combining the defence forces of the Baltic states, the Central European post-communist states and possibly also Ukraine. However, this initiative was abandoned as the Central European states edged closer to NATO. Other plans involving security guarantees from Russia or other CIS states, such as a Baltic-to-the-Black Sea initiative, were never really taken very seriously (Bajarnas, 1995, p. 11). In 1997 the Russian government offered the three Baltic states security guarantees in exchange for abandoning their plans for NATO entry. All three swiftly rejected the offer.

As the Baltic states increasingly integrated with the West from the mid-1990s onwards, a combination of their newly emerging confidence, domestic pro-Russian interests and rising Russian economic power, as well as increased openness to international actors as an inevitable result of globalisation, saw them begin to open up to economic, if not political, cooperation with the East. Dominated by President Vladimir Putin since 2000 – who in his 2005 annual state of the nation address to the Russian parliament called the collapse of the Soviet Union 'the greatest geopolitical catastrophe' of the twentieth century (Osborn, 2005) – twenty-first-century Russia began to pose not just traditional military hard power threats to the Baltic region, but also energy, economic, cyberspace and cultural risks. As the three pushed to 'rejoin Europe', Russia began to pull ever harder to bring them back into its orbit of influence. In 1995 Russian foreign minister Andrei Kozyrev had stated that 'there may be cases when the use of direct military force will be needed to defend our compatriots abroad' (Bajarunas, Haab and Viksne, 1995, p. 8) and the sporadic outbursts of radical nationalist Vladimir Zhrinovsky have also caused alarm.[2] The accession to power of Vladimir Putin began a period of rising Russian influence in the Baltic region that was accompanied by ever sharper rhetoric. A sustained surge in the international price of energy and other raw materials saw the Russian economy boom in the 2000s, and Russia's accompanying newfound economic confidence focused on extending its soft power in the region through economic investment, new print and electronic media, civil society organisations and other support for the Russian-speaking diaspora. Renewed military exercises on the Estonia/Latvia-Russia border, regular fighter-plane incursions into Baltic air space and the invasion of Georgia in the summer of 2008 reminded the Baltic states that Russia remained the major military actor in the Baltic region.

This shared precarious security environment has meant that, in contrast to almost every other policy area, the Baltic states have followed a concentrated and coordinated common foreign and security policy. This began even before independence was achieved, as the three then-Soviet republics harmonised their drives for external legitimacy in the late 1980s and early 1990s. The pro-independence political leaders of the three Soviet republics worked as a troika and intensively lobbied the international community for support in the drive to independence. For example, in June 1991 Baltic leaders travelled together to lobby a session of the Benelux Interparliamentary Council (which subsequently formulated a non-binding resolution calling on the Benelux governments to support the Baltic states' drive for independence) and then moved on to a meeting at NATO headquarters, where they met representatives from Denmark, Iceland and Canada (Tammerk, 1991).[3]

This chapter considers four key dimensions of Baltic foreign and security policy. It begins by looking at Baltic accession to NATO and the EU; it then moves on to evaluate regional cooperation between the three Baltic states, and then within the broader North European region; the final section looks at the complicated and fractious relationship between the Baltic states and Russia. The conclusion considers the successes and failures of Baltic foreign policy.

6.1   NATO

The end of the Cold War fundamentally changed the global-security landscape. The dominant Cold War threat to the West – the Soviet Union – was replaced by a series of smaller and less tangible dangers such as pandemics, terrorism and cross-border refugees. For the Baltic states, however, the Cold War threat remained, and remains, salient. The only significant risk to their newfound statehood was posed by post-Soviet Russia. As a result, they have continued to view the world through a traditional geopolitical security prism. The three are too small and too poor to effectively defend themselves from their large neighbour, which enjoys huge conventional and nuclear military superiority over the Baltic states. With national defence spending only beginning in the early 1990s, and at a time of severe budget restrictions on the purchase of expensive military hardware (and with a poor Soviet material inheritance), it was evident that the Baltic states were entirely reliant on external help in the event of military conflict. They had what was famously known as the CNN defence: 'The region's strategy in the event of a Russian attack was to hold out just long enough for a camera crew to arrive — and then pray for help from the West' (Geary, 2002).

As a result, the initial primary focus of Baltic foreign policy was membership of NATO with its ultimate hard security prize of the common defence shield provided by Article V of the Washington Treaty.[4] In the early 1990s it seemed an almost impossible dream, with Western foreign-policy-makers wishing to avoid antagonising the newly democratic Russia and fearing that the Baltic states, with the large Russophone communities in Estonia and Latvia as well as the heavily militarised Kaliningrad exclave neighbouring Lithuania, could prove potential flash-points. However, as soon as the last Russian troops had withdrawn from the region in 1994 the Baltic states began a concerted drive for NATO membership that was, astonishingly, achieved within a decade.

Initial contact was established through the Partnership for Peace programme, which gave Estonia, Latvia and Lithuania the opportunity to reconstruct their domestic security framework to allow for increased inter-Baltic and Baltic–Nordic military collaboration and ultimately help meet the demands of NATO membership. Just as Estonia surged ahead in negotiations with the EU, Lithuania was initially the best-positioned Baltic state in discussions with NATO. Indeed, there was some concern in both Estonia and Latvia that Lithuania's relationship with the Central European states, and particularly Poland, may lead it to join NATO ahead of Estonia and Latvia. However, Lithuania's hopes of early membership were dashed at the 1997 Madrid Summit when it was not included in the first wave of NATO eastern enlargement. All three Baltic states went on to sign the US–Baltic Charter in 1998 and then NATO Membership Action Plans in 1999 that gave a clear path to membership that culminated with accession to the alliance in 2004. This process occurred at a time of reasonably good NATO–Russia relations, and the Baltic states portrayed their mooted NATO membership as a bridge, rather than barrier, to enhanced Western relations with Russia.

The US-Baltic relationship was central to the Baltic states' drive for NATO accession, and US leadership remains the key motivation for Baltic NATO membership. When the Baltic states felt threatened by Russia in early 2014 they specifically looked to attract US 'boots on the ground'.[5] The relationship with the United States stretches back to well before 1991. Following the Soviet occupation of the Baltic states in 1940 the acting US secretary of state, Sumner Welles, issued a declaration condemning and refusing to recognise the Soviet Union's annexation of the region.[6] This marked a turning point in US attitudes towards the Baltic states. Prior to the annexation, the United States had been rather tepid in its support for Estonia, Latvia and Lithuania as independent states – Aldis Purs (2008, p. 20) described the relationship between Latvia and the United States as 'cordial but limited'. However, the United States became more enthusiastic in its support for the Baltic states when the Baltic region became a potential bulwark and political weapon against the Soviet Union. A month after the Sumner Welles declaration a presidential executive order safeguarded all Baltic financial assets in the United States. This meant that there was both a legal and financial basis for the continued presence of the Baltic diplomatic missions in Washington, DC, throughout the Cold War era. Not only did these missions serve as a constant reminder to other diplomats that the Baltic issue was unresolved, but they also served as a rallying point for the émigré communities and brought together the émigré and Baltic political leaders at various critical points between 1989 and 1991 (Auers, 2008).

After independence in 1991 the Baltic states looked to continue and enhance this bilateral relationship and specifically looked for US security guarantees. Visits to the Baltic states by the presidents Bill Clinton and George W. Bush were interpreted as signals that the Baltic states were allied to the West (as was a visit to Estonia in September 2014 made by president Barack Obama). However, it eventually became clear that the ultimate prize of security guarantees would only come through membership in NATO. Membership was not inevitable. In an influential mid-1990s *Foreign Affairs* journal article, Zbigniew Brzezinski (1995), a giant of the American foreign policy establishment, argued against expanding NATO to the Baltic states. He contended that Baltic membership would have a detrimental effect on attempts to establish democracy in Russia and aid nationalist accession to power with unpredictable results. Baltic membership was also fiercely opposed by Russia. As the then Latvian foreign minister, Valdis Birkavs, pointed out in 1997: 'NATO claims that its door is open, but the Russian dog is guarding the door and barking so as to keep us far away from it' (Ozolina, 2008, p. 84). Consistent Baltic political elite support for NATO accession, as well as sympathetic US presidents and State Department officials in the Bill Clinton and George W. Bush eras, as well as intense lobbying by Baltic diaspora groups in the United States, explain the Baltic states' eventual successful accession (Asmus, 2002).

From 2000 onwards the Baltic states started to restructure and increase their military spending in order to show their commitment to NATO integration. All three military forces were initially based on the Soviet model of mass conscription (and, similarly to the latter years of the Soviet Union, there was mass youth evasion of military service) led by a professional cadre. However, Latvia and Lithuania have switched over to professional forces, with only Estonia retaining the conscription model. The stated aim of defence spending was to eventually reach the NATO recommended defence budget of 2 per cent of GDP. However, neither Latvia nor Lithuania actually achieved this ambition (Latvian defence spending peaked at 1.9 per cent of GDP in 2006 while Lithuania managed a high of just 1.4 per cent in 2001). Moreover, in the case of Latvia at least, not all of this financing was spent on defence. For example, the defence budget was also used to build bridges, to finance state visits made by the Latvian president, to fund the Bank of Latvia's security and even sponsor sports clubs (*TVNET/De Facto*, 2014). Defence spending was then radically cut during the 2008–2010 economic downturn. The biggest cuts took place in Latvia. In 2008 defence spending was approximately 370 million euros, but this was reduced to 190 million euros by 2010, a cut of almost 50 per cent in real terms (Rostoks, 2013, p. 10).[7] In contrast, Estonia has met and regularly exceeded the 2 per cent recommendation since 2007 and President Ilves has regularly criticised Latvia and Lithuania for failing to even approach the 2 per cent recommendation (Raudseps, 2014). In early 2014, after Russian actions in Crimea, both Latvia and Lithuania committed to gradually raising defence spending to the 2 per cent level by 2020.

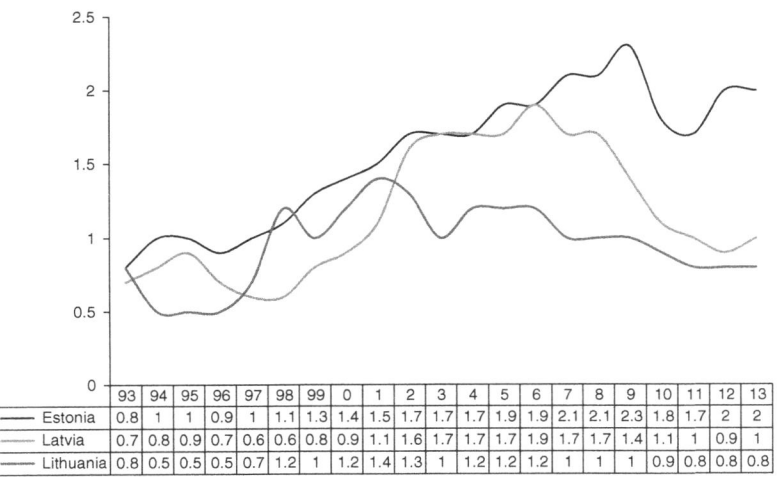

	93	94	95	96	97	98	99	0	1	2	3	4	5	6	7	8	9	10	11	12	13
Estonia	0.8	1	1	0.9	1	1.1	1.3	1.4	1.5	1.7	1.7	1.7	1.9	1.9	2.1	2.1	2.3	1.8	1.7	2	2
Latvia	0.7	0.8	0.9	0.7	0.6	0.6	0.8	0.9	1.1	1.6	1.7	1.7	1.7	1.9	1.7	1.7	1.4	1.1	1	0.9	1
Lithuania	0.8	0.5	0.5	0.5	0.7	1.2	1	1.2	1.4	1.3	1	1.2	1.2	1.2	1	1	1	0.9	0.8	0.8	0.8

Figure 6.1 Military spending (GDP percentage). Baltic states, 1993–2013

Source: Stockholm International Peace Research Institute (2014).

The Baltic states received immediate and tangible security benefits from NATO membership. The most visible aspect was the NATO Baltic air-policing mission that began patrolling the Baltic skies in 2004, providing a jet fighter capability that the Baltic states did not have and could not afford. The three Baltic states also focused hard on lobbying and cajoling within the organisation in order to achieve their core NATO aim of ensuring other states' commitment to collective defence and Article V in particular. They found that the best way to ensure this was to work together with their NATO partners in both international missions and to harmonise and coordinate their own work.

NATO has been the major driver of Baltic cooperation through such common actions as the Baltic Defence College (BALTDEFCOL) and the Baltic Battalion (BALTBAT). The Baltic Defence College was set up in the Estonian university town of Tartu and is equally owned, operated and financed by the three Baltic defence ministries, although much of the initial capital and administrative support was provided by the Danish and Norwegian military forces. BALTBAT is a combined infantry battalion based in Ādaži, Latvia, and is an integrated part of the NATO Response Force.[8] The Baltic states have also initiated joint procurement of military hardware which potentially both cuts costs and makes corruption in the procurement process far more difficult. The reason for this cooperation is clear: They have 'learned that they can succeed within NATO if they act as a group' (Rostoks, 2013, p. 4). Finland's and Sweden's lack of NATO membership has actually eased this process of cooperation by removing any Estonian temptation to cooperate with the Nordic states at the expense of marginalising its Baltic neighbours.

All three states have conducted joint army and navy exercises, harmonised training and cooperated at the decision-making level, with military chiefs of staff and defence ministers discussing common military and security issues on a quarterly basis. The Baltic states have also used NATO instruments to beef up and establish expertise in areas of domestic security that are of particular interest to them. Estonia set up a NATO centre of excellence in cyber security, while Lithuania has set up a similar institution focusing on energy security. Estonia first initiated the creation of a centre for cyber security in 2004 but accelerated its efforts after it was the victim of a cyber attack on government, security, media and financial institutions in 2007. It initiated the Cooperative Cyber Defence Centre of Excellence in Tallinn that has held a number of simulated cyber-attack exercises that have led to the beefing up of NATO members' cyber defences.[9] The Vilnius-based NATO Energy Security Centre of Excellence was set up in 2012, after many years of

Table 6.1   Size of military forces in the Baltic states, (2010)

	Estonia	Latvia	Lithuania
Active military forces	5,250	5,870	7,880
Reserve military forces	11,500	11,000	4,600

Source: Janes Sentinel, 2011.

rising energy insecurity among the three Baltic states.[10] Latvia eventually joined in and set up a centre of excellence in Riga that focuses on the public diplomacy and communication dimension of defence.

All three Baltic states have been active contributors to NATO-led military missions. Indeed, they have contributed at a disproportionately higher level than other European countries as part of a long-term strategy to portray themselves as 'net contributors' rather than 'net consumers' of security. Baltic security planners hope that this then makes them more likely to be supported by other NATO states if the need were to arise. As a result, the Baltic states sent troops to the Balkans in the 1990s as well as to Iraq and Afghanistan in the 2000s as a show of support to the United States (in the case of Iraq) and NATO, even though events in the Middle-East have little direct consequence for them. For example, as Table 6.1 indicates, the total size of the Estonian armed forces is just over 5,000 personnel. Yet 1,500 Estonians served in the Balkans and almost 500 in Iraq and another 2,000 in Afghanistan, taking the second highest number of per capita casualties of any participating NATO state (Coffey, 2013).[11]

Russia has only grudgingly accepted Baltic membership in NATO. Indeed, in a 2014 interview with a German magazine Lithuania's president, Dalia Grybauskaitė, speculated that Russia had recently approached Baltic politicians and offered to substantially lower the price of gas imports in exchange for a Baltic exit from NATO (*Voice of America*, 2014). Russia is discussed in more detail in section 6.4. NATO remains the central pillar of Baltic defence strategy. The United States' 'pivot to the East' under the Obama presidency, as well as Europe's weakness in developing its own security structures as the United States became increasingly uninterested in the region, caused much consternation in the Baltic foreign-policy-making community (Lucas and Mitchell, 2014). After the Crimea events in the first half of 2014 the three Baltic states lobbied hard for greater US involvement in the region and even took to encouraging other Baltic Sea Region states not in the NATO alliance – Finland and Sweden – to reconsider membership. In 2014 Estonian president, Toomas Hendrik Ilves, made a state visit to Finland and laid out the case for Finland joining the NATO alliance. He contrasted EU and NATO security guarantees:

> This is the fundamental difference between the EU solidarity Clause and NATO's collective security commitment in this regard. NATO's core task is to protect and defend its Allies. Since the beginning of the crisis in Ukraine, NATO has emphasised its commitment in this regard. Our defence plans will be reviewed and reinforced. This sends a clear message: NATO will protect every Ally and defend all of the Allied territory, whereas when it comes to the EU, there is no organisation, there are no contingency plans, there is no military command structure. (Ilves, 2014)

In testimony to the US Congress, Ed Lucas, an editor of the *Economist* magazine who has chronicled the development of the Baltic states since the late 1980s, outlined what needed to be done in order to protect the Baltic states in the future:

> That means American and other allies prepositioning military equipment and supplies in the Baltic states. It means NATO creating a standing defence plan – one which assumes that there is a real and present danger of attack. We need to put a major NATO base in Poland, to reassure that country that it can safely deploy its forces to the Baltics as reinforcements in the event of a crisis. We need to boost the NATO presence in the Baltic states with rotating visits by naval vessels, extended air-policing, and ground forces – initially on persistent rotation, but as soon as possible on permanent deployment. (Lucas, 2014, p. 4)

The Baltic states hope and expect that NATO will significantly increase its presence in the region and return to the Cold War era deterrence policies that many US observers believed had become a relic of history. The Baltic states undertook all the reforms that they were expected to undertake in order to join NATO. They proved to be good listeners and keen reformers, both because NATO accession was a high political priority and also because there were no other serious competing domestic-security agendas. They were not torn between East and West like Ukraine or Moldova. The necessary reforms were relatively straightforward because the Baltic military forces were rather small and malleable. Elites and publics alike were largely united in aiming for accession to the West.

These same background conditions explain the comparably swift accession to the EU in 2004.

6.2 The European Union

NATO accession shaped the restructuring of the Baltic states' defence forces and security policy. In contrast, EU accession has had a much broader impact. The demands of the *acquis communautaire* directly shaped the body of law in the Baltic states as well as the administrative and judicial institutions responsible for overseeing and implementing EU law. Participation in various EU bodies as well as the opening up of borders for the increased free movement of goods, services, persons and capital has led to an explicit Europeanisation – the impact of European integration on domestic governance, policy and society – of the Baltic states.[12]

Some of the Europeanisation process has been quite contentious. Many Baltic universities were reluctant to harmonise their teaching programmes and adopt the Bologna 3+2 model, both because four-year undergraduate studies were long-established and because cuts in the length of studies would also affect income.[13] The virulent, albeit ultimately unsuccessful, Latvian opposition to the closure of the last two domestic sugar producing companies is a rather more curious case. In the inter-war period Latvia had famously had three sugar refineries (at that time Latvians were encouraged to have three teaspoons of sugar – one for each refinery – with their coffee or tea), but by 2006 this had been cut to two. The EU's sugar policy at that time was aimed at restructuring and cutting the number of sugar producers in the EU. The owners of the two remaining Latvian sugar refineries were offered almost 50 million euros to effectively close down their businesses. This led to long-running public protests as well as a run on Latvian-produced sugar on the local market because Latvians claimed that only Latvian sugar had the required sweetness and consistency to make jam, marmalade and other preserves. However, these are little more than blips in the surprisingly fast and smooth journey from the Soviet Union to the core of the European Union.

The political foundations for eventual Baltic accession to the EU were laid between 1990 and 1993 as the Baltic states committed to doing whatever was necessary to integrate into the EU. This is also the period when EU member states' positions evolved to considering Estonia, Latvia and Lithuania as realistic potential member states. There is no single convincing theoretical paradigm that explains why the EU member states moved to a position of supporting the accession of three post-Soviet states. As Ainius Lasas (2008) points out, it is likely the result of a combination of some states' economic self-interest (liberal institutionalism), the EU's founding commitment and established practice of continued enlargement (constructivism) and member states' continued rhetorical commitments to the region that eventually forced them to honour these pledges (sociological approaches) as well as Lasas's own argument that the West's 'collective guilt' for the Baltic occupation led the EU to dangle the prospect of membership to the three post-Soviet states. In any case, the road to membership began immediately after independence, when the Baltic foreign ministers, acting together, used a meeting in Brussels to request Europe Agreements as the first step towards eventual EU membership and proceeded in a more or less linear fashion.

The EU initially supported the Baltic states through technical assistance designed to ease the political and economic transformation from authoritarianism to democracy and from planned economies to market. Funding targeted infrastructure improvements as well as raised the capacity of bureaucrats, teachers, professors and judges. The projects were initially quite general, but progressively became more specific and targeted as membership edged ever closer. The Baltic states signed Europe Agreements in 1995 (four years later than Hungary and Poland and two years after other post-communist Central European states), which were followed up by the Agenda 2000 reports on the potential new members states' readiness to join the EU. EU leverage was made possible by regular and detailed monitoring of events in the Baltic states. This initially took the form of regular reports that analysed the degree to which the Copenhagen Criteria were being met (and also offered clear benchmarks of what still needed to be achieved that provided crucial guidance for civil servants and policymakers alike). Later accession reports were shorter documents that indicated both short- and medium-term tasks. The Agenda 2000 reports, as well as the following annual progress reports, provided detailed road maps of what needed to be reformed and also where technical assistance should be directed. The reports were quite contentious in the Baltic states, as Latvia and Lithuania were initially categorised as second-wave countries while Estonia was included in the first-wave group that would immediately begin negotiations on accession in 1998, largely on the strength of its economic reforms. Latvia and Lithuania did not begin negotiations until 2000, although all three states completed the negotiations by December 2002 and joined together in 2004.

Once negotiations were completed, elites had to ensure that the publics would support and vote for membership in the referendums scheduled for 2003. While the government campaigns were officially neutral, there was a clear pro-EU bias in all three, with 'yes' campaigns benefitting from far higher financing and better organisation. The Estonian 'yes' campaign outspent the 'no' campaign by 16 million kroons to 1.5 million kroons (Mikkel, 2003, p. 7). The nature of campaigning was also broadly similar in all three states. The 'yes' campaigns focused on the geopolitical and security dimension as well as the Baltic states' destiny of 'returning' to Europe. The Lithuanian 'yes' campaign's slogan was 'Let's be European!' (Mazylis and Unikaite, 2003, p. 5). The 'no' campaigns, in contrast, focused on more practical issues – potential price inflation, the ability of Baltic farmers and enterprises to compete on the European market, potential immigration, the sale of land and businesses to foreigners, as well as playing on the word 'union' in order to conflate the European Union with the Soviet Union. The slogan for Latvian eurosceptics was 'European Union = Soviet Union' (Pridham, 2003, p. 9). The lack of balance in the debate led one observer to stress that the referendums conferred 'more formal than substantial legitimacy for the EU' (Pridham, 2007, p. 563).

After 2004 the Baltics experienced something of a post-accession lull. The decade-long ambition, after all, had been to join the EU (and NATO). Once this was achieved the Baltic states needed to reconsider *what* they wanted to achieve in the EU and *how* this could be accomplished. This called for a major paradigm shift from the Baltic states being fashioned by the European institutions to their becoming actors that shape the EU.

In broad terms, the Baltic states are supporters of increased European integration. This corresponds to the long-standing strategy of binding themselves into the international community. It is also because they have learned that the European Commission 'is the best friend of the small new members[;] ... [it] can ensure that small members get a fair deal and are not ridden over by the interests of large member states' (Kasekamp, 2013, p. 27). With little domestic fuss the Baltic states supported both the European Constitutional Treaty and then the Lisbon Treaty as well as later initiatives such as the Fiscal Compact law that limits governments' structural budget deficits.

The Baltic states also have three major areas of common interest. First, ensuring continued flows of structural, cohesion and agricultural funds. Second, supporting the EU's Eastern Neighbourhood Policy. Third, developing an EU-wide energy policy that would contribute to the energy security of the Baltic states and Europe more generally.

All three states are among the poorest in the EU and are thus net beneficiaries of EU funds (indeed, the expected inflow of EU money was one of the major selling points during the referendum campaigns in 2003). Common Agricultural Policy funds have become central to the functioning and development of farms and rural communities while structural and cohesion funds have been used to modernise the Baltic infrastructure. In the negotiations for the 2014–2020 EU financial perspective (the seven-year budget) the Baltic states successfully ensured that funding was put aside for two major regional projects: The construction of a Baltic liquefied natural gas (LNG) terminal and the long-planned *Rail Baltica* high speed train that will link the Baltic capitals.

The EU's Eastern Neighbourhood Policy has been another project of joint interest. The broad aim is to Europeanise the Baltic states' eastern neighbours and to transfer Estonia's, Latvia's and Lithuania's accrued knowledge and experience of economic transformation and democratisation to other post-communist states – Armenia, Azerbaijan, Belarus, Georgia, Moldova and Ukraine – and thus create geopolitical security buffers in the same way that the Nordic states did for the Baltic states. From 2009 Lithuania in particular pushed the Eastern Partnership for Belarus and Ukraine and then used its presidency of the European Union in the second half of 2013 to drive for the signing of an EU–Ukraine association agreement at the November Eastern Partnership summit in Vilnius. This initiative failed, triggering the Maidan protests in Kiev that led to the political chaos that engulfed Ukraine in 2014.

Energy security is another common Baltic concern that has found an increasingly central place on the EU agenda. Indeed, between 2004 and 2009 Latvia's EU commissioner, Andris Piebalgs, held the Energy portfolio. In a clear sign of the newly acquired importance of energy after the Russia–Ukraine stand-offs in 2005 and 2006, Piebalgs was moved sideways to the Development commissioner post in 2009, and a German took over the Energy post. Latvia and Lithuania are especially dependent on imports of electricity and fossil fuels from Russia. The EU has been crucial in diversifying energy supply in the region by co-financing and politically supporting two cross-frontier electricity grids (NordBalt, connecting the Baltic and Nordic regions via a link between Lithuania and Sweden and LitPol, which connects the Baltics with the Western European Electricity System via Poland) that will be operational by the end of 2015. As discussed above, the EU has also financially supported the construction of a regional LNG terminal, and EU financing will also be forthcoming to the new nuclear reactor if it is to be built in Visaginas,

Lithuania.[14] The Baltic states also earlier united to (unsuccessfully) oppose the Nordstream pipeline project creating an energy link between Germany and Russia that circumvents the Baltic states. Lithuania has also been prominent in pushing for an EU investigation into Gazprom's monopoly and pricing of gas in the EU and pushed heavily for the EU's Third Energy Package that unbundled domestic energy infrastructures in order to promote competition and weaken Gazprom's influence in the Baltic states' energy markets.

Membership in the EU has also led to a broader, and more difficult to quantify, Europeanisation of the region. This is especially visible in the capital cities, which are lined with European chain fashion retailers (*Zara*, *H&M* and *Mango* are particularly ubiquitous), restaurants, cafes and, increasingly, tourists.[15] Rural areas have also changed, as EU funding has redirected farmers from growing crops and raising livestock to running small hotels and conserving the countryside. After ten years in the EU, the Soros-founded Latvian think-tank Providus assessed that Latvia had become 'more secure and prosperous' (Providus, 2014). More specifically, the authors argued that EU accession had allowed Latvia to increase its diplomatic reach and the share of exports in the economy and increase labour productivity while crime has fallen dramatically and life expectancy has increased. The contrast between the Baltic states and their former Soviet republic neighbours has never been greater. Some strong anti-European public feelings remain. Fringe political parties have campaigned on anti-EU feelings, drawing attention to sharply differing levels of direct payments to Baltic farmers and, in the case of Estonia, presenting the EU as an over-regulator of the economy. However, these are marginal political groupings. The Baltic states have fashioned themselves into EU member states that are in the Schengen area, have adopted the euro and are now very much a part of 'core Europe'.

6.3   Regional cooperation

The third element of the Baltic states' Westernising strategy has been regional integration with Northern Europe. The Baltic states' northern neighbours were active investors and assistance-givers in the 1990s having started their support for the Baltic states in 1990, following free and fair elections to the Baltic SSR Supreme Councils (Archer, 1999). At the same time, however, Sweden and Finland were careful to balance their relationship with Soviet leader Gorbachev with their support for the Baltic states, and were less openly gung-ho, pro-Baltic than Iceland and Denmark. Indeed, in August 1991 the latter were the first states to recognise Baltic independence. Sweden and Denmark have been particularly active actors in all three states while, for geographic and cultural reasons, Finland focused its actions on Estonia. The Finnish military has trained Estonian officers and non-commissioned officers, funded military advisors to the Estonian military and sold arms at favourable rates (Archer, 1999, p. 56).

Initially the Baltic states had few links with the Nordic region, and the early focus was intra-Baltic cooperation. This is despite the fact that until the independence movements of the 1980s, there were few direct contacts between the Baltic states. Indeed, in the Soviet era there were only two direct flights a week between the Baltic capitals (Lieven, 1994, p. 37). The Nordic states assumed greater salience only after independence was achieved in August 1991, and the Baltic states realised that the Nordic states were significant financial supporters and could aid accession into the EU. Later, after 2004, the Baltic states have cooperated with the Nordic states (as the NB6) in pushing for common initiatives, such as the creation of the Baltic Sea Region as the EU's first 'macro region'.

There are parallels between the patterns of Baltic cooperation in both the inter-war and post-Soviet independence eras. The early years in the fights for independence were marked by close cooperation between the Baltic independence movements and a lively intellectual debate on the extent of Baltic cooperation. Between 1918 and 1920, military and political leaders met regularly to discuss tactics for achieving independence. The Estonian delegation at the 1918 Paris Peace Conference had advocated the formation of a Baltic League of eight separate nations: the three Baltic States plus Poland, Finland, Denmark, Sweden and Norway (Kaslas, 1976). The concept of the Baltic states being limited to just Latvia, Lithuania and Estonia was also not yet established at this time as Poland and Finland were often included in their number. Indeed, at the Bulduri Conference from 6 August to 6 September 1920, Latvian, Estonian, Lithuanian, Finnish and Polish delegates agreed on the development of a common monetary and economic union, a Baltic Economic Council and a defensive military accord as well as a non-aggression pact. However, the treaty remained unsigned largely because of the Polish seizure of Vilnius as well as the on-going Polish–Soviet war. A debate on future models of Baltic cooperation was particularly lively among Baltic intellectuals at that time. In 1917 Jaan Tõnisson trumpeted a Nordic–Baltic federation, declaring that it would 'have, as a union of thirty million people, a certain amount of influence during the negotiations at the Peace Conference' (Hiden and Salmon, 1991, p. 63). The Lithuanian-French philosopher Oscar Vladislav de Lubicz-Milosz (1919) argued for a narrower Baltic Union of all three states based on defence and foreign policy considerations. In 1921 Stasys Šalkauskis (1921, quoted in Kaslas, 1976, p. 232) argued for an even narrower cooperation:

> An alliance between Lithuania and Latvia would unite the entire Latvian-Lithuanian stock. ... [Latvia's] interests are identical to those of Lithuania: the union of these two sister nations, uncomplicated by any acute rivalry between them, would serve to increase the importance and strength of each.

There are modern counterparts to this. The high point of modern Baltic cooperation was reached in the late 1980s as the Baltic states wrestled with the Soviet Union for independence. Although the three countries were not entirely unified in their independence tactics – Vytautas Žalys (1996) recounts that a popular Lithuanian joke in this era was that the Estonians would fight for their independence to the last Lithuanian – there was a popular sense of unity of purpose, culminating in the Baltic Way protesting the Molotov–Ribbentrop pact, a unity that had probably never existed before and has not been repeated since. Nevertheless, there was still an undercurrent of mutual distrust. By the time that independence arrived a name was even mooted for a possible confederation of the Baltic states – one that was floated, as seventy years earlier, in Lithuania – Estlalia. However, as in the inter-war era, the strains of nation- and institution-building, as well as the economic crises of the early 1990s, led to Baltic leaders becoming more insular after independence was achieved in August 1991.

While the creation of a Baltic federation has proved to be no more than a pipe dream, there were attempts to institutionalise Baltic cooperation in both eras. However, the 1920s Bulduri conference failed to create a supranational Baltic body, and the Baltic states slipped into an era of bilateral cooperation until the Baltic Entente of 1934. Indeed, there were no Baltic political conferences from 1925 to 1934, and even the Baltic Entente failed to institutionalise cooperation among Baltic foreign ministers, despite envisaging bi-annual meetings of foreign ministers and coordination of Baltic foreign policies. Attempts in the 1990s were far more successful.

Indeed, the 1990s saw the creation of a number of pan-Baltic institutions. First, the Baltic Council was set up on 12 May 1990, at a meeting in which the Baltic Entente of 1934 was also renewed. The aim of the Baltic Council was to ensure regular meetings of both leading Baltic politicians and senior officials. The Baltic Assembly was formed in November 1991 and was composed of 20 representatives from each Baltic parliament. The Baltic Free Trade Agreement was signed in 1993. June 1994 saw the creation of the Baltic Council of Ministers, which was to coordinate, trilaterally, political, economic and cultural policies with the heads of state and to meet every six months. However, these institutions were symbolic and lacking any substantive powers. Indeed, Estonia unilaterally cut its funding for the Baltic Assembly in late 2005. These institutions have been neglected largely because, in the post–Cold War world, the Baltic states focused on accession to existing international organisations (such as NATO, the EU, the Council of Baltic Sea States) rather than the creation of new regional organisations and then, after accession, concentrated their efforts on being heard within these broader organisations (Lehti, 1999).

Thus there has been little serious Baltic political cooperation outside of defence. Rather, the Baltic states have been operating independently, even on issues where there has been a true Baltic interest. In September 1992 Lithuania sought a separate agreement on Russian troop withdrawal with the Russian government and, in 1994, Lithuania was the first to apply for NATO membership. Moreover, the structure of the negotiations and process to enlarge the EU created a race where there was little to be gained by mutual cooperation. To the concern of Latvia and Lithuania, but the delight of Estonia, only the latter was included in 1999 in the first round of negotiations on EU accession. Within the EU the three have also bickered about where to locate the EU-supported LNG terminal and funding mechanisms for *Rail Baltica*. There has even been occasional discord in relations with Russia. In 2005 the Latvian president unilaterally decided to attend the 60-year anniversary celebrations of the end of the Second World War in Europe in Moscow, while the Lithuanian and Estonian presidents stayed away.

Leaders of the Baltic states often feel that their individual identity is submerged beneath a common Baltic one to an extent far greater than that suffered by individual Nordic or Benelux states. After a 2014 visit of the Baltic presidents to the White House, where the US president had a joint meeting with all three, the *Financial Times* quoted an EU ambassador in Washington, DC, as stating that 'they find it frustrating and ask: "Can't we exist in our own right?"' (Milne, 2014).

It is not Baltic cooperation that most leaders oppose. Rather, it is the sense of a Baltic *identity* that pools the three states together. Estonia's president, Toomas Hendrik Ilves, has been the sharpest opponent of this idea.[16] In a landmark speech when Estonian foreign minister in 1999, he emphasised that:

Most if not all people outside Estonia talk about something called "The Baltics". This is an interesting concept, since what the three Baltic States have in common almost completely derives from shared unhappy experiences imposed upon us from outside: occupations, deportations, annexation, sovietisation, collectivisation, russification. What these countries do not share is a common identity. ... I think it is time to do away with poorly fitting, externally imposed categories. It is time that we recognise that we are dealing with three very different countries in the Baltic area, with completely different affinities. There is no Baltic identity with a common culture, language group, religious tradition. For almost four years now, Lithuania has been correctly pointing out that it is a Central European country. Its Catholicism, architecture, history all link it to Poland and the other Visegrad countries. Estonia was and as I will try to point out is, if anything, a member of [the Nordic States]. (Ilves, 1999)

Indeed, Estonia's core Nordic identity has been traced back to the beginnings of the awakening era (Kuldkepp, 2013). Lithuania, as Ilves implied in the speech, is pulled towards Central Europe: In an annual state of the country address the Lithuanian president, Algirdas Brazauskas, (1998) explained:

Lithuania is part of several regions; our historical, religious, cultural and political experience puts us in a somewhat different position from the other two Baltic States, securing for us a natural place among countries of Central Europe. The geopolitical status of Lithuania, as a Central European nation.

It is certainly true that historically the Baltic states have been more disunited that united. As a result, cooperation between the Baltic states has been rather halting. This rhetoric has often left Latvia quite isolated from its Baltic neighbours. However, these weak links between the Baltic states are not a modern feature. Rather, it is a continuation of a long-established pattern of Baltic inter-state relations.

In many ways, the Baltic states have been competing – for investment and external security – rather than cooperating, since independence in 1991. However, accession to the EU may well have led to a greater impetus in Baltic cooperation. After all, there is a history of cooperation between states in the EU. Indeed, Helen Wallace (2000, p. 175) wrote that relationships between European countries have historically been 'of often vigorous regional groupings and intense special partnerships between neighbours'. Regional alliances are particularly important in the Council of the European Union and the European Council, the primary inter-governmental organisations of the EU system. States forge alliances to pursue both narrow national interests (for example in the formation of the seven-year financial perspective), and broader regional ones (the Barcelona process of dialogue with the North African states was largely driven by the southern European member states).

The Benelux and Nordic blocs present particularly relevant, and instructive, models of cooperation. Their success is typically explained by three core commonalities. First, all the countries involved are, on a European scale, a similar size (except Luxembourg, which is exceptionally small). Political cooperation allows them to 'punch above their weight' in the EU. Second, the countries in the Benelux and Nordic groups share a similar modern history that acts as a further motivator for cooperation. Third, they share comparable social models and general levels of economic development, which allows for relative ease of policy coordination. The Baltic states share all three of these features – they are small, with a shared recent history, similar social model and common level of economic development. Thus, the basic prerequisites for Baltic cooperation are in place, although by these measures prospects for deeper cooperation with the Nordic states are not so great.

Nevertheless, the three Baltic states have been far more committed to forging relations with their northern neighbours than with each other. Nordic commitment to the region was conditioned by a number of factors. First, engagement with the Baltic states potentially created a *cordon sanitaire* between the Nordic region and Russia. Not only would this physically put greater distance between the two, but targeted assistance to the Baltic states would allow organised crime, human trafficking and other concerns to be dealt with pre-emptively before they landed on Nordic shores. It would also help to create a secure, democratic neighbourhood and increase the size of the regional economic market and eventually provide business opportunities for Nordic companies (and a glance at the contemporary dominance of Nordic banks and other financial institutions in the Baltic states indicates that these opportunities have been seized upon), as well as a potential springboard into the larger Russian market.

The Nordics supported the Baltic states through a combination of regional financial instruments such as the Baltic Investment Programmes (BIPs) – institutions such as the Nordic Investment Bank and the Nordic Project Fund – as well as bilateral funding. Early forms of cooperation between the Baltic states and the Nordic states typically took the form of technical assistance to the public sector – raising the capacity of the civil service and judiciary as well as higher and further education. The Baltic states themselves were extremely open and positively oriented towards further regional integration with the Nordic states. This is unsurprising, as the Nordic states were often presented as the model of everything that the Baltic states aspired to be (prosperous, safe and peaceful). As well as bilateral assistance, myriad political links have been created across the Baltic Sea, ranging from the Council of the Baltic Sea States (a forum for regional inter-governmental cooperation), the Baltic Sea States Subregional Cooperation, the Baltic Sea Parliamentary Conference and so on. Regional initiatives, such as the Northern Dimension and most recently the creation of a Baltic Sea State 'macro-region' within the EU, have also politically bound the Nordic states ever closer to the Baltic nations. Heavy Nordic investment in the Baltic states, particularly in the finance sector, has increasingly intertwined the economic fortunes of the region. Infrastructure links, such as the *NordBalt*, *Estlink* and *Estlink2* electricity grids have connected the Baltic states with the *Nordpool* North European electric energy market.

The relationship between the Baltic and the Nordic states changed after the double accession of 2004. The balance of power in the BSR moved fractionally eastwards. The Balts, while smaller and poorer, are now more politically equal to the Nordic states. A Nordic Baltic Six (NB6) has gradually emerged as a political bloc with meetings typically held before major summits to coordinate positions. There are also occasional NB8 meetings that include Iceland and Norway, the non-EU Nordic states. However, economic disparities remain both deep and meaningful and broader NB cooperation has yet to replace the intensity of Nordic cooperation. An integrated Northern European bloc comparable to Benelux or existing Nordic cooperation is also yet to emerge, although the increasing frequency with which the media now refers to the Baltic states as 'North European' indicates that this is a process that is occurring. However, research indicates that the primary identity framework for citizens in the Baltic states remains Baltic rather than Nordic, European or something else (Jurkynas, 2007). Perhaps the key thing here is momentum. The Baltic states are gradually shifting north and west, away from Russia, a process that Russia's annexation of Crimea has hastened.

6.4   Cat and mice: Russia and the Baltic states

Relations between the Baltic states and Russia have been fraught throughout the post-1991 era. The loss of hegemony in the Baltic region that was long dominated by Russia (and the Soviet Union) clearly irritated many leading political figures in both the Yeltsin and Putin/ Medvedev regimes. Economic, political and even military tensions have been the norm rather than the exception. As a result:

> The most acute foreign and security policy challenge facing all three Baltic states is the management of their relations with Russia. It is clear that Baltic security will always be in jeopardy as long as Russia is hostile and authoritarian. (Bajarnas, 1995, p. 13)

Almost two decades later, the Russian invasions of Georgia and Crimea and support for insurgents in eastern Ukraine underlined the continued salience of this observation.

The three Baltic states and Russia are neighbours but not friends. While US presidents have made several state and working visits to the Baltic region, Russia's three post-communist presidents have never set foot on independent Baltic soil. Although invitations have been made (and then retracted in light of Russian military incursions into Georgia and then Ukraine), the details have repeatedly proved rather complicated. For example, an established part of every state visit to Latvia is a visit to the Occupation Museum, an effectively grim building in the heart of Riga that recounts Latvia's experience of multiple occupations during the Second World War. While German leaders have visited the museum, it is utterly unimaginable that any Russian leader, representing a state that does not concede that the Baltic states were occupied, would agree to such a visit. Moreover, a Russian president would expect to visit the Victory Monument in Riga, where Russian-speakers celebrate the trium-phant end of the Second World War on 9 May. However, this represents the beginning of Latvia's half-century of Soviet occupation and is a place where Latvian leaders do not lay down flowers. In fact, on the Russian side there is little appetite for a presidential visit to a Baltic state, as this would simply add legitimacy to the Baltic states' existence.

The truth is that there is no love lost on either side. Alongside the United States, the Baltic states have long been regarded as Russia's major enemies.[17] Indeed, the Bronze Solder dispute discussed in Chapter 4 led to a nine-day siege of the Estonian embassy in Moscow that saw a blockade that prevented people leaving or entering and led to physical assaults on the ambassador (who was attacked with pepper-spray by *Nashi* activists) and the embassy building – assaults that were largely tolerated by the Russian authorities (Vark, 2008).

The preconditions for the Russian–Lithuanian relationship initially seemed more promising. Lithuania had a small Russophone community, and it was likely that Lithuania's relationship with Poland would prove more problematic than that with Russia. Both sides had a different view of key historical moments. While the Polish-Lithuanian Commonwealth was the high point of Polish history, Lithuanians remember it as a time when the titular elite and Lithuanian culture was polonised. Deputies representing the Polish minority in Lithuania had abstained from the vote on Lithuanian independence in 1990. Poland was initially seen as a potential threat to the territorial integrity of Lithuania, with latent claims on the Vilnius region. However, Lithuanian–Polish relations quickly normalised in the early 1990s as both set out to join the EU and NATO, ambitions that meant any mainstream nationalist impulses were quickly cast aside.

Lithuanian–Russian relations deteriorated at the same time as the troops withdrew from Lithuania in 1993. The reason for increased tension was Kaliningrad, Russia's smallest region (*oblast*), which was becoming even more militarised at that time, as Russian troops were relocated to the exclave from Germany and then on to the Russian mainland. At the same time, Russian military convoys were also crossing Lithuania from east to west delivering military supplies to Kaliningrad. This 15,100 square kilometre region was long a part of German-speaking East Prussia, but was seized by the Soviet Union at the 1945 Potsdam Conference. In the Soviet era, Kaliningrad was a closed militarised zone and it still contains substantial Russian military forces such as the Russian navy's Baltic fleet. Thus after the troops were withdrawn the position was that 'Lithuania, although free from the Russian troops, was completely encircled by them' (Vitkus, 2006, p. 26). The issue of military transit has continued to dog Lithuania's relations with Russia, particularly as Lithuania prepared to join the EU and had to settle the issue as a precondition for entry. Transit regulations, such as the transfer of toxic fuels from Kaliningrad to mainland Russia, are a frequent form of friction between Lithuania and Russia, despite the pre-EU accession agreement that allowed Russians to transit Lithuania from mainland Russia to the exclave with Facilitated Travel Documents rather than the normal visas that Russians require to enter the EU.

As this case indicates, Baltic–Russian relations often resemble a game of cat and mouse. The Baltic states attempt to pull away from Russia's sphere of influence, but Russia hauls them back in. The double accessions of 2004 did not break the pattern, as Russian soft and hard power has continued to hold sway over the Baltic states. A few short months in late 1991 were probably the high point of the Baltic–Russian relationship. As soon as discussions began to address the tricky issue of troop withdrawal, relations became increasingly fraught. All three Baltic states had been extremely militarised during the Soviet era. Estonia alone had 500 military installations with 132,000 Soviet troops as well as the unique Paldiski strategic nuclear submarine training centre, the only one of its kind in the Soviet Union (Haab, 1995, p. 39).

The Baltic position was that troops could and should be withdrawn fast. Vytautas Landsbergis was quoted as saying that the Soviet Union had 'introduced its army into Lithuania in two days; it could withdraw it equally fast if it wished!' (Mole, 2012, p. 121). The troops were first withdrawn from Lithuania by the end of August 1992 (although no treaty or timetable between the two sides had been signed). This largely reflected Lithuania's tolerance towards its (small) Russophone community. In contrast, the negotiations with Estonia and Latvia were far trickier precisely because of the size of their Russophone communities. Indeed, concerns over Estonian and Latvian treatment of their minorities led President Boris Yeltsin to suspend the continued withdrawal of Russian troops in 1992 and attempt to tie future withdrawals to the fate of the Russophone minorities. President Yelstin also waved the energy card, briefly suspending energy shipments to the three states.

Eventually, however, troops were withdrawn. This came as a result of both external and internal influences. Western diplomats applied pressure on Russia to withdraw its troops. Indeed, the West aided the withdrawal by helping to fund much-needed housing for returning Russian officers and their families. By the mid-1990s Russia was also dealing with a secessionist threat in the Caucasus, which entailed the need for troops to be transferred to this region. Finally, the Russian economy was in free-fall at this time, and the financial burden of maintaining troops in the Baltic, particularly in light of the new Baltic currencies that were in place by then, was quite significant. All this combined to see Russian troops withdrawn from Estonia and Latvia by 1994. Russian military pensioners retained residency permits and social rights in Estonia and Latvia. Latvia also had to agree to a 4-year lease on the Skrunda radar base and give Russia 18 months to dismantle the base. Latvian agreement required intense US lobbying, including the wining and dining of Latvian politicians in Washington, DC, by the Clinton administration.

Thus initial relations between the Baltic states and Russia were dominated by the issue of Soviet/Russian troops on the ground as an immediate legacy of the Soviet era. Then Russia opposed Baltic accession to NATO and attempted to derail Baltic membership through the use of both carrots and sticks. In September 1997, at a conference in Vilnius entitled 'Co-Existence of Nations and Good Neighborly Relations: A Guarantee of Security and Stability in Europe', Viktor Chernomyrdin, the Russian prime minister, offered the Lithuanian government (and later the Estonian and Latvian governments) security guarantees in order to keep them out of NATO (and thus keep them within the Russian sphere of influence). The most frequently used stick that Russia has used is the framing of Estonia's and especially Latvia's ethnic relations as the abuse of Russophone human rights by the titular majorities. In 1997 Alexander Dzasokhov (a member of the Russian Duma and part of the delegation to the Council of Europe's Parliamentary Assembly), stated that Estonia was the number-one oppressor of the Russian-speaking population in the world. And Latvia was number two.

A central problem is the sharply differing view of history (discussed in more depth in Chapter 4), which has led to incompatible 'discursive frameworks' that make negotiations between the two sides all but impossible (Mole, 2012, p. 120). Modern Russian identity is built on a triumphant narrative of Soviet victory over fascism in the Second World War. Indeed, Russia has few other events to draw upon for its great-nation rhetoric. The Russian economy has long performed less impressively than the West and, aside from the Second World War, neither Russia nor the Soviet Union has any great military achievements. Nordic-style social achievements are also few. As a result, the Second World War has been over-emphasised in the Russian identity and any attempts to tarnish this image have been virulently rebuffed by Russian leaders.

Attempts to find common ground on this issue have been unproductive. The Latvian–Russian Committee of Historians first met in Moscow in November 2011, but has made very little progress in finding a common interpretation of history. Sharply contrasting narratives mean that it is even quite difficult for the two sides to talk with each other. There are very few direct meetings between Russia and Estonia, although meetings with Latvian and Lithuanian officials are more frequent. Bilateral visits are rare, with meetings typically taking place on the fringes of other meetings, such as the Council of the Baltic Sea States (of which Russia is a member). Latvia's president, Valdis Zatlers, made a state visit to Russia in December 2010, while Lithuania's president and prime minister both met with then Prime Minister Putin in 2010.

Agreeing on borders has proved equally contentious. The Estonia–Russia border treaty was only signed by the Russian and Estonian foreign ministers in February 2014, while Latvia signed a treaty in 2007. The Lithuanian–Polish border treaty was also similarly delayed by a 1993 Polish amendment to the treaty that referenced Polish 'aggression' against Lithuania in 1920. However, this was amended just as Lithuania's relationship with Russia began to deteriorate from 1993 onwards. Russia had hoped to derail EU and NATO accession by holding out on signing border treaties with Estonia and Latvia. Both treaties faced internal Baltic political opposition. The Estonian and Russian foreign ministers had first signed a border treaty in 2005. However, the Estonian parliament ratified it with a preamble making reference to the Tartu peace treaty of 1920. This prompted the Russian side to reject the deal. In the same way, in 2005 the Latvian parliament had also added an explanatory annex referencing the Treaty of Riga. The Russian side also rejected this treaty. In 2007 the Latvian government reopened negotiations and removed the explanatory annex from the treaty. The radical-right populist All for Latvia! (*Visu Latvijai!*, VL!) party, which at that time had not yet been elected to the Latvian parliament, opposed the signing of the treaty, and at one point in February 2007 15 activists ripped off their shirts in -17c temperatures and stood outside the parliament for 40 minutes protesting the concession of Latvian territory to Russia.

A core challenge to the Baltic states has been power asymmetry with Russia. Estonia, Latvia and Lithuania addressed this issue in the only realistic way that they could, grouping together with other, larger, states in the EU and NATO since 2004, and then attempting to negotiate Baltic–Russian relations through these institutions. This allows the Baltic states to criticise the Russian regime and attempt to nudge it towards democracy, which is in the Baltic interest, but without appearing too censorious. One example is the Baltic states' attitude towards an EU–Russia visa-free regime. The foreign ministries of all three states have used the issue as an opportunity to press for change in Russia, but always emphasising that this is an EU rather than a national position. Latvia's then foreign minister Ģirts Valdis Kristovskis (who served in office from 2010–2011) stated:

> We support the visa-free regime with Russia as much as the whole European Union[,]...but it is a long-term issue[;]...it is a matter of Russia's modernisation, values, economic cooperation, attitude towards the neighbouring countries'. (Bukovskis, 2012, p. 83)

In the same way Estonia's foreign minister, Urmas Paet, talking about this issue, argued:

> Like all other countries, Russia must first demonstrate it respects the principles of democracy and complies with the technical requirements.

> This is the position of both Estonia and the European Commission, as stated by the President of the Commission, Jose Manuel Barroso'. (Lobjakas, 2012, p. 39)

However, this attempt to take the heat out of the relationship has been only partially successful.

There is no doubt that Russia is the key international actor in the post-Soviet space. Until very recently, the governments and policymakers of the Baltic states were not particularly concerned about Russia as a military threat (Corum, 2013, p. 18). Rather, there were concerns about Russian soft power: Its economic pull, particularly in the energy sphere, as well as information campaigns waged through print and electronic media, which would attempt to relocate the Baltic states back into direct Russian influence. Russia's soft power – understood here as 'the ability to get what you want through attraction rather than coercion or payment' (Nye, 2004, p. x) – initiatives in the Baltic region have been particularly expansive on three key dimensions: economic, cultural and political.

Russia's economic influence has rapidly expanded in the region, as Russian businesses have snapped up a number of major Baltic enterprises. For example, in 2000 Russia invested 27.2 million euro in FDI in Lithuania. Five years later this had grown to 704.2 million euro and then 843.3 million by 2010 (Zdanavicius and Volovoj, 2012, p. 211). A similar pattern of increased investment can be seen in Estonia and Latvia. Russia is the fifth biggest source of Lithuanian FDI. However, as is the case in the other Baltic states, Russia's investments may actually be much larger due to the use of offshore vehicles that blur an investments country of origin. These investments have caused consternation in the Baltic capitals because of the close links between Russian business and the Russian state. In other words, Russian businesses are often used as proxies for the illicit influence of the Russian government.

The economic influence is perhaps most visible in the energy sector, where the Russian state-owned Gazprom has had a controlling share in all three national Baltic gas companies (*Eesti Gas, Latvijas Gāze* and *Lietuvos Dujos*). This gives Russia significant energy leverage over the Baltic states, whose energy networks had become fully integrated with Soviet infrastructure over the course of the 50-year occupation, and this was something that would inevitably take plenty of time, lots of money and political commitment to change. Nevertheless, the Baltic states have increasingly focused on decreasing their energy dependence on Russia. Estonia's shale-oil mining means that it only imports some 20 per cent of its energy needs from Russia (shale oil produces over 90 per cent of

Estonia's electricity). However, Estonia's reliance on shale oil is in decline as it seeks to reduce high levels of noxious emissions. As a result, Estonia has planned a joint LNG project terminal with Finland in addition to the 2007 Estlink project that hooked up Estonia's electricity network with Finland. Latvia's Inčukalns facility has the third-largest natural gas storage facilities in Europe, storing gas for all three Baltic states (and the Pskov region in Russia). Before the closure of the Chernobyl-style Ignalina nuclear reactor in 2009, Lithuania had produced much of its own energy needs, even exporting electricity to Latvia. After 2009, however, its energy reliance on Russia reached the same kind of high levels as Latvia's. Lithuania has been most keen to rectify this situation, planning the much-delayed new nuclear facility at Visaginas as well as a new floating LNG terminal (named 'Independence') opened at the end of 2014. Lithuania also opened an oil terminal in Butinge in 1999. The *Nordbalt* project links Lithuania's and Latvia's electricity networks to Sweden.

These numerous energy projects were prompted by fears that Russia would use energy as a political tool against the Baltic states. In her 2013 State of the Union address, Lithuania president, Dalia Grybauskaitė (2013), emphasised that 'energy is the most dangerous geopolitical instrument used to belittle our economic, social and even political independence.' Between 1998 and 2000 *Transneft*, the Russian-owned oil company, cut off oil supplies to Lithuania nine times in an attempt to prevent the sale of Lithuanian oil transit infrastructure to a US company. In the same way, the Russian–Latvian oil pipeline was closed down in 2003 (and is yet to reopen) after the Latvian government rejected the sale of the *Ventspils Nafta* oil business to the same Russian *Transneft* company. Oil supplies to Lithuania's *Mažeikių Nafta* were similarly cut in 2006.

Russia also expanded cultural links across the Baltic states. Naturally, the large Russophone communities as well as a certain level of Soviet nostalgia created a willing audience for Russian culture in the region. Latvia has been particularly susceptible to Russian cultural influence. The Latvian beach resort of Jūrmala has hosted the annual New Wave (*Jaunais Vilnis*) music festival, a bizarre talent show that also showcases popular geriatric Russian singing stars, since the late 1990s. It also brings Russia's economic elite to the region and allows them to mingle with Latvia's economic and political elite. Latvian presidents have been known to attend the concerts. Supporters say that it brings in large amounts of revenue to Riga and Jūrmala, while critics point out that it seems to drag Latvia back into the Russian orbit. In late 2014 organisers announced that the festival would no longer be hosted in Latvia. Similarly, in 2004 the Moscow House was opened in the centre of Riga (Latvia's large Russophone community makes it most open to Russian cultural influence), and it has become a centre of Russian culture in the region. The Russian state also reacted to the declining influence of the Russian language in the Baltic states (young people have preferred to learn English) by setting up Russian language centres in all three states.

The creation of the Kontinental [sic] Hockey League (KHL) to include a Latvian team has been a particularly effective use of Russian soft power in the region. The Russian state has a direct interest in the league. As Stanislav Budnitsky (2013) has pointed out:

> Framing the KHL's expansion in terms of national foreign policy and interests is not a conspiracy theory. Unlike its North American counterpart, the Russian league's leadership is part and parcel of the country's powers that be. KHL Commissioner Alexander Medvedev is a Deputy Chairman of Gazprom's Management Committee and Director General of Gazprom Export. The Russian Federation owns more than fifty percent of Gazprom, the world's largest extractor of natural gas. Gazprom's current Chairman of the Board of Directors, Viktor Zubkov, was Russia's Prime Minister between 2007–2008. Meanwhile, Russia's current Prime Minister, Dmitry Medvedev, held Gazprom's Chairman post in 2000–2001 and 2002–2008. The Head of the KHL's Board of Trustees, Sergey Naryshkin, is also the Chairman of the State Duma.

The Latvian team in the KHL is named Dinamo Riga after a similarly named ice-hockey team from the Soviet era. The team has attracted huge public support, regularly selling out games at the Arena Riga and with a large television following. Even as the Latvian government discussed sanctions on Russia, and Latvians protested the Crimean annexation outside the Russian embassy in Riga, Dinamo Riga continued to play on in the KHL.

Russian media, especially government-owned media, are widely available across the Baltic states. Russian television channels are rebroadcast into Latvia. Russian programmes are very popular among the Russophone communities in the three Baltic states as well as with the older generation of Balts who are fluent in Russian but weaker in the West European languages (and thus find it difficult to watch *Deutche Welle* or BBC News). Russia also financially supports and coordinates the activities of pro-Russia NGOs across the Baltic states. Much of this work is coordinated by the *Russkij Mir Foundation* (Russian World), which was set up in 2007 to coordinate the work of pro-Russian NGOs around the world. However, a series of articles by the *Re:Baltica* (2012) investigative journalism centre identified a significant lack of transparency in the foundation's activities in the Baltic states (particularly in terms of which organisations received funding and the extent of that funding). There is a similar lack of clarity in the ownership of the First Baltic Channel (PBK), the most-watched Russian language television network in the Baltic states.

The Baltic states have not been unified in how to tackle Russian soft power. In April 2014 Latvia and Lithuania introduced temporary bans on *Rossiya RTR*, a Russian public television channel accused by the Latvian security police of dangerously unbalanced reporting of events in Ukraine and Crimea. The previous month Lithuania also suspended broadcasts from Russia's *NTV Mir* for similar reasons (and in 2013 it also suspended broadcasts of PBK for three months). Estonia, however, has refused to adopt any such ban. Its president, Toomas Hendrik Ilves, argued that freedom of speech is one of Estonia's core values, and Russian media cannot be banned in the state (Milne, 2014). All three states have initiated discussions on creating a common Russian–language, pan-Baltic television channel, although Estonia favours an EU-funded Europewide Russian language channel. However, the Baltic states have made it clear that while they will attempt to reduce Russia's cultural and political influence, they will not take a hard line against Russian economic investments in the region.

Russia has also been accused of organising Internet attacks on the Baltic states. Estonia was subjected to a series of cyber attacks, beginning in April 2007, that swamped the websites of banks, news outlets, government ministries and parliament. The pro-Putin youth group in Russia, *Nashi*, took credit for the attacks, which coincided with a dispute between Tallinn and Moscow over the relocation of the Soviet-era Bronze Soldier of Tallinn grave marker. Lithuania experienced a similar cyber attack in 2008, just three days after the legislature passed a new law banning the use of Soviet-era symbols (some of the vandalised websites had hammer-and-sickle symbols graffiti scattered over them) and Internet media outlets in Lithuania were similarly attacked in 2013.

Finally, the Kremlin has also been accused of holding direct influence over the Baltic political systems via the parties that support Russia's interests, such as Harmony Centre (*Saskaņas Centrs*) in Latvia and the Centre Party (*Eesti Keskerakond*) in Estonia, both of which are partnered with Vladimir Putin's ruling United Russia (*Yedinaya Rossiya*) party. In 2003 Viktor Uspaskich founded the Lithuanian Labour Party (*Darbo*

Partija), which was then elected to the Lithuanian Seimas in 2004 and joined the subsequent government coalition. Uspaskich fled to Russia in 2006 amid accusations that his party had received illicit financing from Russia (*Baltic Times*, 2006).[18] Latvia has been particularly torn, thanks to the strength of the transit lobby grouped around the port city of Ventspils and its populist mayor, Aivars Lembergs, who are fierce supporters of the Russian energy giants. In 2014, following the annexation of Crimea, Lembergs spoke out against economic sanctions on Russia, arguing that any sanction on Russia was effectively a sanction on Latvia. Lembergs has also supported the construction of an East-West rail link between Moscow and Riga (and Ventspils) rather than the North-South *Rail Baltica* link supported by the other Baltic states and the European Commission.

The new soft power policies of Russia aim, as Agnia Grigas (2012, p. 2) claims, 'to constrain [the Baltic states'] independence and undermine the political, economic, and civilisational choices they have made'. This ongoing battle means that relations with Russia remain an existential issue for the Baltic states. This is conditioned by the experience of imperial Russian and Soviet occupation as well as disquieting extremist Russian rhetoric about the Baltic states. In 2009 and 2013 Russia held training exercises by the Baltic border simulating an invasion of the Baltic states. Russian actions in Georgia in 2008 and Crimea and eastern Ukraine in 2014 revealed the extent to which it is prepared to use military force in order to achieve its aims. This has radically changed Baltic perceptions of their own security and reinvigorated the post-1991 pattern of ever-increasing integration with the West.

Conclusions

The Baltic states have been ever more deeply embedded in the broad network of international Western organisations since 2004, most recently joining the Eurozone between 2011 and 2015. Latvia and Lithuania have also targeted joining Estonia (which joined in 2010) as members of the OECD. They have seized on contemporary processes of internationalisation and globalisation to strengthen their external security and attract investment. By opening up to trade and FDI they hoped to inextricably bind themselves into the international business and political community. At the same time they attempted to close the door on the East, although the very openness of the Baltic economies has been used by Russia to reassert influence in the Baltic region, bringing new soft and hard threats to Baltic security.

The three states have been remarkably consistent in their foreign policy direction, largely because there has been broad mainstream political agreement that integration with the West is outside the normal competition of politics. Integration with the West, and particularly with the EU, has served as a guide for the macro-level reforms that needed to be undertaken in order to build modern democratic market economies and battle systemic challenges such as corruption and possible ethnic strife. International conditionality was also a convenient replacement for weak or non-existent political ideologies in fledgling political parties in the 1990s.

At the time of writing, Russian military airplanes, ships and submarines regularly encroach Baltic borders. Kremlin political rhetoric against the Baltic states remains fiery. Russia clearly remains the only existing security threat to the sovereignty of the Baltic states. As small countries in an unstable regional environment, the Baltic states have done much to ensure the security of their borders. History will show if it was enough.

Notes

1 A Brief Political History of the Baltic States

1. In April 2007 the Estonian government's relocation of the 'Bronze Soldier' statue (a tribute to Red Army soldiers) from the centre of Tallinn to a military cemetery outside the city led to thousands of Estonia's Russophones running amok in Estonia's only major riot since 1991.
2. Three excellent comparative histories of the Baltic states have been published in recent years (Kasekamp, 2010; Plakans, 2011; Purs, 2012) while Anatol Lieven's (1994) *The Baltic Revolution* remains the best English-language text covering the Baltic states' struggle to break away from the Soviet Union. Richard C.M. Mole's (2012) recent volume on Baltic identities also contains a good comparative overview of the development of the Baltic states. There are also a number of relatively recent fine individual country histories: Estonian histories include: Taagepera (1993), Smith (2002) and Raun (2002), while Latvia is covered by Plakans (1995), Dreifelds (1996), Eksteins (1999), Pabriks and Purs (2001), and Lithuania by Kiaupa (2002) and Lane (2002).
3. Amber is the only other natural resource found in large quantities in addition to north-eastern Estonia's shale oil. However, as Modris Eksteins (1999, p. 9) points out, while amber may well have been sought after in the age of the Greeks and Romans, it now has little monetary value.
4. The most significant celebration is the 'John's Day' midsummer solstice celebration (Jaanipäev in Estonia, Jāņi in Latvia, and Joninės in Lithuania), which still brings the Baltic republics to a beer-sodden halt in late June.
5. Hroch's famous 1985 tome sketches in an explanatory three-stage periodization – (a) scholarly interest; (b) patriotic agitation; and (c) appearance of a mass national movement – that has been used to explain the emergence of nationalism in Estonia, Latvia and Lithuania (see, for example: Raun and Plakans, 1990; Kasekamp, 2010; and Mole, 2012).
6. A term coined by contemporary Baltic Germans and intended as belittlement, rather as the contemporary wealthy, new post-communist elite are mocked for their gaudy, but expensive, style and known as 'new Russians'.
7. One of the key figures in the committee was Janis Čakste, who had previously also been a Duma deputy and was to become the first president of independent Latvia.
8. This confusion is reflected in the *Brāļu Kapi* (Cemetery of the Brethren) in Riga, dedicated to the fallen in the Latvian wars of independence. Latvian Red Riflemen are buried next to soldiers from the self-defence forces, although at some stage they were likely to have fought against each other.
9. Baltic nationalists, Baltic communists, Red Army, Latvian Riflemen, White Russians, the British navy, Finish volunteers and Polish forces (Clemens, 1991, p. 33).

10. Janis Čakste, Alberts Kviesis and Kārlis Ulmanis.
11. In 1921 the Latvian Trade Union Central Committee had 40,000 members. Although the Central Committee split as a result of the different political factions battling to control it, by 1933 there were 50,000 people registered as members of several hundred different trade unions (Šilde, 1976, pp. 560–562).
12. Indeed, the political scientist Rasma Kārkliņš has claimed that her distinguished historian father, Ādolfs Šilde, believed that the Ulmanis coup was carried out because the press was about to break a string of compromising corruption stories concerning Ulmanis and his LZS (Zirnis and Veveris, 2005).
13. For example, Jānis Mežaraugs's (1928) article on 'How the left-wing government fought political corruption' was published by the Latvian Academy of Sciences, although it is more of an angry diatribe against the perceived corruption of the civic parties than an academic investigation of political corruption.
14. In contrast to Andres Kasekamp (1999), Modris Eksteins (1999, p. 116) argued that the members of the Latvian Thundercross styled themselves on Europe's fascists. He wrote that Thundercross 'members wore gray shirts and black berets and adopted a Nazi-style salute accompanied by the greeting "Hail Struggle!" The movement[']s slogan was "Latvia for the Latvians"'.
15. In Latvia, the major changes included reducing the amount of parliamentary seats from 100 to 50 while increasing the term from three years to four; creating a popularly elected, five-year presidency (with a two-term limit) and granting the president increased legislative powers as well as the ability to dismiss parliament. The Estonian government offered almost identical reforms.
16. Laws were passed under Article 81 of the Latvian constitution that gave the Cabinet of Ministers the power to pass laws while the parliament was not in session.
17. The fluctuating fortunes of titular Baltic families under the different occupation regimes is brilliantly captured in William Palmer's little-known 1990 novel, *The Good Republic*.
18. Occupation is here understood as the effective control of a foreign territory by hostile armed forces, as defined in Article 42 of the 1907 Hague Regulations.

2   Elected and Unelected Institutions

1. The new preamble reads as follows:

   The state of Latvia, which was proclaimed on 18 November 1918, has been established by uniting historical Latvian territories and expressing the unwavering desire of the Latvian nation to have its own state and its inalienable right of self-determination in order to guarantee the existence and development of the Latvian nation, its language and culture for centuries, provide freedom and promote prosperity for the people of Latvia and for everyone.

   The people of Latvia won their state in the Fights for Independence. A freely elected Constitutional Assembly served to consolidate the form of government and adopt a Constitution.

   The people of Latvia did not recognise the occupation regimes, resisted them and regained freedom by renewing their national independence on 4 May 1990 on the grounds of continuity of the state. They honour their defenders of freedom, commemorate victims of foreign powers, as well as condemn the Communist and Nazi totalitarian regimes and crimes committed by them.

Latvia is democratic and based on the rule of law, as a social and national state is based on human dignity and freedom; it recognises and protects fundamental human rights and respects minorities. The people of Latvia protect its sovereignty, as well as the independence, territory, territorial integrity and the democratic form of government of the state of Latvia.

Traditionally, Latvia's identity in the European cultural space has been shaped by Latvian and Liv traditions, Latvian folk wisdom, the Latvian language, universal human and Christian values. Loyalty to Latvia, the Latvian language as the only state language, freedom, equality, solidarity, justice, honesty, the work ethic and family are the foundations of a cohesive society. Everyone takes care of one's self, one's relatives and the common good of society by acting responsibly toward other people, future generations, the environment and nature.

Being aware of its equivalence in the international community, Latvia protects its national interests and facilitates the sustainable and democratic development of a united Europe and world.

God, bless Latvia! (Saeima, 2014)

2. Minority government coalitions lack a formal legislative majority but draw on the support of individual deputies or the regular support of a party that, for various reasons, did not enter government. Minimum-winning coalitions collapse when one party withdraws its support. Surplus majority coalitions contain more parties than strictly necessary for a majority.

3. Data are for full electoral terms only. Estonia 1992–2011, Latvia 1993–2011 and Lithuania 1992–2012.

4. Arnold Rüütel won 42% of the vote to Meri's 29.5%. Rein Taagepera came third with 23% and Lagle Parek won 4%.

5. Indeed, even before the first round third-placed Rein Taagepera (who had been nominated by the Popular Front) had expressed his own support for Lennart Meri. In a speech he had said:

    I do not particularly wish to be elected[;] ... if any voters hesitate whether to give a vote for me or Lennart Meri, he or she should vote for Meri[;] ... on the other hand, if any of the voters hesitate whether to vote for me or the person who in 1982 was appointed head of the Estonian government by Yuri Andropov [Arnold Rüütel], then he or she should vote for me. (*Baltic Observer*, 1992, p. 3)

6. In the premier–presidential model the president (a) is selected by popular vote for a fixed term in office; (b) selects the prime minister who heads the cabinet; however, (c) only parliament has the authority to dismiss the cabinet (Shugart and Carey, 1992).

7. Paksas resigned, alongside his Finance and Economics minister's, after failing to negotiate better terms for the sale.

8. If an outgoing prime minister removed by a parliamentary call of no-confidence requests it, the president may, or may not, call an early parliamentary election.

9. A president may call for a referendum on the recall and early election of parliament. However, this is a zero-sum game, with the president having to step down if the public reject the recall of parliament.

10. Only after the prime minister has asked for an early election following a parliamentary vote of no confidence in the government. Moreover, three-

fifths of the resulting newly elected parliament can call for a new presidential election.

11. However, if the president's first and second nominees are not approved by the parliament, the initiative for nominating a prime minister is handed to parliament. All but one of the prime minister candidates nominated by Estonian presidents have been approved at the first nomination. The exception was elected after the president's second nomination. The parliament has never had the opportunity to nominate its own candidate.

12. If the Seimas rejects two presidential nominees in a row, the president can opt to dissolve the legislature and call new elections. This somewhat limits the legislatures options and forces it to take the president's concerns into account.

13. Although this can be over-ridden by a two-thirds parliamentary majority.

14. Although an absolute majority of parliament can override the veto.

15. Only during wartime. At other times the president has the power to nominate the commander-in-chief for parliamentary approval.

16. The president nominates and the Seimas votes.

17. The examination comes before the job interview and has two halves. The first tests candidates' general and legal knowledge, while the second is specific to the job.

18. The research was based on the results of an expert survey that focused on five indicators:

(a) the scope of senior positions that are subject to political appointments ('depth' of politicisation), (b) the size of ministerial cabinets, (c) the turnover among senior officials after elections, (d) the experience of senior officials in politics, for instance, as party functionary, elected representative, and (e) the importance of political contacts including party membership for career progression. (Meyer-Sahling and Veen, 2012, p. 9)

19. In the case of Estonia, more than one-third of the police force in 2012 was female (Valles, 2013).

20. In 2013 Lithuania led the way, with a rate of 322 per 100,000 people. Latvia followed, with 264 and Estonia came third, with 239 (International Centre for Prison Studies, 2014). In contrast, Sweden has a rate of 60 and Finland 58.

21. See Edward Lucas's (2012) detailed chapters on the history and contemporary actions of Russian and Western spying agencies in the Baltic countries.

22. The key tasks of the KaPo are 'combating organised crime and terrorism, protecting territorial integrity and state secrets, protecting secrets related to science, technology and business, securing the safety of national cultural heritage, state agencies, politicians and public officials' (Kaitsepolitseiamet, 2014).

3 Elections, Referendums and Parties

1. The Single Transferable Vote system is much favoured by political scientists because it produces a more proportional result and minimises wasted votes, although votes do take longer to tabulate due to the complex counting procedure.

2. The electoral laws and other relevant legislation, explanations and data can be found on the web pages of the three national electoral authorities: the Estonian Election Commission (http://www.vvk.ee), the Latvian Election Commission (http://cvk.lv), and the Lithuanian Electoral Commission (http://www.vrk.lt).

3. Although the 2002 law was still largely based on the 1992 act.

4. Eleven from 1992–2003.

5. This culture of innovation and experimentation has also helped Estonia set up the world's first nationwide network of fast chargers for electric vehicles as well as to develop e-government (Gerdes, 2013; Tamkivi, 2014).

6. Observers from the University of Michigan claimed that 'Estonia's Internet voting system blindly trusts the election servers and the voters' computers.... Either of these would be an attractive target for state-level attackers, such as Russia' (Independent Report on e-voting in Estonia, 2014).

7. Zatlers later specified that Latvia's three oligarchs are Aivars Lembergs, Andris Šķēle and Ainārs Šlesers. Prior to the 2011 early election, all three were an integral part of the political system. They were known as oligarchs because they combined political office with private business interests. Thus, Lembergs has been the mayor of Latvia's wealthiest city (Ventspils) since the late years of the Soviet era as well as a major shareholder in the transit enterprises that dominate the Ventspils economy. Šķēle is a three-time former prime minister and multi-millionaire businessman, and Šlesers is a former deputy prime minister, economics minister, transport minister and the deputy mayor of the capital city, Riga, in addition to being a successful real estate developer.

8. Turnout in the first round of Lithuania's presidential elections was as follows: 1993, 78.64%; 1998, 73.66%; 2003, 52.65%; 2004, 52.46%; 2009, 51.76%; 2014, 52.17% (Lithuanian Election Commission, 2014).

9. Estonia's Toomas Hendrik Ilves was an MEP when elected president. Lithuania's Dalia Grybauskaitė was a European commissioner before being elected president. Latvia's Valdis Dombrovskis was an MEP before he became Latvia's longest-serving prime minister.

10. The five constitutional mechanisms are: If the parliament changes key articles of the constitution (Article 77); if the president calls for the dissolution of parliament (Article 48); and if there is a substantial renegotiation of Latvia's relationship with the European Union.

    (Article 68). The final two mechanisms are facultative: If the president (acting independently, or at the request of at least one-third of parliamentary deputies) has suspended the proclamation of a law for up to two months, and at least 10% of the electorate have petitioned for a referendum on the issue within this two-month period; or if at least one-tenth of the electorate has petitioned the parliament with a 'fully elaborated draft of an amendment to the Constitution or of a law' (Article 78).

11. For example, a Lithuanian member of parliament in 1992 called for the mass execution of former communists (Lieven, 1994, p.106).

12. Although some of the highest-profile reactionary leaders were banned. Indeed, the reactionary head of the Latvian Communist Party, Alfreds Rubiks, was arrested and eventually sentenced to eight years in prison for his part in

the events of August 1991. He was also banned from holding public office in Latvia. However, he was elected to the European Parliament in 2009.
13. Volatility has been calculated using the Pedersen Index (1979), which measures the cumulated (aggregate) electoral gains and losses of parties winning more than 2% of the vote in a parliamentary election.
14. The mean volatility data for the Baltic states was as follows: Type A, Estonia 30, Latvia 34, Lithuania 56; and Type B, Estonia 17, Latvia 17, Lithuania 14 (Powell and Tucker, 2013).
15. The raw data also reveals this to be the case. For example, 23 parties competed in the 1993 election, but just 13 in the 2010 and 2011 polls).
16. See http://tautastribunals.eu/
17. In 2004 an enterprising young Latvian journalist attempted to join the five Latvian parties that appeared to be the easiest to join (JL, LC, ZZS, LSP, LPP). However, after five months of interviews, attending various rallies and meetings to show good faith, she had only succeeded in joining two – LC and ZZS (Anonymous, 2004).

4 Civil Society, Corruption and Ethnic Relations

1. Dissidents and *samizdat* in the Soviet era are a further example of direct opposition between state and civil society. Cohen and Arato describe the operation of these fledgling groups as 'society *against* the state, nation *against* state, social order *against* political system ...' and so on (Cohen and Arato 1992, p. 31).
2. For example, the Riga Latvian Association, the oldest Latvian NGO, dating back to the nineteenth century, has been successfully revived, as has the inter-war Lithuanian Scouting Association (albeit with a much reduced membership).
3. The year represents the time of the survey rather than the year of the Eurobarometer publication.
4. The protest and lobbying campaign ultimately proved successful, as the European Parliament rejected Ūdre's candidacy.
5. In 2011 one Latvian newspaper, the *Neatkarīgā Rīta Avīze*, even published a long article musing on the correct Latvian term for the agents of Soros (Rozenbergs, 2011). It concluded that '*sorosieši*' rather than '*sorosoīdi*' was grammatically correct. While the article was in essence rather trivial, it was presented as a serious grammatical issue and clearly intended to indicate that discussion of the influence of Soros in Latvian politics was a perfectly normal issue for debate.
6. The core anti-Soros arguments were nicely summed up in a reader's comment to an article on the popular Latvian internet news site '*Apollo*' in 2012. The anonymous comment by 'domāsim' (let's think) charged that Soros/liberals (the two are often conflated) want to take seven things away from Latvians: 1. Family and marriage (to be replaced by partnerships and gay rights), gender (to be replaced by androgynous individuals), nationality (to be replaced by cosmopolitanism), Latvian money (to be replaced by the euro), education in Latvian (to be replaced by English), Latvia itself (to be replaced by a union), and to change the Latvian hymn (Domāsim, 2012).

7. Active civil society is a key part of the open society concept developed by Karl Popper, George Soros's intellectual mentor at the London School of Economics.
8. It also saw Loskutovs receive only a temporary reprieve, as he was then fired by Kalvitis's successor in the prime minister's post in June 2008.
9. The share of Lithuanians who do not participate in anything fell from 40 to 25% between 2007 and 2010 (Leontjeva, 2013).
10. www.rahvakogu.ee (last accessed 15 June 2014)
11. www.aukok.lt. Similar web sites also exist in Estonia and Latvia.
12. When I first began to lecture in politics at the University of Latvia in the 1990s, most students came to lectures with a newspaper in hand. Now students struggle to recall when they last purchased a newspaper.
13. There were similarly high levels of trust in the media at the outset of the transition. The 1992 Central and Eastern European Barometer survey found that 60% of the public in all three states trusted television while 48% of Estonians, 49% of Latvians and 57% of Lithuanians trusted newspapers.
14. Research by the Soros Foundation and Transparency International in Latvia analysed articles in six national and six regional newspapers (Latvian and Russian language) between 10 February and 10 March 2001. Researchers searched for articles that were either one-sided or uncritical as well as for articles that popularised an individual politician or political party. They discovered 189 examples of the latter, 25 of the former and 18 that shared both characteristics. All newspapers were affected. Moreover, they found that these types of article were four times more likely to appear in the national than in the regional presses. (Ločmele 2001) A similar exercise was carried out on the four national television channels between 28 February and 12 March 2001, and 214 cases of hidden party political propaganda were identified.
15. In contrast to the Transparency International Index, the World Bank report is based on interviews and questionnaires with firms in the region – the 1999 Business Environment and Enterprise Performance Survey (BEEPS) commissioned jointly by the World Bank and the European Bank for Reconstruction and Development.
16. Although this was a significant increase over the 26% of Russophones who supported independence in May 1990 (Ott, Kirch and Kirch, 1996, p. 25).
17. This also meant that 40,000 ethnic Latvians who had lived in the Soviet Union during the first era of independence (primarily communists, communist sympathisers and their children) were denied citizenship, while the many and deep-rooted ethnic Russians of the eastern Latgale region (who generally had poor or non-existent Latvian-language skills) were granted citizenship.
18. An example of external influence can be seen through the case of the OSCE. The first official letter to a Latvian foreign minister came from the OSCE High Commissioner on National Minorities, Max van der Stoel, on 6 April 1993, before the parliamentary elections of that year. In this letter the commissioner expressed his recommendation for the 'speedy adoption of a citizenship law', and urged a law that would allow the overwhelming majority of Russian-speakers to gain 'the right to make their views known by participating in the election process (van der Stoel, 1993). Over subsequent years, van der Stoel continued to strongly push this opinion in a succession of letters, speeches and visits to Latvia.

19. The Baltic languages are rarely spoken outside the Baltic states, and it is still considered a novelty when a member of a visible minority learns a Baltic language. Berneen, a singer of Indian origin from South Africa, became famous in Lithuania after she began singing in the local language. In the same way, visible minorities that enter politics also become quite famous. Abdul Turay, a black British citizen, was elected to the Tallinn City Council in 2013 and then campaigned for a seat in the European Parliament in 2014 (McGuinness, 2014).

5 Economic, Social and Welfare Issues

1. *Parex* was the largest domestically owned institution, tracing its history back to the late Soviet era, when its two owners were granted one of the first private foreign-currency exchange licenses in the Soviet Union.
2. The phrase 'neo-liberal' is routinely deployed in a negative sense by critics of the Baltic states' austerity and internal devaluation policies. After much consideration, I have decided to use it throughout this chapter, not because I agree with this criticism, but because I feel that it best captures the open, flexible nature of the modern Baltic economies.
3. Prior to the Russian rouble crisis of August 1998, Russia accounted for 24 per cent of Lithuania's exports, 21 per cent of Latvia's and 15 per cent of Estonia's (Taro, 1999, p. 5).
4. With a fixed peg supported by foreign reserves.
5. The Estonian kroon was pegged to the euro from 1999, the Lithuanian litas from 2002 and the Latvian lat from 2005.
6. See Nasdaq OMX market capitalisation data at: http://www.nasdaqomxbaltic. com/market/?pg=capital&lang=en. 10 June 2014 saw 520 trades with a total turnover of just one million euro. See Nasdaq OMX market statistics at: http://www.nasdaqomxbaltic.com/market/?pg=stats&lang=en.
7. A European Commission (2013) report on the shadow economy in Europe in 2012 used a different methodology and found that Latvia (26.1%) had a smaller shadow economy than Estonia (28.2%) and Lithuania (28.5%).
8. Both Krugman and Roubini held that there were parallels with a previous Argentinian fiscal crisis and believed that a devaluation was the only way to make the Baltic, and especially the Latvian, economies competitive again (Krugman, 2008; Roubini, 2009).
9. Kattel and Raudla (2013, p. 435) point out that this has now become the established pattern for reforms in the Baltic states: '[A] peculiar kind of flying geese pattern of policy transfer and learning, and of growth, in the sense that in most policy reforms as well as growth dynamics, Estonia led the way, with Lithuania being in many cases the last to adopt certain reforms'.
10. The minimum investment amount was raised in 2014 after a polarising political debate that led to the government agreeing to phase out the programme in the medium term.
11. Latvia did experience a riot in the Riga Old Town on the evening of 13 January 2009. As an accidental witness to the events, I can report that it was small in scope and driven by alcohol and testosterone rather than by political or economic demands.

12. Average net migration from Latvia between 2000 and 2007 was 0.5% but increased to an average 1.3% from 2008 to 2011 (Blanchard, Griffiths and Gruss, 2013).
13. Russian tourists made up the biggest share of foreign visitors to the Lithuanian capital of Vilnius in the first half of 2013 (*The Baltic Course*, 2013).
14. In the case of Latvia, '8% of ethnic Latvians and 25% of their minority counterparts said that they (or some family member) would like to work abroad [at least] for some years when their country enters the EU; moreover, 4% of Latvians and 9% of non-Latvians were ready to emigrate permanently' (Zepa and Klave, 2011, p. 78
15. Official government statistics, which are based on people who have registered as leaving the country paint a very different picture, putting net emigration from Latvia at 33,000 individuals. However, research by Mihails Hazans at the University of Latvia uses far more accurate data based on social-security number allocation in the United Kingdom and Ireland and estimates the real emigration number in this period at 194,000 (Hazans, 2013).

6 Foreign and Security Policy

1. This scenario was predicted in American author Tom Clancy's final novel featuring his all-American hero, President Jack Ryan. *Command Authority* opens with an authoritarian Russian president invading Estonia. After (inevitably) being repelled by American-led NATO forces, the Russian army turns to occupy Crimea and eastern Ukraine before again being thwarted by President Jack Ryan's firm leadership. The chilling opening chapters, featuring armed conflict in Estonia, coupled with Russia's actions in Ukraine contributed to the jittery feeling among the Baltic foreign and security policy community in early 2014.
2. Vladimir Zhirinovsky has consistently threatened the Baltic states by a string of outrageous comments since the early 1990s. A typical comment came in 2004, following NATO accession, when he stated:
   Latvia will be destroyed. Empty space will be there. Absolutely nothing will remain from Latvia. Everybody will forget the words "Latvia" and "the Latvian language". There will be nothing in Latvia, forever. We will destroy everything. If you touch Russians and Russian schools. I assure you. Nothing will remain. (*Pravda*, 2004)
3. At the June 1991 NATO meeting Arnold Rüütel stated that in the future the Baltic states could form a demilitarised neutral zone separating NATO from the Warsaw Pact states (Tammerk, 1991). This idea was swiftly abandoned when independence was achieved a few months later.
4. Article V reads:
   The Parties agree that an armed attack against one or more of them in Europe or North America shall be considered an attack against them all and consequently they agree that, if such an armed attack occurs, each of them, in exercise of the right of individual or collective self-defence recognised by Article 51 of the Charter of the United Nations, will assist the Party or Parties so attacked by taking forthwith, individually and in concert with the other Parties, such action as it deems necessary, including the use of

armed force, to restore and maintain the security of the North Atlantic area. (NATO, 2005)

5. In an April 2014 interview with the *Wall Street Journal* Estonia's president, Toomas Hendrik Ilves, stated that US 'boots on the ground is kind of a good idea' in order to show that NATO is 'serious' about defending its member states (Kaminski, 2014).

6. The 23 July 1940 declaration reads in full:

   During these past few days the devious process where under the political independence and territorial integrity of the three small Baltic republics – Estonia, Latvia, and Lithuania – were to be deliberately annihilated by one of their more powerful neighbors, have been rapidly drawing to their conclusion.

   From the day when the peoples of these republics first gained their independent and democratic form of government the people of the United States have watched their admirable progress in self-government with deep and sympathetic interest.

   The policy of this Government is universally known. The people of the United States are opposed to predatory activities no matter whether they are carried on by the use of force or by the threat of force. They are likewise opposed to any form of intervention on the part of one State, however powerful, in the domestic concerns of any other sovereign state, however weak.

   These principles constitute the very foundations upon which the existing relationship between the twenty-one sovereign republics of the New World rests.

   The United States will continue to stand by these principles, because of the conviction of the American people that unless the doctrine in which these principles are inherent once again governs the relations between nations, the rule of reason, of justice and of law – in other words, the basis of modern civilisation itself – cannot be preserved. (US Embassy Vilnius, 2014)

7. Latvia's sharp fall in output meant that the cut was not so radical in terms of the percentage of GDP spent on defence.

8. There are also a number of other pan-Baltic defence cooperative projects such as the Baltic Air Surveillance Network BALTNET) and the Baltic Squadron (BALTRON).

9. See the organisations home page: https://www.ccdcoe.org/history.html

10. See the organisations home page: http://www.enseccoe.org/en/home.html

11. By the end of 2013 Latvia had deployed 2,700 troops to Afghanistan and 1,165 to Iraq. Lithuania had deployed 2,500 in Afghanistan and 930 to Iraq (Coffey, 2013).

12. To be more specific, Europeanisation is defined as 'processes of (a) construction (b) diffusion and (c) institutionalisation of formal and informal rules, procedures, policy paradigms, styles, "ways of doing things" and shared beliefs and norms which are first defined and consolidated in the making of EU decisions and then incorporated in the logic of domestic discourse, identities, political structures and public policies' (Radaelli, 2000, p. 4).

13. The ERASMUS mobility programme for students has brought in ever-rising numbers of international students who have, in turn, internationalised the

universities (while Baltic Erasmus students travelling abroad have had their eyes opened as to how universities function in other European countries).

14. Although the plans for the nuclear reactor were shelved after the Lithuanian public voted against the project in a non-binding referendum in 2012, they were reactivated as concerns for Lithuania's energy security grew in 2014.

15. As small, northern, geographically peripheral states, the Baltic states remain among the least popular tourist destinations in Europe. Among the 28 member states, Estonia ranks 24, Lithuania 26 and Latvia 27 in terms of tourist visits (Eurostat Tourism Statistics, 2014).

16. Andres Kasekamp (2013, p. 20) argues that President Ilves advocated Estonia's Nordic identity at this time in order to differentiate it from Latvia and Lithuania so that it would not have to wait for the other two states to catch up in EU negotiations in order to join the Union.

17. A 1994 Friedrich-Ebert-Stiftung poll of 615 Russian officers placed the following countries as Russia's main enemies: 1. Latvia, 2. Afghanistan, 3. Lithuania, 4. Estonia and 5. United States (Bajarnas, 2005, p. 13). A 2013 Levada poll put them third, fourth and fifth after the United States and Georgia as 'Russia's greatest enemies' (RFE/RL, 2014).

18. He returned to Lithuania in 2007 and was elected once more to the Lithuanian parliament in 2008.

Bibliography

Aasland, A. (2002). Citizenship status and social exclusion in Estonia and Latvia. *Journal of Baltic Studies, 33*(1), 57–77.

Ābols, G. (2003). *The contribution of history to Latvian identity*. Riga: Nacionālais Apgāds.

Agarin, T. (2011). Civil society versus nationalizing state? Advocacy of minority rights in the post-socialist Baltic states. *Nationalities Papers, 39*(2), 181–203.

Agh, A. (2003). Public administration in Central Eastern Europe. In B.G. Peters & J. Pierre, *Handbook of public administration* (pp. 536–548). London: Sage.

Aidukaite, J. (2011). The 'Baltic welfare state' after 20 years of transition. In M. Lauristin, *Estonian human development report 2010/2011: Baltic Way(s) of human development: Twenty years on* (pp. 70–74). Tallinn: Eesti Koostoo Kogu.

Aidukaite, J. (2013). Social policy changes in the three Baltic states over the last decade (2000–2012). *Ekonomika, 92*(3), 89–104.

Alexeyeva, L. (1985). *Soviet dissent: Contemporary movements for national, religious and human rights*. Middletown, CT: Wesleyan University Press.

Anderson, J. (1998). *Corruption in Latvia. Survey evidence*. Washington, DC: World Bank.

Anderson, J.H., Bernstein, D.S., & Gray, C.W. (2005). *Judicial systems in transition economies: Assessing the past, looking to the future*. Washington, DC: The World Bank.

Andresen, M.A. (2011). The impact of accession to the European Union on violent crime in Lithuania. *European Sociological Review, 27*(6), 759–771.

Annus, E. (2012, March). The problem of Soviet colonialism in the Baltics. *Journal of Baltic Studies, 43*(1), 21–45.

Apals, G. (1992). Latvijas Nacionālā Neatkarības Kustība. [The Latvian National Independence Movement]. *Latvijas Vēsture, 3*(6), 26–34.

Archer, C. (1999). Nordic swans and Baltic cygnets. *Cooperation and Conflict, 34*(1), 47–71.

Aristovnik, A. (2012). *Fiscal decentralization in Eastern Europe: A twenty-year perspective*. Retrieved May 18, 2014, from http://mpra.ub.uni-muenchen.de/39316/

Arter, D. (1996). *Parties and democracy in the post-Soviet republics: The case of Estonia*. Aldershot: Dartmouth.

Ashbourne, A. (1999). *Lithuania: The rebirth of a nation 1991–1994*. Oxford: Lexington Books.

Åslund, A. (1994). The case for radical reform. *Journal of Democracy, 5*(4), 63–74.

Asmus, R.D. (2002). *Opening NATO's door: How the alliance remade itself for a new era*. New York: Columbia University Press.

Auers, D. (2006). Potemkin democracy? Political parties and democratic consolidation in post-Soviet Latvia. PhD dissertation. London: School of Slavonic and East European Studies, University College London.

Auers, D. (2008). Salmon, rissoles and smoked eel: The Latvian legation in the Cold War. In D. Auers, *Latvia and the USA: From captive nation to strategic partner* (pp. 51–60). Riga: Academic Press of the University of Latvia.

Auers, D. (2011). The 2009 European Parliament election campaign in Latvia: Europeanizing domestic ethnic discourse. In R. Harmsen & J. Schild, *Debating Europe: The 2009 European Parliament elections and beyond* (pp. 201–216). Berlin: Nomos.

Auers, D. (2012). An electoral tactic? Citizens' initiatives in post-Soviet Latvia. In M. Setala & M. Schiller, *Citizens' initiatives in Europe: Procedures and consequences of agenda-setting by citizens* (pp. 53–68). London: Palgrave Macmillan.

Auers, D. (2012). *Europe and the early Latvian election of September 17, 2011.* European Institute, University of Sussex. European Parties, Referendums and Elections Network.

Auers, D. (2013). Latvia. In S. Berglund, J. Ekman, K. Deegan-Krause, & T. Knutsen, *Handbook of political change in Eastern Europe (3rd edition)* (pp. 85–123). Cheltenham: Edward Elgar.

Auers, D. (2013). Seven democrats and a dictator: Formal and informal powers of Latvia's presidents. In V. Hlousek, *Presidents above parties? Presidents in Central and Eastern Europe, their formal competencies and informal power* (pp. 191–204). Brno: Masaryk University.

Auers, D. (2013). 'We lay claim to him!' Berlin, Rothko, Eisenstein, and the reorientation of Latvian national identity. *National Identities, 15*(2), 125–138.

Auers, D., Krupavicius, A., & Ruus, J. (2009). Referendums and initiatives in the Baltic states. In S. Hug & K. Gilland Lutz, *Financing referendum campaigns* (pp. 81–106). London: Palgrave Macmillan.

Bagenholm, A. & Johansson Heino, A. (2008). Incentives and disincentives for new parties: The cases of Res Publica and New Era. *Midwest Political Science Association 66th Annual Conference in Chicago, April 3–6.*

Bajarnas, E. (1995). Lithuania's security dilemma. In E. Bajarnas, M. Haab, & I. Viksne, *The Baltic states: Security and defence after independence.* Institute for Security Studies of WEU.

Bajarunas, E., Haab, M., & Viksne, I. (1995). *The Baltic states: Security and defence after independence.* Institute for Security Studies of WEU.

Balkelis, T. (2009). *The making of modern Lithuania.* New York: Routledge.

Baltic Independent. (1991, August 2–9). Few Russians master Estonian. *Baltic Independent*, p. 5.

Baltic Independent. (1991A, August/September 30–5). Public opinion supports democracy. *Baltic Independent*, p. 3.

Baltic Independent. (1993, June 18–24). Draft law on aliens arouses strong opposition. *Baltic Independent*, p. 3.

Baltic Institute of Social Sciences. (2001). *Survey of newly naturalised citizens.* Riga: Baltic Institute of Social Sciences.

Baltic News Network. (2012, September 12). Farmers protest: Soviet tractor vs Brussels. *Baltic News Network.* Retrieved June 12, 2014, from http://bnn-news.com/farmers-protest-soviet-tractor-brussels-75024

Baltic Times. (2006, September 18). Uspaskich seeks asylum in Russia. *Baltic Times*, p. 1.

Barr, N. (2005). *Labor markets and social policy in Central and Eastern Europe: The accession and beyond.* Washington, DC: The Word Bank.

Barry, E. (2009, January 16). Baltic riots spread to Lithuania in the face of deteriorating economic conditions. *New York Times.* Retrieved June 11, 2014, from http://www.nytimes.com/2009/01/17/world/europe/17lithuania.html

BBC. (2006, June 7). Dutch envoy flees Estonian abuse. BBC News. Retrieved February 16, 2014, from http://news.bbc.co.uk/2/hi/europe/5057142.stm

Bennich-Björkman, L. (2007). The cultural roots of Estonia's successful transition: How historical legacies shaped the 1990s. *East European Politics and Societies, 21*(2), 316–347.

Berglund, S. & Dellenbrant, J.A. (1994). *The new democracies in eastern Europe: Party systems and political cleavages.* Cambridge: Edward Elgar.

Bergson, A. (1984). Income inequality under Soviet socialism. *Journal of Economic Literature* (23), 1052–1099.

Bertoa, F.C. (2014). Party systems and cleavage structures revisited: A sociological explanation of party system institutionalization in East Central Europe. *Party Politics, 20*(1), 16–36.

Bertoa, F.C. & Spirova, M. (2013). Get a subsidy or perish! Public funding and party survival in Eastern Europe. The legal regulation of political parties. Working paper No. 29. Retrieved April 10, 2014, from http://www.partylaw. leidenuniv.nl/uploads/wp2913.pdf

Bērziņš, A. (1963). *Labie gadi. [The good years].* New York: Grāmatu Draugs.

Bērziņš, V. (2000). *20. gadsimta Latvijas vēsture – Latvija no gadsimta sākuma līdz neatkarības pasludināšanai. [Twentieth century Latvian history – Latvia from the beginning of the century to independence: 1900–1918].* Riga: Latvian Historical Institute.

Bicakova, A. (2010). Gender unemployment gaps: Evidence from the new EU member states. *CERGE-EI Working Paper Series, 20*(2).

Biezen, I. (2005). On the theory and practice of party formation and adaptation in new democracies. *European Journal of Political Research, 44,* 147–174.

Blackburn, R.M., Jarman, J., & Brooks, B. (2000). The puzzle of gender segregation and inequality: A cross-national analysis. *European Sociological Review, 16*(2), 119–135.

Blanchard, O., Griffiths, M., & Gruss, B. (2013). *Boom, bust, recovery: Forensics of the Latvia crisis.* Washington, DC: Brookings.

Blanchard, O., Hamid, F., & Das, M. (210). The initial impact of the crisis on emerging market countries. *Brookings Papers on Economic Activity,* 263–323.

BNS. (2014, July 15). Prime Minister Butkevi⊠ius: No bilingual signs in Lithuania. *Delfi: The Lithuanian Tribune.* Retrieved July 16, 2014, from http://en.delfi. lt/lithuania/society/prime-minister-butkevicius-no-bilingual-signs-in-lithuania.d?id=65298092

Board, L.N. (2000). *On the way to a civic society – 2000: Survey of Latvian inhabitants.* Riga: Baltic Institute of Social Sciences.

Bohle, D. & Greskovits, B. (2009). East-Central Europe's quandary. *Journal of Democracy, 20*(4), 50–63.

Bottolfs, H. (2000). Latvia. In F. Aarebot & T. Knutsen, *Politics and citizenship on the eastern seaboard.* Kristiansand: Nordic Academic Press.

Bower, T. (1989). *Red Web: MI6 and the KGB master coup.* London: Aurum.

Brazauskas, A. (1998, February 19). State of the country address to the Lithuanian parliament.

Brzezinski, Z. (1995). A plan for Europe: How to expand NATO. *Foreign Affairs,* 26–42.

Budnitsky, S. (2013, February 14). *Kontinental Hockey League: Soft power of the tough game.* Retrieved April 18, 2014, from USC Center on Public Diplomacy:

http://uscpublicdiplomacy.org/blog/kontinental_hockey_league_soft_power_of_the_tough_game

Bukovskis, K. (2012). Latvia. In A. Lobjakas & M. Mölder, *EU-Russia Watch 2012* (pp. 77–84). Tartu: Tartu University Press.

Bush, G.W. (2002, November 24). Text of speech in Lithuania. *New York Times*, http://www.nytimes.com/2002/11/24/international/europe/24LITHU-WIRE.html. Retrieved June 2, 2014

Caramani, D. & van Biezen, I. (2007). Cleavage structuring in Western vs. Central and Eastern Europe: State formation, nation-building and economic modernisation. *ECPR Joint Sessions*. Helsinki, 7–12 May.

Ceccato, V. (2008). Expressive crimes in post-socialist states of Estonia, Latvia and Lithuania. *Journal of Scandinavian Studies in Criminology and Crime, 9*(1), 2–30.

Chenet, L., Britton, A., Kalediene, R., & Petrauskiene, J. (2001). Daily variations in deaths in Lithuania: The possible contribution of binge drinking. *International Journal of Epidemiology, 30*(4), 743–748.

Civitas. (2006). *Undiscovered power: Map of the civil society in Lithuania.* Vilnius: Civil Society Institute.

Clemens, W.C. (1991). *Baltic independence and Russian empire.* New York: St. Martins Press.

Coffey, L. (2013). *The Baltic states: Why the United States must strengthen security cooperation.* Washington, DC: The Heritage Foundation. Retrieved May 22, 2014, from http://www.heritage.org/research/reports/2013/10/the-baltic-states-why-the-united-states-must-strengthen-security-cooperation#_ftn26

Cohen, J. & Arato, A. (1992). *Civil society and political theory.* Cambridge, MA: MIT Press.

Corum, J.S. (2013). *The security concerns of the Baltic states as NATO allies.* Carlisle, PA: US Army Strategic Studies Institute.

Craddock, T. (2006, March 14). Lennart Meri: Keeping Estonia alive in times of freedom and oppression. *The Guardian.* Retrieved March 15, 2014, from http://www.theguardian.com/news/2006/mar/15/guardianobituaries.mainsection

Crime, U.N. (2014, March 17). *Crime and criminal justice statistics.* Retrieved from http://www.unodc.org/unodc/en/data-and-analysis/statistics/crime.html

Crime, U.N. (2014). *UNODC homicide statistics 2013.* Retrieved June 1, 2014, from https://www.unodc.org/gsh/en/data.html

Davoliute, V. (2012, May 11). Mob justice in Lithuania: Who can stand up to the madding crowd? *Open Democracy.* Retrieved June 12, 2014, from https://www.opendemocracy.net/od-russia/violeta-davoliute/mob-justice-in-lithuania-who-can-stand-up-to-madding-crowd

Davulis, G. (2013). Concept of fiscal decentralization and its development in the Baltic countries. *Review of Contemporary Business Research, 2*(2), 18–27.

de Lubisz-Milosz, O.V. (1919). *L'alliance des etats Baltiques.* Paris: Desmoineaux.

Deegan-Krause, K. (2004). Slovakia. In S. Berglund, J. Ekman, & F. Aarebot, *The Handbook of political change in Eastern Europe (2nd edition).* Aldershot: Edward Elgar.

Delfi (2005, June 11). Nodibināta partija 'Jaunie demokrāti'. *Delfi.* Retrieved March 10, 2014, from http://www.delfi.lv

Dellenbrant, J.A. (1994). The reemergence of multi-partyism in the Baltic States. In Sten Berglund and Jan Ake Dellenbrant, *The new democracies in Eastern Europe: Party systems and political cleavages.* Aldershot: Edward Elgar.

Domāsim (2012, November 24). A reader's comment. *Apollo*. Retrieved June 15, 2014, from http://apollo.tvnet.lv/komentari/zinas/541656/3

Donskis, L. (2006). Another word for uncertainty: Anti-semitism in Lithuania. *Nord Europa Forum* (1), 7–26.

Dreifelds, J. (1996). *Latvia in transition*. Cambridge: Cambridge University Press.

Duvold, K. & Berglund, S. (2014). Democracy between ethnos and demos: Territorial identification and political support in the Baltic states. *East European Politics and Societies, 28*(2), 341–365.

Dzintars, R. (2010). *Ceturtā atmoda*. Riga: Lauku Avīze.

Eberhardt, P. (2003). *Ethnic groups and population changes in twentieth-century Central-Eastern Europe: History, data, and analysis*. Armonk, NY: M.E. Sharpe.

Egle, I. (1998, December 22). Gorbunovs izraisa diskusiju par prezidenta vēlēšanām. *Diena*. Retrieved March 15, 2014, from http://www.diena.lv/arhivs/gorbunovs-izraisa-diskusiju-par-prezidenta-velesanam-10374410

Egle, I. (2004, April 15). Opozīcijā Jaunais Laiks pievērsas partijas stiprināšanai. *Diena*, p. 5.

Eglitis, A. (2004, September 2). Minister: Soros trying to overthrow cabinet. *Baltic Times*. Retrieved 17 May 2014, from http://www.baltictimes.com/news/articles/10786/#.U9JAd7nlpD8

Eksteins, M. (1999). *Walking since daybreak – A story of Eastern Europe, World War II, and the heart of our century*. New York: Houghton Mifflin Company.

Erixon, F. (2010). Baltic economic reforms: A crisis review of Baltic economic policy. Brussels: ECIPE Working Paper.

Estonia.eu. (2014, March 7). *Citizenship*. Retrieved May 28, 2014, from Estonia.eu: http://estonia.eu/about-estonia/society/citizenship.html

Estonian Internal Security Service. (2014). *Annual review 2013*. Tallinn: Estonian Internal Security Service. Retrieved June 16, 2014, from https://www.kapo.ee/cms-data/_text/138/124/files/kapo-annual-review-2013-eng.pdf

Estonian National Election Committee. (2012). *Elections in Estonia, 1992–2011*. Tallinn: Estonian National Election Committee.

Estonian National Election Committee. (2014). *Statistics about Internet voting in Estonia*. Retrieved May 19, 2014, from http://www.vvk.ee/voting-methods-in-estonia/engindex/statistics

Estonian Public Broadcasting. (2014, June 2). NGOs hit back after independent MEP says they are propped up by state. Estonian Public Broadcasting News. Retrieved June 21, 2014, from http://news.err.ee/v/society/22afa1b5-da1c-4c8e-ae72-0f9f436d32d8

European Bank for Reconstruction and Development. (1997). *Transition report*. London.

European Commission. (2002–2004). *Candidate countries Eurobarometer*. Brussels: European Commission. Retrieved February 12, 2014, from http://ec.europa.eu/public_opinion/archives/cceb2_En.htm

European Commission. (2012). *Convergence programme of the Republic of Latvia, 2012–2015*. Riga.

European Commission. (2013). *Shadow economy and undeclared work*. European Commission. Retrieved April 14, 2014, from http://ec.europa.eu/europe2020/pdf/themes/07_shadow_Economy.pdf

European Commission. (2014). *EU anti-corruption report*. Brussels: European Commission.

Eurostat Tourism Statistics. (2014, June). *Tourism statistics – top destinations.* Retrieved June 22, 2014, from Eurostat: http://epp.eurostat.ec.europa.eu/statistics_Explained/index.php/Tourism_statistics_-_top_destinations

Evans, G. & Whitefield, S. (1998). The structuring of political cleavages in post-communist societies: The case of the Czech Republic and Slovenia. *Political Studies, 46*(1), 115–139.

Ezergailis, A. (1996). *The holocaust in Latvia: The missing center.* Riga: Historical Institute of Latvia.

Farkas, B. (2011). The Central and Eastern European model of capitalism. *Post-Communist Economies, 23*(1), 15–34.

Feldman, M. (2001). The fast track from the Soviet Union to the world economy: External liberalization in Estonia and Latvia. *Government and Opposition, 36*(4), 537–558.

Finbalt Health Monitor. (2011). *Social determinants of health behaviours: Finbalt Health Monitor 1998–2008.* Tampere: Juvenes Print.

Fish, M. & Kroenig, M. (2009). *The handbook of national legislatures: A global survey.* New York: Cambridge University Press.

Fleming, A., Chu, L., & Bakker, M.-R. (1996). The Baltics – banking crises observed. World Bank Policy Research Working Paper 1647.

Freivalds, O. (1961). *Latviešu politiskās partijas 60. Gados. [60 Years of Latvian political parties].* Stockholm: Imanta.

Galbreath, D. (2003). The politics of European integration and minority rights in Estonia and Latvia. *Perspectives on European Politics and Society, 4*(1), 35–53.

Gallagher, M. (2014, May 15). *Election indices dataset.* Retrieved from http://www.tcd.ie/Political_Science/staff/michael_gallagher/ElSystems/index.php

Gallagher, M., Laver, M., & Mair, P. (1992). *Representative government in Western Europe.* San Francisco: McGraw Hill.

Galzons, E. (2005, April 11). Lemberga paziņojums Dienai redzama saikne ar Preses namu. *Diena,* pp. 1 and 4.

Geary, J. (2002, November 17). Yes, we have no army. *Time.* Retrieved June 3, 2014, from http://content.time.com/time/magazine/article/0,9171,901021125–391500,00.html

Gellner, E. (1983). *Nations and nationalism.* Ithaca, NY: Cornell University Press.

Gerdes, J. (2013, February 26). Estonia launches nationwide electric vehicle fast-charging network. *Forbes.* Retrieved May 10, 2014, from http://www.forbes.com/sites/justingerdes/2013/02/26/estonia-launches-nationwide-electric-vehicle-fast-charging-network/

Girnius, K. (1991). The party and popular movements in the Baltic. In J.A. Trapand, *Toward independence: The Baltic popular movements* (pp. 57–69). Boulder, CO: Westview Press.

Greeley, B. (2012, July 20). *Krugmenistan vs. Estonia.* Retrieved from *Bloomberg Businessweek*: http://www.businessweek.com/articles/2012–07–19/krugmenistan-vs-dot-estonia#p2

Grigas, A. (2012). *Legacies, coercion and soft power: Russian influence in the Baltic states.* Chatham House.

Grybauskaitė, D. (2013, June 11). *State of the nation address, 2013.* Retrieved June 2, 2014, from President of the Republic of Lithuania: http://www.president.lt/en/activities/state_of_the_nation_address/2013.html

Gutterman, S. (2013, October 7). Russia halts Lithuanian dairy imports before EU summit. Reuters. Retrieved June 2, 2014, from http://www.reuters.com/article/2013/10/07/us-russia-lithuania-dairy-idUSBRE99604Y20131007

Haab, M. (1995). Estonia and Europe: Security and defence. In E. Bajarnas, M. Haab, & I. Viksne, *The Baltic states: Security and defence after independence*. Institute for Security Studies of WEU.

Haas, A. (1996). Non-violence in ethnic relations in Estonia. *Journal of Baltic Studies, 27*(1), 47–76.

Hanovs, D. & Tēraudkalns, V. (2013). *Ultimate freedom – No choice: The culture of authoritarianism in Latvia, 1934–1940*. Leiden: Koninklijke Brill.

Hansen, M. (2013, July 29). More on Latvian growth and convergence. *Ir*. Retrieved May 28, 2014, from http://www.ir.lv/2013/7/29/more-on-latvian-growth-and-convergence

Hansson, A. & Ranveer, M. (2013). Economic adjustment in the Baltic countries. Tallinn: Bank of Estonia Working Paper Series. 1.

Hazans, M. (2013). Emigration from Latvia: Recent trends and economic impact. In OECD, *Coping with emigration in Baltic and East European countries* (pp. 65–110). OECD Publishing.

Hecking, C. (2013, October 8). EU immigration: Only the rich are welcome. *Spiegel*. Retrieved May 28, 2014, from http://www.spiegel.de/international/europe/immigrants-buy-visas-in-latvia-as-europe-locks-out-the-poor-a-926543.html

Helasoja, V., Lahelma, E., Prattala, R., Kasmel, A., Klumbiene, J., & Pudule, I. (2006). The socio-demographic patterning of health in Estonia, Latvia, Lithuania and Finland. *European Journal of Public Health, 16*(1), 8–20.

Hiden, J. & Salmon, P. (1994). *The Baltic nations and Europe: Estonia, Latvia, and Lithuania in the twentieth century*. London: Longman.

Hobbes, T. (1651 (republished 1991)). *Leviathan*. Cambridge: Cambridge University Press.

Hõbemägi, T. (2013, April 29). Latvia's largest daily paper still losing money. *Baltic Business News*. Retrieved May 18, 2014, from http://www.balticbusinessnews.com/default.aspx?PublicationId=42b816df-e1b1–49a8-a05f-53fdfe37884a

House, F. (2014). *Freedom of the Press 2014*. Freedom House. Retrieved July 2, 2014, from http://freedomhouse.org/report/freedom-press/freedom-press-2014#.U9ijOLnlo5s

Howard, M.M. (2002). The weakness of post-communist civil society? *Journal of Democracy, 13*(1), 157–169.

Hroch, M. (1985). *Social preconditions of national revival in Europe*. Cambridge: Cambridge University Press.

Huang, M. (2002). *Wannabe oligarchs: Tycoons and influence in the Baltic states*. Camberley, Surrey: Conflict Studies Research Centre.

Huntington, S. (1996). *The clash of civilizations and the remaking of world order*. London: Simon & Schuster.

Ibenskas, R. (2012). Activists or money? Explaining the electoral persistence of political parties in Lithuania. *Party Politics*, 1–18.

Ilves, T.H. (1991). Reaction: The intermovement in Estonia. In J.A. Trapans, *Toward independence: The Baltic popular movements* (pp. 71–83). Boulder: Westview Press.

Ilves, T.H. (2014, May 14). *Security in Northern Europe after the collapse of the Helsinki Final Act.* Retrieved May 16, 2014, from Estonian World Review: http://www.eesti.ca/toomas-hendrik-ilves-security-in-northern-europe-after-the-collapse-of-the-helsinki-final-act/article42179

Ilves, T.H. (1999, December 14). Estonia as a Nordic Country. Speech to the Swedish Institute for International Affairs. Retrieved December 10, 2013, from www.vm.ee/eng/index

International, T. (2014, June 18). *Corruption Perceptions Index.* Retrieved from Transparency International: http://www.transparency.org/research/cpi/overview

Jacobbson, B. (. (2010). *The European Union and the Baltic states: Changing forms of governance.* New York: Routledge.

Jamestown Foundation. (1996, September 17). State department plan will need improvements. *Monitor, 2*(172). Retrieved 11 June 2014, from http://www.jamestown.org/single/?tx_ttnews%5Btt_news%5D=14140&tx_ttnews%5BbackPid%5D=210&no_cache=1#.U84Tabnlo5s

Janes Sentinel. (2011). *Country risk assessments: Central Europe and Baltic states.* London: HIS Global Limited.

Jansons, A. (2004, October 20). A public spat. *Transitions Online.* Retrieved May 17, 2014, from http://www.tol.org/client/article/13002-a-public-spat.html?print

Jegelevicius, L. (2011, July 20). Wikileaks report reveals corruption in Lithuanian newspapers. Retrieved May 18, 2014, from http://ejc.net/magazine/article/wikileaks-report-reveals-corruption-in-lithuanian-newspapers#.U9dWiLnlo5s

Jegelevicius, L. (2013, March 11). The Baltics: Making sense of the journalism next door. *European Journalism Centre.* Retrieved May 17, 2014, from http://ejc.net/magazine/article/the-baltics-making-sense-of-the-journalism-next-door#.U9iR_Lnlo5s

Johannsen, L. & Pedersen, K.H. (2011). The institutional roots of anti-corruption policies: Comparing the three Baltic states. *Journal of Baltic Studies, 42*(3), 329–346.

Jonusaite, R. (2004). Providing for parliamentary oversight: The case of Lithuania. In Y. Korobovsky & J. Powers, *Defence reform in the Baltic states: 12 years of experience* (pp. 12–21). Geneva: Centre for the Democratic Control of Armed Forces.

Jurkynas, M. (2007). *How deep is your love? Baltic brotherhood reexamined.* Vilnius: University of Vilnius Press.

Jurkynas, M. (2009). The parliamentary election in Lithuania, October 2008. *Electoral Studies, 28*, 329–333.

Kaitsepolitseiamet. (2014, June 8). *Re-establishment of the security police.* Retrieved from Kaitsepolitseiamet: https://www.kapo.ee/eng/general-information/history/re-establishment

Kaktins, A. (2014, February 24). Vēlme pēc tautas vēlēta Valsts prezidenta (kā aizvien) janvārī bija nemainīgi augsta. *Twitter.* Retrieved May 21, 2014, from https://twitter.com/ArnisKaktins

Kallaste, E. & Woolfson, C. (2013). Negotiated responses to the crisis in the Baltic countries. *Transfer: European Review of Labour and Research, 19*(2), 253–266.

Kalniņš, B. (1956). *Latvijas sociāldemokrātijas piecdesmit gadi. [Fifty years of Latvian social democracy].* Stockholm: LSDSP Foreign Committee.

Kalnins, V. (2004, August 19). Lukashenko atblazma Latvijas Prezidentē. *Diena,* p. 2.

Kaminski, M. (2014, April 4). An American ally in Putin's line of fire. *Wall Street Journal*. Retrieved June 10, 2014, from http://online.wsj.com/news/articles/SB1 0001424052702304441304579481731492686664

Kangsepp, L. (2013, January 10). Ilves-Krugman spat to be turned into 'Financial Opera'. *Wall Street Journal*. Retrieved May 25, 2014, from http://blogs.wsj.com/emergingeurope/2013/01/10/ilves-krugman-spat-to-be-turned-into-financial-opera/

Karklins, R. (1994). *Ethnopolitics and transition to democracy: The collapse of the USSR and Latvia*. Washington, DC: Woodrow Wilson Center Press.

Karklins, R. (2005). *The system made me do it: Corruption in the post-communist region*. New York: M.E. Sharpe.

Kasekamp, A. (1993). The Estonian Veterans' league: A fascist movement? *Journal of Baltic Studies, 24*(3), 263–268.

Kasekamp, A. (1999). Radical right-wing movements in the North-East Baltic (Interwar period, fascism, Estonia, Latvia). Journal of Contemporary History, 34(4), 587–600.

Kasekamp, A. (2010). *A history of the Baltic states*. Basingstoke: Palgrave Macmillan.

Kasekamp, A. (2013). In A. Grigas, A. Kasekamp, K. Maslauskaite, & L. Zorgenfreija, *The Baltic states in the EU: Yesterday, today and tomorrow* (pp. 16–32). Paris: Jacques Delors Institute.

Kasemets, A. & Lepp, U. (2010). *Anti–corruption programmes: Studies and projects in Estonia 1997–2009. An overview*. European Research Centre for Anti-Corruption and State-Building.

Kask, P. (1996). Institutional development of the parliament of Estonia. In P. Norton & D.M. Olson, *The new parliaments of Central and Eastern Europe* (pp. 193–212). Portland, OR: Frank Cass & Co.

Kaska, V. (2013). Emigration from Estonia: Recent trends and economic impact. In OECD, *Coping with emigration in Baltic and East European countries* (pp. 29–44). OECD Publishing.

Kaslas, B.J. (1976). *The Baltic nations: The quest for regional integration and political liberty*. Pittston, PA: Euramerica Press.

Kastrand, K. (2007). *Countering narcotics and organized crime in the Baltic Sea region*. Uppsala: Central Asia – Caucasus Institute: Silk Road Studies Program. Retrieved June 17, 2014, from http://www.silkroadstudies.org/new/docs/publications/20 07/0703Karrstrand.pdf

Kattel, R. & Raudla, R. (2013). The Baltic republics and the crisis of 2008–2011. *Europe–Asia Studies, 65*(3), 426–449.

Keane, J. (1998). *Civil society: Old images, new visions*. Cambridge: Polity Press.

Kiaupa, Z. (2002). *The history of Lithuania*. Vilnius: Baltos Lankos.

King, A. (1969). Political parties in Western democracies: Some skeptical reflections. *Polity* (2), 111–141.

Kirby, D. (1995). *The Baltic world 1772–1993: Europe's northern periphery in an age of change*. London: Longman.

KNAB. (2013). *Publiskais Parskats*. Riga: KNAB.

Koker, P. (2013). Presidential activism in Central and Eastern Europe (CEE): A statistical analysis of the use of presidential vetoes in the CEE EU member states, 1990–2010. 63rd Political Studies Association Annual International

Conference, Cardiff. Retrieved April 17, 2014, from http://www.psa.ac.uk/sites/default/files/52_30.pdf

Kopocek, L. (2007). The far right in Europe. A summary of attempts to define the concept, analyze its identity, and compare the Western European and Central European far right. *Central European Political Studies Review, 9*(4), 280–293.

Kovalenko, J., Mensah, P., Leoncikas, T., & Zibas, K. (2010). *New immigrants in Estonia, Latvia and Lithuania.* Talinn: Legal Information Centre for Human Rights.

Krugman, P. (2008, December 23). *Latvia is the new Argentina .* Retrieved from *New York Times* Blog: http://krugman.blogs.nytimes.com/2008/12/23/latvia-is-the-new-argentina-slightly-wonkish/?_php=true&_type=blogs&_r=0

Krupavicius, A. (2013). Lithuania's president: A formal and informal power. In V. Hlousek, *Presidents above parties? Presidents in Central and Eastern Europe, their formal competencies and informal power* (pp. 205–232). Brno: Masaryk University.

Krupavicius, A. & Zvaliauskas, G. (2001). Lithuania. In A. Auer, & M. Butzer, *Direct democracy: The Eastern and Central European experience* (pp. 109–128). Aldershot: Ashgate.

Kuldkepp, M. (2013). The Scandinavian connection in early Estonian nationalism. *Journal of Baltic Studies, 44*(3), 313–338.

Kuris, G. (2012). *Surmounting state capture: Latvia's anti-corruption agency spurs reforms, 2002–2011.* Princeton: Innovations for successful societies. Retrieved May 28, 2014, from http://www.knab.gov.lv/uploads/eng/policy_note_id215.pdf

Laakso, M. & Taagepera, R. (1979). 'Effective' number of parties: A measure with application to west Europe. *Comparative Political Studies, 12*(1), pp. 3–27.

Laar, M. (1996). Estonia's success story. *Journal of Democracy, 7*(1), 96–101.

Lagerspetz, M., Hinno, K., Joons, S., Rikmann, E., Sepp, M., & Vallimae, T. (2007). *Unequal treatment on grounds of individual or social characteristics: Attitudes, experiences and awareness of the population in Estonia.* Tallinn: Tallinn University Press.

Lane, T. (2002). *Lithuania: Stepping westward.* London: Routledge.

Lasas, A. (2008). Guilt, sympathy and cooperation: EU Baltic relations in the early 1990s. *East European Politics and Societies, 22*(2), 347–372.

Latvijas Avize. (2014, March 18). Straujuma: ekonomisko saišu saraušana ar Krieviju Latvijas IKP var mazināt par 10%. *Latvijas Avize.* Retrieved June 2, 2014, from http://www.la.lv/straujuma-ekonomisko-saisu-sarausana-ar-krieviju-latvijas-ikp-var-mazinat-par-10/

Ledeneva, A.V. (1998). *Russia's economy of favours: Blat, networking and information exchange.* Cambridge: Cambridge University Press.

Lehti, M. (1999). Sovereignty redefined: Baltic cooperation and the limits of national self-determination. *Cooperation and Conflict, 34*(4), 413–433.

Leon, D.A. (2011, March 17). Trends in European life expectancy: A salutary view. *International Journal of Epidemiology,* pp. 1–7.

Leontjeva, K. (2013). *Lithuania 2013: Nations in Transit.* Freedom House. Retrieved June 22, 2014, from http://freedomhouse.org/report/nations-transit/2013/lithuania#.U9dE2fmSz_n

Lewis, P. (2000). *Political parties in post-communist Europe.* London: Routledge.

Lewis, P. (2006). Party systems in post-communist Central Europe: Patterns of stability and consolidation. *Democratization, 13*(4), 562–583.

Licmane, O. & Voronova, I. (2013). Problems and perspectives in pension system: Case of Baltic states. *Regional Formation and Development Studies, 7*(2), 99–109.

Lieven, A. (1994). *The Baltic revolution: Estonia, Latvia, Lithuania and the path to independence (2nd edition)*. New Haven: Yale University Press.

Lipset, S.M. & Rokkan, S. (1967). Cleavage structures, party systems and voter alignments: An introduction. In S.M. Lipset & S. Rokkan, *Party systems and voter alignments*. New York: Free Press.

Lobjakas, A. (2012). Estonia. In A. Lobjakas & M. Mölder, *EU–Russia watch 2012* (pp. 36–43). Tartu: Tartu University Press.

Lucas, E. (2012). *Deception: Spies, lies and how Russia dupes the West*. London: Bloomsbury.

Lucas, E. (2014). Testimony of Mr. Edward Lucas senior fellow and contributing editor, Center for European Policy Analysis Senate Foreign Relations Committee Subcommittee on European Affairs. Washington, DC. Retrieved July 11, 2014, from http://www.foreign.senate.gov/imo/media/doc/Lucas_Testimony1.pdf

Lucas, E. & Mitchell, A.W. (2014). *Central European security after Crimea: The case for strengthening NATO's eastern defenses*. Center for European Policy Analysis.

Magone, J.M. (2011). *Contemporary European politics: A comparative introduction*. Abingdon, Oxon: Routledge.

Mair, P. & van Biezen, I. (2001). Party membership in twenty European democracies, 1998–2000. *Party Politics, 7*(1), 5–21.

Mana Balss. (2014, May 19). Retrieved from Mana Balss: https://manabalss.lv/

Maslauskaite, K. & Zorgenfreija, L. (2013). Economic miracle in the Baltic states: An exemplary way to growth? In A. Grigas, A. Kasekamp, K. Maklauskaite, & L. Zorgenfreija, *The Baltic states in the EU: Yesterday, today and tomorrow*. Studies & Reports No 98, Notre Europe. Jacques Delors Institute.

Masso, J., Espenberg, K., Masso, A., Mierina, I., & Philips, K. (2012). *Growing inequalities and its impacts in the Baltics*. Gini growing inequalities' impacts. Retrieved May 29, 2014, from http://gini-research.org/system/uploads/437/original/Baltics.pdf?1370077200

Mazylis, L. & Unikaite, I. (2003). *The Lithuanian EU accession referendum: 10–11 May 2003*. University of Sussex: European Parties, Elections and Referendums Network.

Mazylis, L. & Unikaite, I. (2004). *The 2004 European Parliament election in Lithuania*. European Parties, Elections and Referendums Network.

McGuinness, D. (2014, April 22). Black Briton aims to be Estonian MEP. BBC News. Retrieved April 24, 2014, from http://www.bbc.com/news/blogs-eu-27103706

McLaughlin, N. & Trilupaityte, S. (2013). The international circulation of attacks and the reputational consequences of local context: George Soros's difficult reputation in Russia, post-Soviet Lithuania and the United States. *Cultural Sociology, 7*(4), 431–446.

Meyer-Sahling, J.-H. (2009). *Sustainability of civil service reforms in Central and Eastern Europe five years after EU accession*. OECD Publishing.

Meyer-Sahling, J.-H. & Veen, T. (2012). Governing the post-communist state: Government alternation and senior civil service politicisation in Central and Eastern Europe. *East European Politics, 28*(1), 4–22.

Mikkel, E. (2003). *The Estonian EU accession referendum: 14 September 2003.* University of Sussex: European Parties, Elections and Referendums Network.

Mikkel, E. (2006). Patterns of party formation in Estonia: Consolidation unaccomplished. In S. Jungerstam-Mulders, *Post-communist EU member states: Parties and party systems* (pp. 23–50). Aldershot: Ashgate.

Millard, F. (2011). Electoral-system change in Latvia and the elections of 2010. *Communist and Post-Communist Studies* (44), 309–318.

Milne, R. (2014, April 22). Russian threat prompts Baltics to try to solve squabbles. *Financial Times.* Retrieved April 28, 2014, from http://www.ft.com/intl/cms/s/0/2f627e7a-ca20–11e3-ac05–00144feabdc0.html?siteedition=intl#axzz2zd9qCga3

Misiunas, R. & Taagepera, R. (1983). *The Baltic states: Years of dependence, 1940–1990.* London: Hurst & Company.

Missiunas, R. (1994). National identity and foreign policy in the Baltic states. In S.F. Starr, *The legacy of history in Russia and the new states of Eurasia.* London: M.E. Sharpe.

Mole, R.C. (2012). *The Baltic states from the Soviet Union to the European Union.* London: Routledge.

Moller, J. & Skaaning, S.-E. (2010). From each according to his need, to each according to his ability: A comparative analysis of post-communist corruption. *Acta Politica, 45*(3), 320–345.

Muižnieks, N. (1997). Latvia: Restoring a state, rebuilding a nation. In I.B. Taras, *New states, new politics: Building the post-soviet nation* (pp. 376–397). Cambridge: Cambridge University Press.

Muižnieks, N. (2010). Conclusion. In N. Muižnieks, *How integrated is Latvian society? An audit* (pp. 279–284). Riga: University of Latvia Press.

Myllyntaus, T. (1992). Standard of living in Estonia and Finland in the 1930s. *Proceedings of the Estonian Academy of Sciences, 41*(3), 184–191.

NATO. (2005, February 18). Retrieved June 2, 2014, from NATO and the scourge of terrorism: http://www.nato.int/terrorism/five.htm

Nichol, J.P. (1995). *Diplomacy in the former Soviet Republics.* Westport, CT: Praeger.

Nimmo, B. (2007, April 19). Baltic universities grapple with rising racism. *Deutsce Presse Agentur.*

Nørgaard, O. (1995). *The Baltic states after independence: Why different?* Aldershot: Edward Elgar.

Norkus, Z. (2008). Carl Schmitt as a resource for democratic consolidation studies: The case of the president's impeachment in Lithuania. *East European Politics and Societies, 22*(4), 784–801.

Norton, P. (1998). *Parliaments and governments in Western Europe.* London: Frank Cass.

Nye, J. (2004). *Soft power: The means to success in world politics.* New York: Public Affairs.

Oberlenders, E. (2003). Instruments of sovietization in 1939/40 and after 1944/45. In *The soviet occupation regime in the Baltic States 1944–1959: Policies and their consequences.* Riga: Latvian History Institute Press.

OECD. (2000). *OECD economic surveys: Baltic states 2000 .*

Osborn, A. (2005, April 26). Putin: Collapse of the Soviet Union was 'catastrophe of the century'. *The Independent.* Retrieved April 20, 2014, from http://www.

independent.co.uk/news/world/europe/putin-collapse-of-the-soviet-union-was-catastrophe-of-the-century-6147493.html

Ott, A.F., Kirch, A., & Kirch, M. (1996). Ethnic anxiety: A case study of resident aliens in Estonia (1990–1992). *Journal of Baltic Studies, 27*(1), 21–46.

Paas, T., Hinnosaar, M., Masso, J., & Szirko, O. (2004). *Social protection systems in the Baltic states*. Tartu: Tartu University Press. Retrieved March 17, 2014, from http://www.mtk.ut.ee/sites/default/files/mtk/toimetised/febawb26.pdf

Pabriks, A. & Purs, A. (2001). *Latvia: The challenges of change*. London: Routledge.

Page, S. W. (1949). Social and national currents in Latvia, 1860–1917. *American Slavic and East European Review, 8*(1), 25–36.

Palmer, W. (1990). *The good republic*. London: Minerva.

Pannebianco, A. (1988). *Political parties: Organization and power*. Cambridge: Cambridge University Press.

Park, A. (1994). Turning points of post-communist transition: Lessons from the case of Estonia. *Government and Opposition, 29*(3), 403–413.

Parliament and Government Composition Database. (n.d.). Retrieved May 15, 2014, from Parliament and Government Composition Database: http://parlgov.org/stable/index.html

Pedersen, M. N. (1979). The dynamics of European party systems: Changing patterns of electoral volatility. *European Journal of Political Research, 7*(1), 1–26.

Peniķis, J. (n.d.). Par Saeimas vēlēšanām: skats atpakaļ un uz priekšu. *Academic Life* (47), 43–52.

Petrova, A. (2011, October 12). Slesers, Skele and Lembergs may have bought Diena via Rigas tirdzniecibas osta. *The Baltic Course*. Retrieved April 10, 2014, from http://www.baltic-course.com/eng/transport/?doc=47109

Pettai, V. & Kreuzer, M. (1999). Party politics in the Baltic states: Social bases and institutional context. *Eastern European politics and societies, 13*(1), 150–191.

Pettai, V. & Madise, U. (2006). The Baltic parliaments: Legislative performance from independence to EU accession. *The Journal of Legislative Studies, 12*(3–4), 291–310.

Pettai, V., Auers, D., & Ramonaite, A. (2011). Political development. In M. Lauristin, *Estonian Human Development Report 2010/2011: Baltic way(s) of development twenty years on* (pp. 144–164). Tallinn: Estonian Cooperation Assembly.

Plakans, A. (1995). *The Latvians: A short history*. Stanford: Hoover Press.

Plakans, A. (2011). *A concise history of the Baltic states* . New York: Cambridge University Press.

Poguntke, T. & Webb, P. (2005). *The presidentialization of politics: A comparative study of modern democracies*. Oxford: Oxford University Press.

Polsby, N. (1968). The institutionalisation of the US House of Representatives. *American Political Science Review* (62), 144–168.

Popova, S., Rehm, J., Patra, J., & Zatonski, W. (2007). Comparing alcohol consumption in Central and Eastern Europe to other European countries. *Alcohol & Alcoholism, 42*(5), 465–473.

Postimees. (2013, November 22). Editorial: Breaking silence is golden. Postimees in English. Retrieved April 21, 2014, from http://news.postimees.ee/2606224/editorial-breaking-silence-is-golden

Prattalla, R., Helakorpi, S., Sipila, N., Sippola, R., & Saaksjarvi, K. (2011). *Social determinants of health behaviours: Finbalt health monitor 1998–2008*. Tampere: Juvenes Print.

Pravda. (2004, March 27). Latvia will be destroyed. *Pravda*. Retrieved June 11, 2014, from http://english.pravda.ru/world/ussr/27–03–2004/5157-latvia-0/

Pray, L., Cohen, C., Makinen, I.H., Varnik, A., & MacKellar, F. (2013). *Suicide in Eastern Europe, the Commonwealth of Independent States, and the Baltic countries: Social and public health determinants*. Vienna: Remaprint.

Preisvergleich. (2013). *Salary atlas in the 27 EU countries*. Retrieved May 22, 2014, from http://www.preisvergleich.de/presse/customs/uploads/2013/05/PVG_Pressemappe_Abgeordneten-Geh%C3%A4lter_EN.pdf

Pridham, G. (2003). *Latvia's EU accession referendum: 20 September 2003*. University of Sussex: European Parties, Elections and Referendums Network.

Providus. (2014). *Latvia in the EU. Ten years later. A different Latvia?* Riga: Providus. Retrieved June 14, 2014, from http://politika.lv/article_files/2610/original/Latvia_in_the_EU_10_years_brief.pdf?1401281421

Przeworski, A. (1995). *Sustainable democracy*. Cambridge: Cambridge University Press.

Puisāns, T. (2000). *Okupācijas varu nodarītie postījumi Latvijā, 1940–1990. [Damage caused by the occupation: 1940–1990]*. Stockholm: Memento.

Purfield, C. & Rosenberg, C.B. (2010). *Adjustment under a currency peg: Estonia, Latvia and Lithuania during the global financial crisis 2008–2009*. IMF Working Paper WP/10/213. Washington, DC: IMF.

Purju, A. (2013). *Economic and social development in the Baltic states: Estonia*. Brussels: European Economic and Social Committee.

Purs, A. (2007). Working towards 'an unforeseen miracle' redux: Latvian refugees in Vladivostok, 1918–1920, and in Latvia, 1943–1944. *Contemporary European History, 16*(4), 479–494.

Purs, A. (2008). 'Weak and half-starved peoples' meet 'vodka, champagne, gypsies and drozhki': Relations between the republic of Latvia and the USA from 1918 to 1940. In D. Auers, *Latvia and the USA: From captive nation to strategic partner* (pp. 19–32). Riga: Academic Press of the University of Latvia.

Purs, A. (2012). *Baltic facades*. London: Reaktion Books.

Purs, A. & Pabriks, A. (2001). *Latvia: The challenges of change*. London: Routledge.

Putnins, T.J. & Sauka, A. (2014). *Shadow economy index for the Baltic countries: 2009–2013*. The Centre for Sustainable Business at SSE Riga.

Racius, E. (25–27 March, 2010). The place of Islamophobia among the radical Lithuanian nationalists – the neglected priority? Conference on Far Right Networks in Northern and Eastern Europe. Uppsala University.

Racko, G. (2011). On the normative consequences of economic rationality: A case study of a Swedish economics school in Latvia. *European Sociological Review, 27*(6), 772–789.

Radaelli, C.M. (2000). *Whither Europeanization? Concept stretching and substantive change*. European Integration Papers Online. Retrieved June 5, 2014, from http://eiop.or.at/eiop/pdf/2000–008

Radio Free Europe / Radio Liberty. (1954, July 21). OSA Archives. *Life in Latvia*. Munich, Germany: Radio Free Europe/Radio Liberty Research Institute. Retrieved April 14, 2014, from OSA Archives: http://hdl.handle.net/10891/osa:71f85791–60f0–406e-a1f3-e8b5beadc5fe

Rae, D.W. & Taylor, M. (1970). *The analysis of political cleavages*. New Haven: Yale University Press.

Rajevs, I. (2004). Modernization in the Latvian armed forces. In Y. Korobovsky & J. Powers, *Defence reform in the Baltic States: 12 years of experience* (pp. 25–28). Geneva: Centre for the Democratic Control of Armed Forces.

Ramonaite, A. (2006). The development of the Lithuanian party system: From stability to perturbation. In S. Jungerstam-Mulders, *Post-communist EU member states: Parties and party systems* (pp. 69–90). Aldershot: Ashgate.

Randma-Liiv, T. (2008). New public management versus neo-Weberian state in Central and Eastern Europe. Trans-European Dialogue 1: Towards the neo-Weberian State? Europe and beyond: Tallinn. Retrieved April 22, 2014, from http://iss.fsv.cuni.cz/ISS-50-version1-080227_TED1_RandmaLiiv_NPMvsNWS.pdf

Randma-Liiv, T., Nakrosis, V., & Gyorgy, H. (2010). Public sector organization in Central and Eastern Europe: From agencification to de-agencification. *Transylvanian Review of Administrative Sciences*, 160–175.

Rauch, G.V. (1974). *The Baltic states: The years of dependence 1917–1940*. London: C. Hurst & Co.

Raudseps, P. (2014, July 9). Es gatavojos karam. *Ir*. Retrieved July 14, 2014, from http://www.ir.lv/2014/7/9/es-gatavojos-karam-2

Raun, T. (1979). The development of Estonian literacy in the 18th and 19th centuries. *Journal of Baltic Studies, 10*(2), 115–126.

Re:Baltica. (2012, March 11). *Money from Russia*. Retrieved June 10, 2014, from The Baltic Centre for Investigative Journalism: http://www.rebaltica.lv/en/investigations/money_from_russia

Regelmann, A.-C. (2014). Introduction – Minority participation in Estonia and Latvia. *Journal on Ethnopolitics and Minority Issues in Europe, 13*(1), 1–18.

Reif, K. & Schmitt, H. (1980). Nine second order national elections: A conceptual framework for the analysis of European election results. *European Journal of Political Research, 8*(1), 3–44.

Reuters. (2014, March 17). Lithuania accuses Russian diplomat of spying. *Reuters*. Retrieved May 28, 2014, from http://www.reuters.com/article/2014/03/17/us-lithuania-russia-spy-idUSBREA2G14520140317

Riigi Arhiiv. (2014, April 10). *Eesti Vabariigi lipu ja vapi kavandeid 1919–1922*. Retrieved from Estonian State Archive: http://riigi.arhiiv.ee/est/eesti-vabariigi-lipu-ja-vapi-kavandeid-1919–1922/

Rommele, A. (1999). Cleavage structures and party systems in East and Central Europe. In K. Lawson, A. Rommele, & G. Karasimeonov, *Cleavages, parties and voters: Studies from Bulgaria, the Czech Republic, Hungary, Poland and Romania*. Westport, CT: Praeger.

Rose, R. (n.d.). *New Baltic barometer surveys I-VI*. Retrieved February 10, 2014, from Baltic Voices: http://www.balticvoices.org/nbb/surveys.php

Rostoks, T. (2013). *Baltic states and NATO: Looking beyond the article V*. Helsinki: National Defense University: Department of strategic and defense studies.

Roubini, N. (2009, June 10). Latvia's currency crisis is a rerun of Argentina's. *Financial Times*. Retrieved March 11, 2014, from http://www.ft.com/intl/cms/s/0/95df08fe-55f3-11de-ab7e-00144feabdc0.html?siteedition=intl#axzz33s8bAHe9

Rozenbergs, R. (2011, July 29). Valodnieki: latviski labāk teikt sorosieši, nevis sorosoïdi. *Neatkarīgā Rīta Avīze*, p. 2.

Ruin, P. (2012, June 27). Mergers have become a necessity. *Baltic Worlds*. Retrieved May 25, 2014, from http://balticworlds.com/mergers-have-become-a-necessity/

Rutland, P. (1994). The economy: The rocky road from plan to market. In A.P. Stephen White, *Developments in Russian and post-soviet politics*. London: Macmillan.

Ruutsoo, R. (1996). The emergence of civil society in Eastern Europe 1987–1994. In R. Bloom, H. Melin, & J. Nikola, *Between plan and market: Social change in the Baltic states and Russia* (pp. 97–122). Berlin: Walter de Gruyter.

Ryals Conrad, C. & Golder, S.N. (2010). Measuring government duration and stability in Central Eastern European democracies. *European Journal of Political Research*(49), 119–150.

Saar, J. (1999). *Criminal justice system and process of democratization in Estonia.* Tallinn: NATO Democratic Institutions Research Fellowship Final Report. Retrieved March 7, 2014, from http://www.nato.int/acad/fellow/97–99/saar.pdf

Saarts, T. (2011). Comparative Party System Analysis in Central and Eastern Europe: The case of the Baltic states. *Studies of Transition States and Societies, 3*(3), 83–104.

Saeima. (2014, June 20). *Saeima expands the Constitution with a preamble.* Retrieved from Saeima: http://www.saeima.lv/en/news/22361-saeima-expands-the-constitution-with-a-preamble

Sakkov, S. (2014). Towards Nordic-Baltic defence cooperation: A view from Estonia. In A.-S. Dahl & P. Järvenpää, *Northern security and global politics: Nordic-Baltic strategic influence in a post-unipolar world* (pp. 155–168). Abingdon: Routledge.

Salmon, J.H. (1994). *The Baltic nations and Europe.* London: Longman.

Satversmes Aizsardzibas Birojs. (2014). *Annual review.* Riga: Satversmes Aizsardzibas Birojs. Retrieved June 18, 2014, from http://www.sab.gov.lv/downloads/2013_parskats.pdf

Saukauskis, S. (1921). *Sur les confins de deux mondes.* Geneva: Atar.

Scarrow, H. (1967). The function of political parties: A critique of the literature and the approach. *Journal of Politics* (29), 770–790.

Ščerbinskis, V. (2005). The Latvian student corps and politics in the inter-war period of the twentieth century. *Journal of Baltic Studies, 36*(2), 157–177.

Schafer, R.B. & Schafer, E.A. (1993). Latvia in transition: A study of change in a former republic of the USSR. *Journal of Baltic Studies, 24*(2), 161–172.

Schattschneider, E.E. (1975). *The semisovereign people.* Hinsdale, IL: Drysden Press.

Schopflin, G. (1993). *Politics in Eastern Europe.* Oxford: Blackwell.

Schulze, J.L. (2014). The ethnic participation gap: Comparing second generation Russian youth and Estonian youth. *Journal on Ethnopolitics and Minority Issues in Europe, 13*(1), 19–56.

Sczerbiak, A. (2001). *Poles together? The emergence and development of political parties in post-communist Poland.* Budapest: Central European University Press.

Senn, A.E. (1958). The sovietization of the Baltic states. *The annals of the American Academy of Political and Social Science*, 123–129.

Shugart, M.S. & Carey, J.M. (1992). *Presidents and assemblies: Constitutional design and electoral dynamics.* Cambridge: Cambridge University Press.

Sikk, A. (2004). Successful new parties in the Baltic states: Similar or different? Paper prepared for the conference, 'The Baltic States: New Europe or Old?', University of Glasgow, 22–23 January 2004.

Sikk, A. (2005). How unstable? Volatility and the genuinely new parties in Eastern Europe. *European Journal of Political Research*(44), 391–412.

Sikk, A. (2006). From private organizations to democratic infrastructure: Political parties and the state in Estonia. *Journal of Communist Studies and Transition Politics, 22*(3).

Sikk, A. (2006). From 'sexy men' to 'socialists gone nuts'. In P.G. Lewis & Z. Mansfeldova, *The European Union and Party Politics in Central Eastern Europe* (pp. 40–63). Basingstoke: Palgrave.

Sikk, A. (2009). *The 2009 European elections in Estonia.* European Parties, Elections, Referendums Network.

Sikk, A. (2012). Newness as a winning formula for new political parties. *Party Politics, 18*(4), 465–486.

Sikk, A. (2014). *Elections in the Baltic states, 1992–2012.* Retrieved from http://http://www.homepages.ucl.ac.uk/~tjmsasi/

Sikk, R. (2007, December 17). Rassisti ootab jõulupakis neeger. *Eesti Paevaleht.*

Sildam, T. & Mattson, T. (2001). Spies in the Baltics: Are they still active? *Baltics Worldwide.* Retrieved June 12, 2014, from http://www.balticsworldwide.com/spies.htm

Šilde, Ā. (1976). *Latvijas Vēsture: 1914–1940 [A History of Latvia 1914–1940].* Stockholm: Daugava.

Šilde, Ā. (1982). *Pirmā republika. [First republic].* New York: Grāmatu Draugs.

Sipaviciene, A. & Stankuniene, V. (2013). The social and economic impact of emigration on Lithuania. In OECD, *Coping with emigration in Baltic and East European countries* (pp. 45–64). OECD Publishing.

Skultans, V. (1997). The expropriated harvest: Narratives of deportation and collectivization in north-east Latvia. *History Workshop Journal* (44), 172–188.

Skulte, J. (2005). Returned diaspora, national identity and political leadership in Latvia and Lithuania (PhD Dissertation). College Park: University of Maryland. Retrieved March 18, 2014, from http://drum.lib.umd.edu/bitstream/1903/2475/1/umi-umd-2347.pdf

Smith, A.D. (1991). *National identity.* London: Penguin Books.

Smith, D.J. (2002). *Estonia: Independence and European integration.* London: Routledge.

Smith, G. (1994). The resurgence of nationalism. In G. Smith, *The Baltic states: The national self-determination of Estonia, Latvia and Lithuania.* New York: St. Martin's Press.

Smith, G. (1996). Latvia and the Latvians. In G. Smith, *The nationalities question in the post-soviet states.* London: Longman.

Smith, K.W. (2007). Determinants of Soviet household income. *The European Journal of Comparative Economics, 4*(1), 3–24.

Smith-Sivertsen, H. (2004). Why bigger party membership organizations in Lithuania than in Latvia 1995–2000? *East European Quarterly, 38*(2), 215–259.

Smith-Sivertsen, H. (2004). Latvia. In S. Berglund, J. Ekman, & F.H. Aarebrot, *Handbook of political change in Eastern Europe. (2nd edition)* (pp. 95–131). Cheltenham: Edward Elgar.

Snyder, T. (1995). National myths and international relations: Poland and Lithuania, 1989–1994. *East European Politics and Societies, 9*(2), 317–343.

Solvak, M. & Pettai, V. (2008). The parliamentary elections in Estonia, March 2007. *Election Studies* (27), 574–577.

Spekke, A. (1952). *Latvia and the Baltic problem.* London: Latvian Information Bureau.

Standard Eurobarometer. (2014, May 20). *Eurobarometer surveys.* Retrieved from http://ec.europa.eu/public_opinion/archives/eb_arch_En.htm

Stockholm International Peace Research Institute. (2014). *Military expenditure database.* Retrieved June 10, 2014, from http://milexdata.sipri.org/files/?file=SI PRI+military+expenditure+database+1988–2013.xlsx

Stranga, A. (1991). Sociāldemokrāti K. Ulmaṇa režīma gados: 1934–1940. [The Social Democrats under Kārlis Ulmanis: 1934–1940]. *Latvijas Vesture, 1*(3), 15–20.

Studies, I.C. (2014, June 10). *Highest to lowest: Prison population rate.* Retrieved from http://www.prisonstudies.org/highest-to-lowest/prison_population_rate

Šulmane, I. (2010). The media and integration. In N. Muižnieks, *How integrated is Latvian society? An audit* (pp. 223–252). Riga: University of Latvia Academic Press.

Swain, G. (1999). The disillusioning of the revolution's praetorian guard: The Latvian riflemen, summer-autumn 1918. *Europe–Asia Studies, 51*(4), 667–686.

Taagepera, R. (1990). The Baltic states. *Electoral Studies, 9*(4), 303–311.

Taagepera, R. (1993). *Estonia: Return to independence.* Boulder, CO: Westview Press.

Taagepera, R. (2011). Albert, Martin and Peter too: Their roles in creating the Estonian and Latvian nations. *Journal of Baltic Studies, 42*(2), 125–141.

Tamkivi, S. (2014, January 24). Lessons from the world's most tech-savvy government. *The Atlantic.* Retrieved May 10, 2014, from http://www.theatlantic.com/international/archive/2014/01/lessons-from-the-worlds-most-tech-savvy-government/283341/

Tammerk, T. (1991, June 6–12). Stop Western aid in face of Soviet violence, say Baltic leaders. *Baltic Independent,* p. 1.

Taro, L. (1999). *Baltic economies in 1998–1999: Effects of the Russian financial crisis.* Helsinki: Bank of Finland Institute of Economies in Transition.

Tavits, M. (2008). On the linkage between electoral volatility and party system instability in Central and Eastern Europe. *European Journal of Political Research, 47*(5), 537–555.

Tavits, M. (2010). Why do people engage in corruption? The case of Estonia. *Social Forces, 88*(3), 1257–1279.

Taylor, N. (2006, March 15). Lennart Meri obituary. *The Independent.* Retrieved February 25, 2014, from http://www.independent.co.uk/news/obituaries/lennart-meri-469918.html

Temperley, H. (1924). *A history of the peace conference of Paris,* vol. VI. London: Frowdy, Hodder and Stoughton.

Thatcher, M. (1994, May 10). *Speech introducing the prime minister of Estonia (Mart Laar).* Retrieved June 11, 2014, from Margaret Thatcher Foundation: http://www.margaretthatcher.org/document/108333

The Baltic Course. (2013, August 28). Biggest number of tourists visiting Lithuania's capital is from Russia. *The Baltic Course.* Retrieved May 28, 2014, from http://www.baltic-course.com/eng/good_for_business/?doc=79691

Toomla, R. (2013). The presidency in the Republic of Estonia. In V. Hlousek, *Presidents above parties? Presidents in Central and Eastern Europe, their formal competencies and informal power* (pp. 167–190). Brno: Masaryk University.

Transmission. (2013, June 19). United States once again Russia's worst enemy. *RFE/RL.* Retrieved June 17, 2014, from http://www.rferl.org/content/russia-us-worst-enemy/25021735.html

Trapans, J.A. (1991). Introduction. In J.A. Trapans, *Toward independence: The Baltic popular movements* (pp. 3–8). Boulder, CO: Westview Press.

Trapans, J.A. (1991). The sources of Latvia's Popular Front. In J.A. Trapans (ed.), *Toward independence: The Baltic popular movements* (pp. 25–41). Boulder, CO: Westfield Press.

Trechsel, A.H., Alvarez, R.M., & Hall, T.E. (2008). *Internet voting in Estonia*. Working Paper, Caltech/MIT Voting Technology Project.

Trofimoviene, L. (2008). Overview of trafficking in human beings in Lithuania. In P. Downes, A. Zule-Lapimaa, L. Ivanchenko, & S. Blumberg, *Not one victim more: Human trafficking in the Baltic states* (pp. 155–180). Tallinn: Living For Tomorrow.

TVNET/De Facto. (2014, March 30). Augošais aizsardzības budžets daudzus gadus bijusi vien izlikšanās. *TVNET*. Retrieved June 9, 2014, from http://www.tvnet.lv/zinas/latvija/503670-augosais_aizsardzibas_budzets_daudzus_gadus_bijusi_vien_izliksanas

Ugaine, A. (2011, June 22). Vairums Saskaņas centra deputātu neatzīst okupāciju . *Diena*. Retrieved 03 08, 2014, from http://www.diena.lv/sodien-laikraksta/vairums-saskanas-centra-deputatu-neatzist-okupaciju-13889368

United Nations Development Programme. (1996). *Latvia: Human development report 1996*. Riga: UNDP.

University of Michigan Open Rights Group. (2014). Press Release. Retrieved May 19, 2014, from Independent report on e-voting in Estonia: https://estoniaevoting.org/press-release/

Urban, W.L. (1998). Victims of the Baltic crusade. *Journal of Baltic Studies, 24*(3), 195–212.

Urbonas, R. (2009). Corruption in Lithuania. *The Quarterly Journal* (Winter), 67–94.

US Embassy in Vilnius. (2014, June 10). *Sumner Welles declaration*. Retrieved from http://vilnius.usembassy.gov/welles_declaration.html

USAID. (2013). *2012 CSO Sustainability Index for Central and Eastern Europe and Eurasia*. Washington, DC: USAID.

Vajda, M. (1988). East-Central European perspectives. In J. Keane, *Civil society and the state: New European perspectives*. London: University of Westminster Press.

Valles, L., Cande, M., & Bande, M. (2013). *Women in police services in the EU 2012*. Barcelona: Institute of Public Security for Catalonia. Retrieved March 22, 2014, from http://www20.gencat.cat/docs

van der Stoel, M. (1993, April 6). *Latvia and the OSCE*. Retrieved February 17, 2014, from Minority Electronic Resources: http://www.minelres.lv/count/latvia/930406r.htm

Vanags, E. & Vilka, I. (2008). Local government in the Baltic states: Similar but different. In A. Coulson & A. Campbell, *Local government in Central and Eastern Europe: The rebirth of local democracy* (pp. 82–96). New York: Routledge.

Vark, R. (2008). The siege of the Estonian embassy in Moscow: Protection of a diplomatic mission and its staff in the receiving state. *Juridical International* (XV), 144–153.

Vasilyeva, K. (2012). *Nearly two-thirds of the foreigners living in EU member states are citizens of countries outside the EU–27*. Eurostat. Retrieved March 3, 2014, from http://epp.eurostat.ec.europa.eu/cache/ITY_OFFPUB/KS-SF-12–031/EN/KS-SF-12–031-EN.PDF

Vedler, S. (2014, January 27). Free public transit in Tallinn is a hit with riders but yields unexpected results. *Citiscope*. Retrieved March 10, 2014, from http://citiscope.org/story/2014/free-public-transit-tallinn-hit-riders-yields-unexpected-results

Velykis, D. (2010). *A diagnosis of corruption in Lithuania*. European Research Centre for Anti-Corruption and State-Building.

Verheijen, T.J. (2003). Public administration in post-communist states. In B.G. Peters & J. Pierre, *Hanbook of public administration* (pp. 489–499). London: Sage.

Vēveris, E.Z. (2005, April 2–8). Blēdību pasaule: Korupcija pirmskara Latvijā un mūsdienu Eiropā. [A deceitful world: Corruption in interwar Latvia and modern Europe]. *sestdiena*, pp. 8–11.

Viilmann, N. & Soosaar, O. (2012). Eesti Tööturu Ülevaade. *Eesti Pank*. Retrieved May 25, 2014, from http://www.google.com/url?sa=t&rct=j&q=&esrc=s&source=web&cd=2&ved=0CCgQFjAB&url=http%3A%2F%2Fwww.eestipank.ee%2Fpublikatsioon%2Ftooturu-ulevaade%2F2012%2Ftooturu-ulevaade-1 2012&ei=1emaU8atMczgsATF0IGwDQ&usg=AFQjCNHI9fd27p0BKBsWO-SqazhnMWlOxg&bvm=bv.68911

Vīķe-Freiberga, V. (2007, June 21). *Valsts prezidentes Vairas Vīķes-Freibergas uzruna Saeimā 2007.gada 21.jūnijā*. Retrieved May 21, 2014, from President of Latvia: http://www.president.lv/pk/content/?cat_id=605&art_id=11232

Vilpisauskas, R. & Kuokstis, V. (2010). Economic adjustment to the crisis in the Baltic Republics in comparative perspective. Paper presented at the 7th Pan-European International Relations Conference, Stockholm.

Vitkus, G. (2006). *Lithuanian-Russian relations in 1990–1995: A study of Lithuanian foreign policy*. University of Mannheim. Retrieved May 23, 2014, from http://www.uni-mannheim.de/fkks/fkks12.pdf

Voice of America. (2014, June 23). Source: Russia offered Baltics cheaper gas for NATO exit. *Voice of America News*. Retrieved July 10, 2014, from http://www.voanews.com/content/source-russia-offered-baltics-cheaper-gas-for-nato-exit/1943109.html

von Beyme, K. (1996). *Transition to democracy in Eastern Europe*. Basingstoke: Palgrave Macmillan.

Voorman, R. (2009). Gender segregated labour markets in the Baltics: What are prevailing – similarities or differences? *Studies of Transition States and Societies*, 1(1), 66–80.

Wallace, H. (2000). Flexibility: A tool for integration or a restraint on disintegration. In K. Neunreither & A. Wiener, *European integration after Amsterdam: Institutional dynamics and prospects for democracy* (pp. 175–192). New York: Oxford University Press.

Watts, L.L. (2007). Intelligence reform in Europe's emerging democracies: Conflicting paradigms, dissimilar contexts. *Studies in Intelligence*, 48(1). Retrieved June 18, 2014, from https://www.cia.gov/library/center-for-the-study-of-intelligence/csi-publications/csi-studies/studies/vol48no1/article02.html

Weisbrot, M. & Ray, R. (2011). *Latvia's internal devaluation: A success story?* Washington, DC: Center for Economic and Policy Research.

Woolfson, C.A. (2010). The race equality directive: 'Differentiated' or 'differential' Europeanisation. *European Societies*, 12(4), 543–566.

World Bank. (2000). *Anticorruption in transition: A contribution to the policy debate.* Washington, DC: World Bank.

Zake, I. (2002). The people's party in Latvia: Neo-liberalism and the new politics of independence. *Journal of Communist Studies and Transition Politics, 18*(1), 109–132.

Zake, I. (2010). *American Latvians: Politics of a refugee community.* New Brunswick, NJ: Transaction Publishers.

Zake, I. (2010). Soviet campaigns against 'capitalist ideological subversives' during the cold war. *Journal of Cold War Studies, 12*(3), 91–114.

Zalys, V. (1996). The prospects for Baltic cooperation at the end of the twentieth century. In E. Demm, R. Noel, & W. Urban, *The independence of the Baltic States: Origins, causes and consequences: A comparison of the crucial years 1918–1919 and 1990–1991* (pp. 249–252). Lithuanian Research and Studies Center.

Zarina, Z. (2009, November 12). Latviju pamet Gobziņa grupas „Los Amigos" nigērietis. *Kas Jauns.* Retrieved February 22, 2014, from http://www.kasjauns.lv/lv/zinas/11777/latviju-pamet-gobzina-grupas-los-amigos-nigerietis

Zepa, B. (2004). *Etniska Tolerance un Latvijas sabiedribas Integracija.* Riga: Baltic Social Science Institute.

Zepa, B. & Kļave, E. (2011). *Latvia human development report 2010/2011: National identity, mobility and capability.* Riga: Advanced Social and Political Research Institute of the University of Latvia.

Zile, R. & Steinbuka, I. (2001). Latvia on the way to the European Union. *Finance and Development, 38*(2). Retrieved June 2, 2014, from http://www.imf.org/external/pubs/ft/fandd/2001/06/zile.htm

Index